KJLH-FM and the Los Angeles
Riots of 1992

KJLH-FM and the Los Angeles Riots of 1992

Compton's Neighborhood Station in the Aftermath of the Rodney King Verdict

P H Y L I S   J O H N S O N

McFarland & Company, Inc., Publishers
Jefferson, North Carolina, and London

LIBRARY OF CONGRESS CATALOGUING-IN-PUBLICATION DATA

Johnson, Phylis, 1957–
    KJLH-FM and the Los Angeles Riots of 1992: Compton's
neighborhood station in the aftermath of the Rodney King
verdict / Phylis Johnson.
        p.   cm.
    Includes bibliographical references and index.

    ISBN 978-0-7864-4386-4
    softcover : 50# alkaline paper ∞

    1. KJLH-FM (Radio station : Los Angeles, Calif.)   2. African
Americans in radio broadcasting — California — Los Angeles.
3. Radio broadcasting — Social aspects — California — Los Angeles.
4. Riots — California — Los Angeles.   5. Los Angeles (Calif.) —
Race relations.   I. Title.
PN1991.8.A35J64   2009
791.44089' 96079494 — dc22   2009024871

British Library cataloguing data are available

Cover image: Smoke rises from a shopping center burned by rioters
early Thursday, April 30, 1992, as the Los Angeles skyline is partially
obscured by smoke. More than 300 fires were reportedly set after four
police officers were acquitted Wednesday of the beating of motorist
Rodney King (AP Photo/Paul Sakuma)

Manufactured in the United States of America

McFarland & Company, Inc., Publishers
  Box 611, Jefferson, North Carolina 28640
  www.mcfarlandpub.com

Acknowledgments

Special thanks to Kay McCrimon, Aisha Cool, and Jennifer Johnson for assisting in transcribing the interviews for this book. Thank you to KJLH for its hospitality and providing documentation, interview time with management and staff—and sharing the kindness, joy, love and happiness that permeates its airwaves. I would like to acknowledge Karen Slade, Carl Nelson, Eric Rico Reed, and E. Steven Collins, in particular, for the many hours that they shared with me. I thank the many others I interviewed for this book, and their stories are included in this book as well.

Special thanks to my dissertation committee — Dr. Joseph A. Brown, S.J., Dr. William Coscarelli, Dr. Candis S. Isberner, Dr. Donna M. Post, and my chair and advisor, Dr. Sharon Shrock. Thank you to Brenda Cooley, Jean Elder and Theresa Strack for their editorial assistance. Thank you to Tejai Maxwell and Jon Pluskota for helping in the interview process at KJLH in 2002. Thank you to Dr. Thomas A. Birk for his collaboration in the early years of this project. And of course, last not but least, my family, especially my father, Dr. Philip T. West; husband, James C. Johnson, and my children, Nick, Jenny and Julie — thank you for your inspiration and encouragement.

This book is dedicated to my mother, Dr. Joan West, who passed away in 2003 — only months after I was awarded my Ph.D. And I thank God for divine inspiration!

Table of Contents

Introduction

All of a sudden, the streets went wild. The helicopters, National Guard, and media converged onto one station, one community. In a moment, one verdict had transformed a community into a state of confusion. One station stayed tuned to its community in the dark hours of anger, madness, and grief. After listening to days of KJLH-FM's broadcast tapes and reviewing transcripts of its coverage of the 1992 Los Angeles Riots, I thought the best way to enter this story is smack in the middle, and then go back and tell you a bit about KJLH's history, its founders, its legacy, and its future. This introduction serves to draw you into the relevance of the KJLH story, and the station's impact on its community during the riots through the eyes and ears of its staff and community.

Smack in the Middle

On Wednesday, April 29, 1992, KJLH-FM, Compton, Los Angeles, halted its regular programming for days to report, as well as to open a dialogue, on the events surrounding the acquittals of four Los Angeles police officers by a Simi Valley jury in the case involving the beating of Rodney King. From the moment the acquittals of the Los Angeles police officers were announced, KJLH not only reported on the events that followed but attempted to relieve the anger and frustration that had been building over several months. KJLH's commitment to informing its audience always went beyond the rip-n-read style of many music-oriented radio stations. During the L.A. Riots, the station became an information hub to the

1

African American community and to the world. Media representatives from throughout the nation camped out at KJLH, and by Friday, May 1, the events happening at the KJLH studio were transmitted all over the world via satellite.

KJLH introduced the world to South Central, Los Angeles — a story that could be told only by those that lived and worked there. For this reason, this book relies heavily on interviews and station documentation. One such person that played a significant role in the coverage of the riots in 1992 was Carl Nelson, then KJLH-FM news director. He began his broadcast career in 1971 at WYNT-AM in New York, and within four years he was working for the legendary WLIB-AM and WBLS-FM. In 1980, he became the KJLH-FM news director, and responsible for the birth and expansion of its daily news show *Front Page* in the early 1990s. *Front Page* is the vehicle that Nelson used to propel KJLH's news department into a global arena. He was named the 1996 News Director of the Year by *Black Radio Exclusive* magazine. This award was perhaps the culmination of all his successes through the years. He no longer hosts *Front Page*, but the show continues to air on KJLH. Eric "Rico" Reed, his co-host in 1992, has remained a West Coast radio personality, working at various stations over the years. His perspective at the helm of *Front Page*— along with Nelson — tells a powerful story, as revealed in the transcripts of KJLH's live broadcast during the critical hours of the unrest.

A number of KJLH and media personalities helped them answer phones, coordinate news reports, and keep the dialogue going. What emerges is a portrait of a radio station that knows and cares for its audience, as evidenced by staff members who remained on-air on the battleground in an effort to help the community survive this crisis. The following segments from KJLH's transcripts provide an overview to the station's coverage of the events, and the listeners' on-air response to what was going on around them during and after the riots.

> *Rico Reed*: Good evening, KJLH — you're on the special edition of *Front Page*. Good evening KJLH — you're on the special edition of *Front Page*. What is your name and where are you calling from?
>
> *Caller*: I'm [Brad] calling from Westchester. I just want to say that I was disgusted beyond words when I heard about that verdict coming back this afternoon, and it sends a message out to all African-Americans that you do not have a say in the way that this country is run. Your voice means nothing so far. People we have to get out there; we have to vote. We have to get these clowns out of office who say they'll represent us and they're not representing us at all. Our best interests are not their top priority —

it's the rich White people who are supporting their campaigns — they're doing what they want to do.

Brandon Bowlin: Exactly.

Tyrone: And when you get that literature in the mail, that tells you how to vote and tells you about the issues, do not throw it away.

Rico Reed: Read it.

Tyrone: Read that stuff and vote intelligently. Know what you're voting for.

Rico Reed: It's not just the President, it's not just the councilmen, it's the issues, the propositions that you are missing out on.

Tyrone: Exactly, you go to the polling place and you just fill in the little holes and just punch right down without even knowing what we're voting for. I've done that myself. I've been guilty of it.

Brandon Bowlin: You know, the person who was talking about political puppets — Malcolm X in his book, *By Any Means Necessary* — it's a companion to the *Malcolm X Speaks*. He calls them "chicken wing" politicians because they go wherever the food is. That means wherever the money is, they're right behind them, and if you want to make a difference, hey — vote, learn, educate yourself on the issues and go out and take care of that business.

Rico Reed: Alright, let's go to another phone call. 10:03 on 102-3, KJLH — Good evening, what is your name, and where are you calling from?

Caller: I'm [Macy] calling from Inglerock and I just want to say, "thank you KJLH," and I want to say how devastated I was when the decision was handed down, but by the same token, had we united in peace, the way that we united to violate ourselves in our community, a whole lot, that would have made a tremendous statement to the world.

Rico Reed: It certainly would have —

Caller: It just sickens me beyond belief, the devastation that is happening in our own community. But thank you to KJLH that we can voice these opinions and you guys are doing an awesome job.

Rico Reed: Thank you so much for calling. Here's a number to call if you're looking for someplace to register to vote or you need more information, write this number down — 7-2-1-1-1-0-0. That is 721-1100. You must be registered by May the 4th — that's coming up. What is that, Monday?

J. Anthony Brown: Monday.

Rico Reed: Monday, you must be registered by Monday to vote in the June election. If *anything* can move you to vote, this should do it right here.

J. Anthony Brown: If we could get as many people out who are rioting right now to go out and register to vote....

Rico Reed: It would make a big difference.

A Bird's Eye Perspective

Stevie Wonder purchased KJLH in 1979, and the station remains a social and political force in South Central Los Angeles. KJLH's history goes back to 1965, with the original owner having dabbled in radio for many years prior to his purchase of the station. KJLH had been owned by an African American funeral director, John Lamar Hill, Jr., since 1965. He made a commitment to sell KJLH only to another African American so that the programming would continue to serve the Black community in ways that mainstream radio did not do. In the those early years of Black radio in Los Angeles, KGFJ-AM had established itself as a strong and credible voice for the African American community; its Black-oriented format was tested in the midst of the 1965 Los Angeles Watts Riots. Stations such as KGFJ, with such authority and outreach to its South Central listeners, would provide KJLH with insight into its on-air responsibility to the community.

Nearly three decades later, KJLH opened its phone lines and became an information hub to its neighborhoods during the riots of 1992, reaffirming Black radio's civic role during a crisis, especially for those who remembered the riots of 1965, to a new generation of station listeners. In 1992, KGFJ briefly stopped its music and turned to talk during the riots; however, KJLH had developed a strong community and news presence by then and took the lead in the coverage, while calling for peaceful solutions.

The station's history began as one of serving the Long Beach area, but through the years, its license was upgraded to fully serve South Central, primarily Compton and Hollywood, under the leadership and ownership of Hill, Jr., and Wonder. Formatted as adult rhythm and blues (or urban adult contemporary), KJLH's audience represents more of a minority mix than most Los Angeles stations, although primarily African American. KJLH has reflected the diversity of the surrounding neighborhoods in its programming of issues.

The station in 1992 was located a few yards from where the unrest occurred. From the studio window, the KJLH staff witnessed the 1992 riots unfold before their eyes and ears — and through their voices we begin to see and hear what they experienced:

> *Carl Nelson*: L.A. police advise us some 200 people have gathered near Sunset Boulevard and Gardner Street in Hollywood, where members of Queer Nation and Act Up L.A. are staging a protest, and uh, those two groups

have been violently opposed to Chief Gates and the LAPD. Also, an angry mob converged on the Hall of Justice in the Criminal Courts Building downtown tonight, hurling rocks and bottles, setting small fires and taunting deputies before moving on. Mobs set fires in the Criminal Courts Building lobby and in the exterior courtyard.

Rico Reed: Alright. 520-KJLH. 977-KJLH — for the 7-1-4. Our phone lines are jammed up, but let's try to take as many calls as we can. Good evening, you're on the special edition of *Front Page*, what is your name and where are you calling from? Hel-lo? Are you there?

Caller: Hel-lo.

Rico Reed: Hi, go right ahead, you're on the special edition of *Front Page*.

Caller: Yes, I'm [Len] from Culver City.

Rico Reed: Alright, [Len], go right ahead.

Caller: I just want to articulate the hypocrisy in the situation. I'm watchin' TV right now as we speak and they are sitting, what I mean by "they" are the TV stations — are sitting with mini cams or whatever, cameras pointed at places that are being looted and people are like robbing or whatever. And on the other side of that, the hypocrisy of it all, is they said these four men were just doing their job by beating Rodney King the way they did. So what I'm wondering is, where the hell are they doing their job and [why aren't they] stopping the people who are looting these businesses in the community?

Brandon Bowlin: One of the ... like I said, one of the tactics we saw — we talked about this earlier, we've been talking about this all through the night, is not to show the authoritative figure in hopes of quelling anything that might happen: an explosion that might be the spark to the flame or to the gasoline to have this bomb that goes off. But it almost backfired because, like I said before, if you noticed earlier today, on Normandy and Florence that cars were continually going down the street and they were getting pummeled. Not brothers, now, 'cause our own van went down there and the brothers were cheering all the African Americans on. But anybody else, any other race, any other color was getting destroyed, and that almost backfired.

Rico Reed: I saw African Americans get pulled out of their cars.

Brandon Bowlin: You saw one, that's right, you saw the sister.

J. Anthony Brown: When the mob, when it gets out of hand, it doesn't have a mind.

Rico Reed: It doesn't matter.

Tyrone: It's an insanity that goes places, just like I was telling the guys when we were off the air, there's people, just for the sake of lootin' — they're runnin' down the street with mismatched shoes that they stole, just 'cause they stole them. They just — their eyes are all big and glassy; they look insane.

Rico Reed: What really bothered me, I'm sure everybody saw this — the guy with the double, the two-tiered truck, the red truck; they pulled him out, they beat him, they hit him over the head with a fire extinguisher, some piece of pottery or something. The guy is lying down, blood is comin'— I hate to be so graphic but blood is coming out all on the street and there's a guy standing there with a video camera filming the whole thing.

J. Anthony Brown: Filming the whole thing. The violence also breaks out in terms of Blacks who try to help this guy. I mean, you could get beat up just trying to help this guy out.

Rico Reed: Yeah. And there was a guy on a motorcycle, pulls out a shotgun, looks up at the helicopter and shoots at cars. Puts his helmet on and rides away like nothing happened.

Brandon Bowlin: So what's happening? What's going to go on? Where are we gonna take this? We know what's going on. We go in our basements; we go in our living rooms and talk with our children, make them understand what happened with Rodney King, make them understand what's happening. Where do we go from here? It's not just to the voting polls, but we have to see what other strategies we have to do to make sure this type of thing does not happen in this fair city again.

Into the Night

As the evening progressed, the KJLH crew attempted to comprehend the events happening around them and translate the experiences to the audience. An endless stream of calls into the studio affirmed the audience's search for answers throughout the night.

Rico Reed: Alright.102-3 KJLH, a special edition of *Front Page*. Good evening, you're on Front Page, what is your name and where are you calling from?

Caller: Good evening this is [Mindy], I'm calling from Compton.

Rico Reed: Okay, [Mindy], go right ahead.

Caller: Ok, I just wanted to say that the verdict today shows that the life of a Black man in America is worthless. It shows that they can just take advantage of us and do us any type of way and they expect us to be passive and just accept what they do to us. The Latasha Harlins case, they had — I mean there's no justice anywhere. I mean, Latasha Harlins, there was evidence, I mean, a video tape — that was rare. They had evidence that it was murder, but they gave her [the Korean store clerk] probation, no just sentence. You kill a dog, you go to jail. You kill a Black teenager — nothing.

Rico Reed: I know you're right — you beat a man and nothing happens. You're in Compton. Is anything happening out there that you know about?

Caller: No, I'm really sorry because I live right across the street from [Martin Luther King Elementary School] and it's like very quiet over here, but on my way home....

Rico Reed: Very ironic.

Caller: ... down Imperial, there were like crowds like Avalon, Central, all those streets, there were crowds of people on corners throwing bottles at the cars and stuff and I was like, "why don't you take it elsewhere." You know, I was screaming out the car and then we seen three cars with six police officers in helmets — they were doing U-turns, blocking off streets and everything. So they need to just go in the house. All they're gon' do is hurt 'em or kill 'em. Why are they doing this to their own community?

Rico Reed: I don't know. Thank you for your call this evening. 10:14. We have another bulletin.

Securing the Community

Administrators from area schools began calling into the station to announce the cancellation of classes. It became evident that life would never be the same for the families of South Central. KJLH's on-air narrative depicted a human drama that images could not convey across television.

Carl Nelson: Ok, Rico. Several L.A. Unified School District campuses will be closed tomorrow due to the rioting by the verdict in the Rodney King beating trial. Superintendent William Hampton has called for the closure of all schools and offices tomorrow within the area of Adams Boulevard to the north, Imperial Highway to the south, La Cienaga Boulevard to the west and Alameda to the east. So we'll give you those directions again a little later on.

Rico Reed: That's all the high schools, elementary schools, everything.

Carl Nelson: All high schools, everything — even district buildings, school district buildings.

Rico Reed: I wonder what's going to happen with the banks. Anything on the banks? I guess we'll find out.

Carl Nelson: We'll find out.

J. Anthony Brown: Everything's going to follow, probably.

Rico Reed: Yeah, probably so.

Brandon Bowlin: You know, we were talking about historical references. Remember when the Watts riots took place, a lot of the Jewish businesses were burned — and here, a lot of the Korean businesses are burned, and then there, the lines were drawn over what the Black community actually was, and now you've just seen, when you discussed the schools, it almost draws the exact block of the Black community that's in the riotous state.

Carl Nelson: Ok, Rico, we've got a couple of bulletins here. I'll take the first one. A fire fighter was wounded tonight in a shooting in Los Angeles.

Rico Reed: Awww.

Carl Nelson: ... shooting occurred at 35th and Western about 9:50. The wounded fire fighter whose condition is not immediately available was taken to Cedars Sinai. Also, police have cordoned off the area around Foothill Division, where a few shots were fired and rocks and bottles thrown earlier this evening. However, no major action appears to be continuing in that area. This time, of course, Foothill is the division where those four officers worked out of— who were acquitted today in the Rodney King beating trial.

Rico Reed: 520-KJLH, 977-KJLH for the 7-1-4. We're still taking calls. Vent your frustration out over the radio. Stay indoors if you're in the South Central Los Angeles. If you can, stay off your telephone unless it's an actual emergency because I think they've basically turned the phone lines off or they're just jammed. You'll get a steady busy signal.

J. Anthony Brown: We're saying we need calmness in our own neighborhood 'cause that's where the problem is right now. We're not saying, leave here and go up to Hollywood or to some other area. We need calmness right here where we are.

Rico Reed: We're saying violence is unnecessary and what makes it even worse is you're being violent right in your own neighborhood. That is ridiculous. That's what we're trying to say.

The Onslaught of Media

The national and world media were captivated by KJLH's coverage and its direct access to celebrities and political leaders. As a new day emerged — on the dawn of the second day of the uprising, Nelson and Reed attempted to sort out what was happening around them. They engaged in dialogue with Russ Parr, a Dallas radio personality at KJMC 100.3 FM. The escalating death toll framed much of the discussion that would air throughout the second day.

Rico Reed: Well they pulled African Americans out of cars. Carl was over there when it first erupted on Florence and Normandy and it was hell. That's what we were just saying a few minutes ago on the air.

Russ Parr: And I think part of the problem is, I know you have got TV cameras sitting in your face right now, and I'm sure ABC and NBC, everybody's there, but I think right now we don't need that kind of exposure. I know it's sweeps week and everybody wants the ratings and everything, but where is the responsibility? Where are journalists, when are the journalists there going to take responsibility for what they're doing? They're whoring the public and to me, I think that's a travesty. You're only inciting, and it's wrong. You know, forget your ratings. You know, because these people are not represented — I've been trying to tell people here, these people that you see running like animals in the streets are not representative or indicative of the kind of people that are in Los Angeles.

Rico Reed: Well Russ, just to reiterate on what you're saying and add something. No, the people that are running the streets are not the total view of what Los Angeles is all about. There are good people out there. We have hundreds of phone calls, I guess by now, thousands of phone calls we've fielded over the air and talked to people off the air that are concerned. They don't like the violence in the streets; yes they're upset about the King verdict. You know, I know people in Dallas probably feel the same way. Somebody should have been guilty; I mean, out of all of it, I would have been personally satisfied if Powell was guilty of excessive force. That would have satisfied me. But to have everybody basically acquitted, not guilty and have Powell just on a hung jury. Yes, they can retry him, but wait a minute. How can you look at a video tape and tell me that you can't see it.

Russ Parr: Well let me say this Rico. In perspective, I would love for the people in Los Angeles to look at the loss of life. What is the death toll now Carl?

Carl Nelson: The death toll is 29.

Russ Parr: 29 people.

Rico Reed: What's the injury total now? That's important too.

Russ Parr: 200.

Rico Reed: It's over 300.

Russ Parr: Well look at those police officers that got off. If you look at those people and then look at people who have died behind these police officers, it's not worth it.

Rico Reed: No, not at all. Not at all, Russ. It certainly isn't.

Celebrity Voices

A number of celebrities could be heard across those Los Angeles radio stations targeting the African American community, and some dropped into the KJLH studios at risk to their own life. The celebrity voices, many of which were African American, reached out to listeners to call out for peace on Black radio during the bleakest hours of South-Central Los Angeles.

Christian Slater: I've been watching daily, I've been in contact with everybody back in Los Angeles. My girlfriend, she just went and did the A.M.E. (African Methodist Episcopal Church) thing that Sinbad is running for the homeless? You know handing out cans of food and everything. She wanted me to say that it's safe down at Adams and Western, and that area.

Arsenio Hall: That's my church man. First A.M.E. God is always down there. You're safe if you're anywhere near First A.M.E.

Christian Slater: That's right. That's right. That's the church. So people are making a positive change there. Yeah I guess I just wanted to reiterate what Barbara was saying about make a change, change is something that I feel everyone is afraid of, but we've gotta develop courage to face this fear in a positive and peaceful way. We all gotta come together. We know positive changes were never made by using excessive force and the thing that we can do is register to vote and put people in office that can make positive change.... That is the key point that I want to make.

Other celebrities would encourage listeners to consider ways to redirect their time and energy away from complaining toward helping with solutions — and commending those already involved in the process of healing the community:

Denzel Washington: You know, listen. The money is not the important thing. Those who have, give. But everybody has time and effort and everybody should have concern and the important thing is to give your time and to show up and to come down and to be a part, be a part of the solution, instead of sitting back complaining about the problem. Be a part of the solution.

Jody Watley: I just wanted to make a comment as I'm sitting here, I just think it's pretty incredible as much as the media was here when everybody was looting and they were calling everybody savages and thugs, there's no media right now. There are people bringing food down here, there are people cleaning up. And I don't see any of the major ... stations that were down here covering all the devastation. They're not covering the positive actions that are going on.

Many KJLH radio personalities and African American deejays across Black America challenged the perspective of mainstream media and its coverage of the unfolding events. While Black radio called out for peaceful resolution and change in the political and justice system, many mainstream outlets seemed to fan the flames with sensational headlines and images offering little contextualization regarding the complexities of the issues involved and the events happening, particularly giving little to no voice to African Americans in South Central Los Angeles who struggled physically and emotionally to make sense out of what was occurring around their homes.

Ear to the Ground

KJLH is a station that advocates family, community, and abundant life. Its ownership and legacy in Los Angeles — and as part of the greater story of African American radio-laid a foundation of trust and credibility among its audience. The cornerstone of KJLH is a gospel of community service embodied by the African American song and struggle, actualized through faith and empowered, and at best, by a network of Black business owners. Historically, Black radio became the vehicle to express cultural and spiritual renaissance in the heart of South Central, and African American business leaders envisioned radio as a way to elevate the community, politically and socially. To grasp KJLH's role in its community is to understand its location, examining it within a social and geographic soundscape. KJLH is a station with its programming fashioned to address the daily concerns of its audience as well as those critical moments that no one can be fully prepared to comprehend or to explain to listeners. KJLH is a station that has its metaphorical ear to the ground; it is a station that listens to its audience, partly due to its location.

Information Is Power

Dick Gregory, long-time supporter of KJLH, has watched the station handle social and political unrest across the airwaves while touching the hearts, minds and souls of its listeners and community on a daily basis. Richard Claxton "Dick" Gregory was born October 12, 1932, in St. Louis, Missouri. He is a highly influential African American comic and commentator, author and speaker, actor and philosopher, nutritionist and overcomer, and long-time civil rights leader and activist. Gregory points out that the small independent station with a big voice has continually reached out to its community of listeners and further connected them to the larger Black community across America and the world. KJLH has empowered them through the station's mission of bringing relevant cultural information and perspective to its audience, filling in the gaps and sometimes contrasting with that of mainstream media. During a May 13, 2002, interview, Gregory explained, "I don't know how any area could function without a radio station like KJLH.... Every day for an hour and a half, they deal with issues on a worldwide level, local level and national level, and they call the people who are involved. So if something happens in ... the Black community, you can be guaranteed that the issue is going to be discussed within a matter of days." He continued, indicating that KJLH is one of those rare full-service stations that still exist in the U.S.:

KJLH is a music station that has talk, and it has one of the largest audiences of any station I know. It's amazing. I think one of the thrills for me is waking up every morning and knowing that there is a station on the planet that deals with issues. You see, I love it. I read about 600 hours worth of newspapers every 10 days. I'm not only a news junkie, but I'm a junkie for putting it out to the masses of the people to hear. And I have a personal feeling [for KJLH] because it gives me an outlet of information.

Gregory understands KJLH's mission as one of empowerment to its community of listeners: "So I've always felt that money is not power, education is not power, but information is power. If you get bad information, you have bad power. And this is a story of a station that gives you information." He frames his perspective against the increasing consolidation of media, where the Black voice is diminished and disempowered, and entrance into the radio business as a minority is nearly impossible:

There's almost nothing you can do when you're talking about consolidation. You still got banks that are not loaning Black people money. You've got White organizations that have done the research that say a Black person who's got an education is 85 percent less likely to not get a loan for a mortgage as a White who drops out of high school. So you're at the mercy of a White racist system. And when the prices move up to out of your range, you're in trouble.

For Gregory, the social, political, and economic issues behind consolidation are similar to those that drive the market of every business within the U.S.: "You can sit and blame an agency like the FCC. But what about the agency that regulates oil (laugh), or the agency that regulates safety (laugh), or regulates our food? All of them serve at the whim of big business. So why would you expect one not to serve that way when the rest don't?" He continues, "Look at all the medicine that they end up taking off the market after people died, after everything's already been approved. It would be lovely if everything functioned right." Gregory offers no immediate solution other than to offer a glimpse into the reality that independently Black owned stations like KJLH confront daily in order to survive against market forces and governmental regulation that does little in the way of ensuring transmission of culturally relevant information and programming across the airwaves. He concludes, "So the FCC is not an example of where you can go to get help. You've never been able to get help [from it]. Any time a president of the United States spends over 400 million dollars in a campaign to get a job that pays less than 300,000, you don't have to be too smart to know what that's about. That's America" (Gregory, personal communication, 2002).

In 2001, FCC chairman William Kennard stepped down as the chief of the top communications regulatory agency in the U.S. As the first African American to lead the organization, he was committed toward improving diversity in station ownership and employment in the media industry ("Black FCC," 2001), a priority that was continually undermined by the financial interests of larger media corporations. In 1999, he had called for the reestablishment of tax certificates favorable to minority groups and women to boost ownership in response to rampant consolidation within the industry prompted by the 1996 Telecommunications Act ("FCC chief," 1999). He left office before he was able to achieve his goals, but he did provide an opportunity for owners like Stevie Wonder to tell their story in a 1999 FCC hearing investigating localism, challenging requests by major corporations for continued deregulation of communication legislation and community outrage to blatant abuse of media corporate power evidenced, in part, by a decline in independent radio ownership by African Americans.

Outline of the Book

Chapter 1 positions KJLH geographically and socially within its community, introduces the primary storytellers and relevant literature, and elaborates on the methods used for this study. The city of KJLH's license, after its technical upgrade in recent years, extends its reach beyond Compton to Hollywood, Los Angeles. In Chapter 2, the author, referencing her 10-year qualitative study of the station, examines how community-centric themes have consistently inspired KJLH's programming decisions to date. The primary themes of community empowerment, unity, and service that came forth from this investigation were pivotal toward understanding KJLH's role in preserving and serving the multitude of voices that comprise its listener base. Themes of unification and empowerment are not contained to only KJLH's listeners but seemingly benefit the larger community of South Central. The idea that radio can be perceived as a public sphere as well as a counterpublic sphere is discussed in Catherine Squires' (2000) article on "Black Talk Radio" in the *Harvard International Journal of Press/Politics*. Nancy Dawson (1994a/b) elaborates on this idea of a Black counterpublic which provides the means toward alternative viewpoints to mainstream thought in the journal *Public Culture* and examines race and class in African American politics in her book *Behind the*

Mule, published by Princeton University Press. It becomes evident that KJLH has served as a counterpublic sphere through its ability to connect with a culturally specific community of listeners; particularly this is revealed within the *Front Page* transcripts of the 1992 civil unrest as well as through its sponsored events and daily discussions. KJLH is thus a safe haven that provides oppositional opportunity for otherwise neglected communities of thought and action.

Chapters 3 and 4 contextualize KJLH's mission within the heritage of Black radio, with the former providing an overview of the early history of African American radio and its evolution on the West Coast. The work of Nelson George's (1988) *The Death of Rhythm & Blues*, Louis Cantor's (1992) *Wheelin' on the Beale*, and William Barlow's (1999) *Voice Over: The Making of Black Radio* reveal a portrait of African American radio as it progressed, developed, and was absorbed within mainstream corporate infrastructures. Regardless, Black radio has a story to tell today as well as in the past.

Chapter 4 begins with some issues that remain unresolved for the radio and recording industry and its community, particularly the upsurge of street violence and controversial lyrics promoted by the market strategies of major corporate players in the radio and recording industry. Black and urban radio stations that are White owned and some that are part of Black owned large media corporations succeed at times through sensational tactics and strategies, rather than connecting listeners through issues. Radio talk host and political activist Al Sharpton, as well as some prominent African American musicians and radio programmers, have been outspoken against this trend, calling for community friendly stations. In *Black Journalism Review Online*, Earl Ofari Hutchinson (1999) in the article "Endangered Black Radio" called attention to a national decline in Black and urban radio ownership and how that would lead to a continual downward spiral away from culturally specific programming that tapped into the needs of its audience. Hutchinson is a political and social issues analyst and commentator that can be heard weekly on KJLH's *Front Page*. KJLH management remains committed to serving in the public interest in a respectful manner, keeping in mind its mission to cater to its audience as a family and community station.

Chapter 5 examines KJLH's economic role in the community, as well as the ongoing struggle of independent Black-owned radio against corporate media consolidation. Kofi A. Ofori (1999; 2002) prepared reports for the Minority Media & Telecommunications Council and the FCC critical to understanding minority ownership as impacted by industry advertising practices and local market consolidation — economic forces that have created hardships for independent minority owned stations. The FCC has a checkered history when it comes to promoting diversity on the airwaves through legislation and policies favorable to women and minority groups, even when research demonstrates best practices by minority and female broadcasters.

Chapters 6 and 7 bring us into the heart of the riots — KJLH's coverage and response to its community under duress. The chapters follow the story of KJLH in its coverage of the issues, the creation of *Front Page*, and the station's response to the civil unrest. Chapter 8 draws upon the community dialogue behind KJLH's message of empowerment directed to listeners as a means toward peaceful change within the political system. This message was put forth across the airwaves during the unrest and echoed in the aftermath and remains a mission today for the station. Interestingly, information and promotion by Black-targeted local media, as with community-centric stations like KJLH, increases the likelihood of a greater voter turnout among African Americans, according to Oberholzer-Gee and Waldfogel (2001) in their investigation of the effect of minority population on minority turnout.

Chapter 9 commemorates the 10th anniversary of the Los Angeles civil unrest in 2002, reviewing the station's on- and off-air response to the crisis at hand. This chapter takes a look at KJLH's efforts to help rebuild its business community and maintain its role in the community as a business and service — a dual responsibility critical to Black radio, as espoused in Mark Newman's *Entrepreneurs of Profit and Pride: From Black Appeal to Radio Soul* (1988). KJLH's role as a legacy station, still independently and African American owned, is contrasted to the increasingly competitive radio environment.

Chapter 10 offers some concluding remarks related to keeping the peace within the African American community by ensuring preservation of Black-owned stations like KJLH. The chapter provides a summary and retrospective of where the station has been and why it must march forward. The book concludes with an epilogue from E. Steven Collins, director of urban marketing and external relations for Radio One. He is a 30 year broadcast veteran and still works in the Philadelphia market. He was the national sales manager of WDAS-AM/FM when I interviewed him near the 10th anniversary of the Los Angeles Riots. He had worked with KJLH to transmit its signal across the East Coast and then to the world.

Collins describes what he believes to be the soul of Black radio, the essence of which cannot be packaged and sold to African Americans en masse, but rather must be appreciated and preserved for its historical significance and continued relevance to daily life.

Note: The names of listeners who called into the station during the traumatic series of events during the Los Angeles Riots were changed to provide them with privacy and anonymity. The original audio recordings are stored at KJLH-FM studios.

CHAPTER 1

KJLH on Location

Soundscapes from South Crenshaw

The anguished cries of families whose members were sold away; the repetitive crack of the master's or overseer's whip; these were emblematic sounds for captive African Americans, stark "aural reminders." — White & White, *The Sounds of Slavery: Discover African American History through Songs, Sermons, and Speech* (p 3).

An important event occurred on April 29, 1992, in America's second largest media market when a Simi Valley jury acquitted four members of the Los Angeles Police Department accused of beating Rodney King. Within hours of the verdict, vivid scenes of a public uprising in the streets of South Central Los Angeles were beamed around the world. By nine o'clock that evening, the mayor of Los Angeles declared a state of emergency. This book is not about the trial, the Los Angeles Police Department or Rodney King, although each plays a key role. It is about the actions of one small Compton, California, radio station in the wake of this historical event.

It is also about how a subset of United States broadcasting — Black radio — reacts during critical issues and events in American history. It wasn't merely what was seen on the streets of South Central Los Angeles that is etched as memories in the minds of those who lived through the events. Anger, tears, and voiced fears filled the air, accompanied by an overwhelming roar from the buildings engulfed in flames and a low rumble emanating from beneath the blaze. On their car radios and inside their homes in the neighboring districts, listeners tuned into KJLH to hear what was going on and to find solace through their calls into the station. They listened to KJLH day and night, and they knew they were not alone. These have

17

become the "emblematic sounds" and the "stark 'aural reminders'" that compose a significant piece of the soundscape from the Los Angeles riots (White and White, 2005, p 3).

In 1992, KJLH was one of a hundred or so FM radio stations in the United States owned by a Black American; in the case of KJLH that owner was best known by his stage name, Stevie Wonder. The radio station was at the time located on Crenshaw Boulevard in the heart of South Central Los Angeles, the epicenter of the riots. The station's geographic location, of course, gave its staff a (sometimes all too dramatic) bird's eye view of the events following the verdict, but it also was critical to *why* KJLH intervened. Karen Slade was the company's vice president and general manager in 1992 and remains at the helm today. Though it is located within the number two U.S. radio market, she told me that her station remains in many ways much like a small-market station: "My location is such that I am the community station. My listeners believe they own me. They can trust me, and I have a large degree of credibility."

News that affects the community therefore is extremely important for a station like KJLH. However, in 1992, news departments were being reduced or eliminated because of the bottom line, but not at KJLH. According to Slade, "Small independent stations cannot afford two full-time news people, but I consider it an investment." So while Slade was defying the corporate logic of the time, she was also occasionally seen by her staff as stepping on the mores of broadcast journalism. "My news people see themselves as journalists first and foremost, and they hate for me to mention 'you are also a black male and a black female. You can bring that to the story and enrich the story without embellishing it and not lose your objectivity.'" Such ideals were tested in 1992.

3847 South Crenshaw Boulevard: Compton Studios

Two former students, Jonathan Pluskota and Tejai Maxwell, who were familiar with the Los Angeles area joined me for a site visit to the original KJLH-FM studios. Gathering information regarding the approaching 10th anniversary of the Los Angeles riots topped our agenda. A visit to the former site helped me to visualize the April 1992 events. It was here on South Crenshaw Boulevard in Spring 1992 that two station deejays looked out the studio window to watch the civil unrest unfold before their microphones. Driving through the South Central neighborhood a decade later, it was difficult for us to imagine the massive destruction that had taken place in the community around the original KJLH location. Some buildings were still crumbled around West Boulevard and Florence, but they were not obvious at first glance when we drove into the neighborhoods. The boulevard had a steady pace of cars and trucks during the days that we visited KJLH. From our vantage points, only a few people here and there walked down the sidewalk or crossed the boulevard to a store. The neighborhood was a mix of bungalows sandwiched in between businesses, and in some instances these businesses were once homes. Many of the houses had iron bars secured across the windows and doors, but that practice among residents seemed to be fairly common within many of the business districts throughout southern Los Angeles.

161 N. La Brea Avenue: Inglewood Studios

The station was relocated in Inglewood (about five minutes away from its original location) after its lease had expired on the 3847 South Crenshaw property in the late 1990s. It was a Monday afternoon that we visited the former KJLH studios, which once shared space with a funeral home. That story, too, is forthcoming. Much earlier that day, we headed toward the new KJLH studios; the streets were quiet — not a car in sight. I sat in the passenger seat and soaked in my surroundings. After a 20 minute drive, including a quick stop for doughnuts along the way, it was about 4 A.M. when we arrived at the Inglewood studios. We parked in the gated parking garage under the KJLH offices. The station's garage is located directly in front of the Inglewood Police Station. This is not really the ideal place to situate the station given the acrimonious relationship between some police officers and residents in the nearby neighborhoods and the somewhat historical hostility toward news and public affairs personnel armed with an investigative spirit. We entered KJLH through the back door, went up the stairs past the front door to the lobby and then turned left and kept walking until the hallway ended. Ten years earlier, the KJLH staff could look out the big picture window to observe the looting and then burning of the Crenshaw Square Mall that was directly across the street. Now at the Inglewood location, radio personalities and reporters were tucked away in a rear corner of the building. Was this coincidental? Or perhaps, it was merely the best use of the space. The overnight gospel deejay welcomed us, and we spoke to him for about 20 minutes. He was a schoolteacher who was about to go home long enough to eat and change before he headed for his full-time job.

I was scheduled to meet Jamaal Goree, then co-host and producer of the weekday news magazine program *Front Page* that preceded the morning drive-time show. He arrived about 5 minutes before his show was scheduled to begin that morning at 4:30. I spent the next two hours in the on-air studio, observing Goree coordinate all the programmatic elements. On this particular day, he was dressed casually in an oversized shirt with jeans. His comfortable appearance reflected his on-air style and presentation. He seemed very relaxed and natural as he conversed with lead host Carl Nelson and the morning's guest, Dr. Vicki Hufnagle. Consistent phone and e-mail response to the show indicated that a number of people were listening; Goree added that Los Angeles reporters typically tuned into the show looking for a news scoop on particular issues impacting the African American and larger community.

Nelson hosted *Front Page* live from his newly acquired Florida station, while Goree simultaneously produced the show from KJLH's on-air studio. Goree worked the phones locally in Inglewood and coordinated the e-mails across the United States. The show had developed an impressive East Coast audience via the Internet. Nelson, long-time KJLH news director, had purchased a Caribbean-formatted station; however, he agreed to host *Front Page* from afar. Nelson, along with others, was instrumental in transforming the show's content from light entertainment chatter to serious investigative discussion with call-ins in 1992 (leading up to and during the riots and subsequent years).

Nelson and Goree have moved on to pursue other work, both leaving KJLH several years ago. Nevertheless, the 10th anniversary of the 1992 civil unrest invited a moment to pause and reflect on KJLH's role within the local community and among its African American audience; it was as if time had stood still for this critical analysis. On this particular Monday, January 29, 2002, it was as if the Los Angeles riots, and all those events leading up to it, might happen again at any moment. Many issues that had trigged the rebellion had not been resolved. Emotions were intense on the streets and airwaves, and there were calls for community discussions and activism. The station crew was only months away from a historical retrospective of the unrest. I spent much of the morning with Goree, who started working with the show in 1992 after the uprising. He told me:

I guess I was brought in to put a different spin on the show, an edge on the show, that wasn't here prior to the rebellion. The show was a little different, it was a little more, I would say, entertainment oriented and after the rebellion nobody wanted to talk about subjects that you could get on MTV or E-TV. Our community was burning — and our community wanted something; they wanted a forum where they could express their rage, their anger, and obviously, we had a voice that wasn't getting the kind of airplay or getting the forum that they needed — and so KJLH began to become that forum.

Issues discussed on KJLH regularly provide an alternate viewpoint to those broadcast on the mainstream media. Today's show featured Dr. Hufnagle, a female physician who appeared to have blown the whistle on the medical community, noting questionable ethical practices and social justice concerns. The theme presented an intriguing perspective, one proposing a sort of conspiracy theory in which political institutions and the media cannot be trusted for complete and accurate information related to the concerns and issues of the African American community. The topic is not directly relevant to the 1992 civil unrest, but it does shed light on the investigative, civic, and interactive nature of *Front Page* (as well as the lack of culturally specific information available on mainstream media).

The discussion involved her attempt to expose unethical and illegal gynecological care provided to African American women in the U.S. Hufnagle was not in the studio and neither was Nelson. In an amazing display of electronic coordination, Goree connected Nelson, Hufnagle, and listeners via phone lines and the Internet. The KJLH hosts communicated with each other through traditional broadcast and computer technology during the entire program. The studio seemed small because it was crammed with equipment, but in reality it was fairly large (approximately 15 by 25 feet).

I sat on a wooden stool facing Goree as he stood behind an expansive radio console that cut across the width of the studio; the console was connected to multiple computers, phone lines and, let's just say, lots of buttons. As he kept the show moving along swiftly, he never missed a beat. The fast interaction between Nelson and Goree seemed to intensify the pacing of the show, and it sounded as if both hosts were in the same room. Perhaps it was just the topic that was engaging — like something from a spy thriller:

> *Dr. Hufnagle:* Well they didn't want you to give women options. They wanted everybody to have a hysterectomy and they wanted everyone to shut up

about it and just let it go on. Well what would happen is, if a patient I operated on and saved her uterus, I would be flagged. The insurance company would take the records, send them to the attorney general's office, not pay me, so that I wouldn't make any money, and then use the records against me to try to bring me down. Meanwhile, the patient never signed a consent [form], never released the records, and this is what the scam was — how they controlled the practice of medicine because they can control policy this way. Now I have the audio cassette tape.... Well guess what? They broke down my door. They took my things; they terrorized me; they took my own mammogram — thank God that the Watts Community Center took care of me. I was destitute. They took great care of me and, you know, I'm [a] white-Caucasian woman. I'm going into Watts to be helped by the Black community — by the Black community. The Medical Board (I had an abnormal mammogram) took my records so I couldn't even get medical care [*Front Page*, 2002a].

Hufnagle's story could be potentially heard across the world. *Front Page* had matured since the civil unrest of 1992. Goree (personal communication, 2002) explained that through the Internet, the program had extended its ability to empower with information the larger African American community across the U.S. Its primary goal is to serve its South Central audience, but it is providing an alternative forum to listeners across the country that is virtually untapped in other radio markets:

We are cultivating a national audience, you know, because as you were saying, for this type of programming — it's not on mainstream radio. People are searching for it, and so they're finding it on the Internet, but our show started to become really familiar to folks across the country just by audiotape. People will buy a copy of the show or they would make their own copy and send it across country. And this was happening.... [O]h it still happens, you know, and then you got the bootleggers out there who make copies; they have to have a career. I know some guys that have built homes on our show, you know. But, nevertheless, it's helped to build a national audience, and so maybe syndication is in the future ... I think that New York, New Orleans, Chicago, Atlanta, Washington, D.C., and Philadelphia, these are areas where we have our larger listeners on the Internet, especially in New York.... It's great for them because it's 7:30 there — it's still hell for us 'cause it is 4:30 [Goree, 2002].

Goree (2002) points out that *Front Page* gets "calls from the [*Los Angeles*] *Times*. On many days, some of its reporters want to follow up on something, or find out who our guest was, or how to contact them. We were on ABC World News ... years ago during the O.J. Simpson trial."

The show ended at approximately 5:50 A.M., and then Goree and Nelson related a few reminders about upcoming station promotions and quizzed listeners on history trivia. In this brief excerpt, the commitment to its primarily but not exclusively African American audience appears evident:

> *Jamaal Goree:* Just a couple of announcements. Carl and the *Front Page* family — we want everybody to join our authors' study club. They're going to be hosting a free Black history bus tour and that will be taking place this Saturday, February 2nd, leaving from the Consolidated Reality Board, 3725 Don Felipe Drive. It is free and there's plenty of free parking. Also, for those of you that want to go with us to Africa, now the seats may be taken. I didn't get the final tally on that.... And as always, if you have any information for the *Front Page*, or topics for discussion, you need to e-mail us at *Front Page* at kjlhradio.com. That's it for the announcements, Carl.
>
> *Carl Nelson:* Alright, we have a pair of passes to give away to see the new movie, *Collateral Damage* that stars Arnold Schwarzenegger at the Howard Hughes Promenade, that's around by the Fox Hills area — and this is for Thursday, February 5th; it starts at 7:30, and you can win these passes if you know the answer to Jamaal's question. What's the question, Jamaal?
>
> *Jamaal Goree:* Okay, *Front Page* family, let's put on those thinking caps and all think "Black" this morning. Name the African American NASA mission specialist who was killed when the space shuttle *Challenger* exploded on this day in the year 1986 — name this man [Ronald McNair].
>
> *Carl Nelson:* 5-2-0 K-J-L-H is the number to call if you know the answer to Jamaal's question. I want to remind you that the comments expressed on the *Front Page* are not necessarily those of our advertisers or the management staff of KJLH. *Front Page* is the property of KJLH Radio, which retains the rights to rebroadcast these programs [*Front Page*, 2002a].

Then, Nelson closed the show, by quoting author Kamau Ramsey, "From her book, '*No' Means Find Another Way To Do It!: And Other Mental Morsels*: 'Evil thoughts when met by opportunity become evil deeds.' You stay strong, stay positive, Cliff and Janine are coming up next, God willing."

I continued my conversation with Goree after the show ended. He pointed out that the word rebellion, not riots, more accurately depicted the intent or original motivation of some South Central residents involved in the civil strife. Once the violence erupted, the streets went wild. For many, anger was birthed from a series of escalating circumstances, and the intention of many participants was to rebel against governmental infrastructures that offered no solution or recourse. South Central has not recovered economically and spiritually, Goree explained. Near the end of the interview, one of my assistants, accompanying me at the station, asked, "What did it feel like to be in the middle of a riot?" Goree repeated the question, and sighed. You could read his expression: "Didn't we understand? Did we not get what he was saying, or what happened to this community?" Then he boldly and authoritatively asked, "Do you really want to know what it's like to be in a riot? From a bird's eye point of view?" He explained that he had been on the streets of South Central in the middle of all the craziness and the images still haunt him. He continued:

> Do you want to know what it's like to be in one of those stores as it's burning and seeing people literally turning into animals as they are scrounging for goods, and, I mean, do you really want to know what it's like to see someone dragged out of their car, beaten, and their car turned over and lit on fire. I saw this with my own eyes. I was shocked at how comfortable some people were in that environment [Goree, personal communication, 2002].

That morning he described the mayhem on the streets that first night of the civil unrest, and reminded us that the streets and certain areas of South Central were still scarred by the violence. That discussion is for a later chapter. Goree was one of several personalities, among others, interviewed for this book. The interviewees recorded for this project, though their words and emotion, help reveal the collective voice behind the KJLH microphone.

The Ordinary and Extraordinary Community of Listeners

A long line of people stood outside the KJLH studios as they waited for the city bus. KJLH is situated on a busy street that runs through the heart of town, a location that fits its role in the city. It is part of the pulse of the community. Politicians, celebrities and listeners have walked in and out of the station, past the glass doors and into the reception area. The famous and ordinary comprise the listener base of KJLH, whether online or on the dial. KJLH understands its role as a community advocate; beyond that, KJLH personnel do not view themselves as objective observers. They understand the issues because they invite the community to help shape the programming. KJLH is not unique in its ability to hear beyond the majority viewpoints. African American radio has historically served as a social institution within its respective communities. It has offered a venue for conversations often unheard across mainstream media. KJLH is a dramatic example of how Black radio works for the community, by being part of the community.

Oral Contextualization

For two decades, I have conducted site visits to African American stations in Philadelphia, Memphis, Houston, and Los Angeles. In the early 1990s, KJLH station manager Karen Slade and *Front Page* host Carl Nelson agreed to some initial phone conversations, and that would spring forth into a series of interviews with them and other staff employees. In those early years, I worked collaboratively with a professorial colleague, Thomas A. Birk, who also taught at Southern Illinois University. It would be nearly 10 years later before that dialogue would trigger this larger study of KJLH's role in the civil unrest of 1992 and its subsequent community involvement. I have since kept in touch with the station, following the people and stories behind the microphone.

The bottom line is that a commercially licensed, low watt radio station played a significant role in its community and the world during the Los Angeles Riots. On April 29, 1992, KJLH opened its airwaves to its listeners, the community, and world media to assuage fear and speak peace into the lives of those of South Central. I have had the opportunity to review archives, scrapbooks, memorandums, and other materials within KJLH's offices and on-air studio. A significant portion of the data collected for this study was transcribed from audio recordings of KJLH's 1992 coverage, particularly the Extended Edition of *Front Page,* as it was referred to during the on-air broadcast. The decision to open the airwaves to listeners, and the subsequent interactive nature of the dialogue between KJLH's moderators and listeners, was evaluated within the context of the station's organizational mission, institutional setting and unique experiences. The larger context of culturally specific media, in this instance Black radio, was especially relevant to understanding why the station decided to drop all regular programming and offer continuous coverage of the events, including ongoing dialogue between listeners and station hosts. Transcripts from *Front Page* recordings (20 cassette tapes) added another dimension to what originally aired on Wednesday, April 29, 1992, through Saturday, May 2, 1992. The *Front Page* transcriptions offer a play-by-play account of the civil uprising and the subsequent events, as broadcast live on KJLH. The on-air exchange was initiated by KJLH's moderators and shaped by the ongoing influx of calls into the studio. A written record of this dialogue is captured through transcription.

Meeting the many station personnel for the first time was a memorable experience. Although my list of contacts grows longer daily, what follows is a profile of the primary people who have helped me to tell the story of KJLH.

Karen Slade began working at KJLH in 1989. Years earlier, she had earned an undergraduate degree in broadcasting and telecommunications from Kent State, and a Masters of Business Administration from Pepperdine University. Before becoming general manager at KJLH, she worked her "way up through product launches and project management" (Slade, personal communication, 2001) to regional sales manager at the Xerox Corporation. As the vice president and general manager of KJLH, she directly oversees every aspect of the station's operation, including personnel, from sales, programming, and engineering to community outreach. She is the front line person for KJLH, entrusted by the owner to create and execute policy.

Carl Nelson, former KJLH news director, began his broadcast career in 1971 at WYNT-AM in New York, and within four years he was working for the legendary WLIB-AM and WBLS-FM. In 1980, he became the KJLH news director and was responsible for the birth and expansion of its daily news show *Front Page* in the early 1990s. *Front Page* is the vehicle that Nelson used to propel KJLH's news department into a global arena. He was named the 1996 News Director of the Year by *Black Radio Exclusive* magazine. This award was perhaps the culmination of all his successes through the years. For a brief stint, while hosting KJLH's *Front Page*, Nelson owned Mystik WSRF (1580 AM), a local Caribbean music-talk station in Ft. Lauderdale. WSRF talk programs included *South Florida Speaks Out* that aired weekdays from 11 A.M. to 1 P.M. and *Feedback* on Mondays from 7 P.M. to 9 P.M. Other programming included *The International Link with Lance O*, a call-in show that encouraged listeners to send link-ups worldwide to family and friends from New York, London, and Jamaica. The station has since been sold, and Nelson has moved on to other business ventures. He has not been part of KJLH for nearly five years, but his contributions to the news department have been part of the station's legacy.

Several local newspapers in Los Angeles over the years, and others across the U.S. (i.e., in Florida and Ohio), have quoted Nelson regarding his perspective on a number of topics, including the Rodney King and Reginald Denny trials ("L.A. Enjoys," 1992; Rollins, 1993), the Simpson case ("Simpson," 1996; Michaelson, 1995), and the Central Intelligence Agency's alleged involvement in the spread of crack cocaine (Hawkins, 2002). In these articles, he had shared his perspective on the significance of Black radio as an important social and political institution within the U.S., calling forth well-deserved acknowledgment of the format's legacy in community service and empowerment.

Radio personality Eric "Rico" Reed has worked in Los Angeles radio for many years, bringing to KJLH his on-air experience. He most recently worked for Radio One, until the company sold its urban station in 2008. He played a critical role in the coverage of the 1992 uprising that cannot be ignored. He offered depth in emotion and keen observation of the events that surrounded him and Nelson; his coverage of the story as it unfolded on the air offered a first-hand account of what transpired during those critical hours, and it is still available on tape. His perspective at the helm of *Front Page*—along with Nelson—is a powerful story. Reed and Nelson share their story of the L.A. unrest, along with Slade and Stephens, as primary gatekeepers of the news and information flow, from coverage of the trials to the aftermath of the rioting. All four interviewees were key players in the coverage of the 1992 events; they merely had to look and listen outside the KJLH studio in some instances.

In 1992, Jacquie Stephens was working as a news reporter and anchor at KJLH. At that time, she reported to News Director Carl Nelson. Prior to her arrival, Stephens had performed similar jobs in Iowa and Denver. Since Nelson's departure several years ago, she has served as the public affairs and news director, and hosts the weekly show *L.A. Speaks Out* on Saturday mornings. The 60-minute program has featured California Supreme Court judges as well as politicians and community leaders. Through the years, Stephens has organized and hosted a number of high-profile KJLH forums, including a two-hour radio forum called *Rhythm Rap Session* that created an opportunity for listeners and several rap artists — Dr. Dre, Ice Cube, Snoop Doggy Dog, King T, and Queen Latifah, among others — to discuss the theme of violence in rap music. In September 1992, Stephens interviewed Los Angeles Police Department (LAPD) officer Ted Brisano and a community reporter from the *Los Angeles Sentinel*. In 1994, Stephens' program made headlines in the *Los Angeles Sentinel* for her interview of Mayor Richard Riordan on the earthquake damage in southern Los Angeles. Ten years after the 1992 Los Angeles Riots, Stephens hosted a special anniversary edition of *Speaks Out*, in which community leaders gathered to discuss the city's progress and problems. In 2008, she has had much success with her health forums, drawing men and women from greater Los Angeles together for information and screenings, with one event attracting more than 3,000 women. Another well attended event for men only involved coordinating 22 barbershops from Compton to Wilshire, across South Central, to serve as centers for health information and screenings.

Other Storytellers

Jamaal Goree was co-host and producer of *Front Page* with Nelson after the uprising, and long before that he was a community activist. He has hosted the issues program *Talking Drum Community Forum*, a neighborhood town meeting that had regularly aired on KJLH at one time. The show continues as a forum to gather and inform community members in South Central neighborhoods on a variety of critical social, economic and spiritual issues. The show once stirred the curiosity of CBS' *60 Minutes* because of its producers' keen understanding of concerns relevant to the African American community, its behind-the-scenes investigative team and its alleged informal link to the Black Panthers that had provided insights into issues not readily available to mainstream media. Goree's accomplishments include being the president and owner of African Renaissance Productions, a company that produces educational materials, co-founder of a video documentary company called Kemet Nu Productions, and manager of a Web based radio station called Inner Light Radio. On October 31, 2008, *Talking Drum* offered a pre-election day public forum and a free screening of Peter Joseph's film *Zeitgeist: Addendum* to provoke social thought. Goree moderated the discussion.

"Well-known around the community as a marketing person, I work with a lot of churches, that's actually ... where my base is," is how Greg Johnson, KJLH marketing director, describes his relationship with the community. He spoke of the station's philosophical mission and its strong partnership with area churches. Before KJLH, he was involved with the Community Development Corporation "doing everything from feeding the homeless to literacy programs and all of that, and I produce a banquet for them every year, and that's what really started making me interact with politics and everything." He started in radio as a national radio syndicator "so he was flying all over the country, Chicago, New York, Miami, all these places, doing sales and marketing."

Other interviews included political activist Dick Gregory, who lives in Washington, D.C., and lectures at campuses across the U.S. E. Steven Collins was the former news director and promotions director at long-time

Black-owned WDAS-AM/FM before it was purchased by Clear Channel Communications. He worked as the WDAS-AM/FM national sales manager before becoming director of urban marketing and external relations for Radio One in Philadelphia.

I also interviewed Tracy Marrow, who is better known as the rapper and movie actor Ice-T. His aunt in South Central raised him after his parents died in a car accident. He attended Crenshaw High School. I interviewed Ice-T during his appearance at the Shryock Auditorium at Southern Illinois University, Carbondale, in the spring of 2002. Many other voices contributed to this project, especially the hundreds of listeners who called into the station during the heat of the unrest.

Mending the Gaps

Oral narratives fill in information gaps when an event is undocumented, ignored, or examined through a narrow lens by reporters or historians. Passage of time might also allow for reinterpretation of the events; details sometimes become muddied as time passes and as people age (Watson, 1989). Sometimes, voices once overlooked contribute new perspectives and information. Data collected through archives and transcripts can be used to enrich and provide credibility to oral history as a methodological tool. Oral history is significant to the African American culture, and therefore is relevant to this study of a Black-owned radio station that caters to a mostly Black audience. Of particular importance to this study is the use of interview and transcription of the on-air interaction between hosts and their primarily African American audience during KJLH's response to the uprising in April 1992.

The extent to which one should revise, reconstruct, and interpret historical events within an African American perspective has been extensively examined and debated among social scientists (Hoover, 1970; Watson, 1989). In the past 60 years, oral histories have attempted to elaborate on events, and even to question and reexamine the facts, so to speak, through primary sources. There is more than one side to every story, and there are numerous untold stories that come to surface years after an event, as demonstrated by a number of books written by White and African American historians, journalists, and laymen: *Deep South* (Davis, Gardner and Gardner, 1941); *Growing Up in the Black Belt: Negro Youth in the Rural South* (Johnson, 1941); *You Gotta Deal with It* (Kennedy, 1980); *Praise the*

Bridge That Carries You Over: The Life of Joseph L. Sutton (Krech, 1981); *Drylongso: Self Portrait of Black America* (Gwalthney, 1981); *Book of Negro Folklore* (Hughes and Bontemps, 1983); *Tell My Horse* (Hurston, 1983); *The Village* (Watson, 1989); *Twilight, Los Angeles, 1992: On the Road: The Search for American Character* (Smith, 1994); *All We Had Was Each Other* (Wallis, 1998); and *Martin Luther King, Jr.* (Moldovan, 1999).

In his *Radio Free Dixie*, Timothy Tyson (1999) conducted four interviews with Robert E. Williams, a leading activist in the Black Power movement of the civil rights era, as well as with a number of others who knew him. The interviews were conducted over a three-year period (1993 to 1996). Tyson also reviewed interviews conducted by other writers, as well as transcripts and government documentation spanning nearly a century. He researched a number of articles pertaining to Williams' life and the Black freedom struggle itself. Williams inspired and narrated the 90-minute *Radio Free Dixie* series of the 1960s that emanated from a station in Havana, Cuba. The series could be heard across the Southern states, along the East Coast, and even reached Saskatchewan, Canada. But the message was directed at the South, "calling upon the oppressed Negroes to rise and free themselves" (p. 287), a message so strong that it troubled some officials within the Federal Bureau of Investigation:

> Radio Free Dixie was both innovative and rooted in African American cultural traditions.... Williams mixed music with news about racial violence in Albany, Georgia, or voter registration campaigns in McComb, Mississippi, coverage from clippings that readers would send to and from a wide array of magazines and newspapers funneled through the Olsens in Toronto. Even after the CIA jamming and Cuban censorship eventually hobbled Radio Free Dixie, WBAI in New York and KPFA Radio in Berkeley, California, often rebroadcast the tapes. Bootleg copies circulated in Watts and Harlem [Tyson, 1999, p. 288].

According to Tyson (1999), the transcripts of these tapes were "more powerful" (p. 289) than the actual broadcasts. The transcripts were compiled into the book *Negroes with Guns* and represented the "storytelling tradition" (p. 289) that was important to the South. The book became one of "the classic documents of the black freedom struggle" (p. 289). Frank Greenwood's *If We Must Live*, a play adapted from *Negroes with Guns*, opened in July 1965 in Los Angeles' Watts area. Only one month later, a civil uprising broke out in Watts that resulted in the death of "at least 34 people, injured approximately 1,000 others, destroyed $200 million worth of property, and required 16,000 law enforcement agencies to subdue. Many far right observers, overstating their evidence and overlooking local realities, blamed Williams' influence in Los Angeles for the destruction" (Tyson, 1999, pp. 289–290).

Such oral testimony, according to Watson (1989), is "especially useful for documenting events and event sequences about places, people, and periods ... about which predecessors left no formal records except scattered newspaper clippings" (p. 151). William Barlow's (1999) *Voice Over: The Making of Black Radio*, an outgrowth of a chapter in *Split Image: African Americans in the Mass Media* (Dates and Barlow, 1993), was based on more than 150 interviews:

> Oral testimony was crucial to the project because the written material and recorded programming I uncovered on black radio showed significant historical gaps; probing the public memory was the only way to reconstruct the missing history. Yet I also had a methodological rationale for pursuing this line of research. I wanted the project to privilege the local and grassroots nature of black radio — to tell the story from the bottom up, and to do so as much as possible in the words of those who were involved [Barlow, 1999, p. xii].

In addition, Barlow's collection of oral histories was pivotal in the making of the Peabody Award-winning radio documentary *Black Radio: Telling It Like It Was*. The nature of oral history is to provide context to community at a particular point of time as well as over time. In doing so, the concept of community is defined in the context of serving a culturally specific audience: "This is what true community does. It creates and sustains a legacy of character handed down through the generations, a set of values that the members of the community inherit, honor, and enact in their lives" (Watson, 1989, p. xviii).

Some popular press books (Bunting and Diaz, 1999; Cannon, 1999) have been written on the social and political impact of the 1992 civil uprising, with Smith (1994) and Williams and Alan-Williams (1996) using oral narrative as the primary research technique. Anna Deavere Smith (1994) brought her novel's oral narrative to life on stage as a one-woman theatrical production throughout the U.S., and *Twilight: Los Angeles, 1992* was subsequently recorded and aired on the national Public Broadcasting Service (PBS). Mainstream television has attempted to capture the social and political meaning of an event, with varied success. This book documents the civic role of KJLH through the voices of its on-air presenters, station and community leaders, and listeners. It is a story that thrives on the power of oral testimony.

Black radio's role in high profile situations has not been sufficiently documented in scholarly journals. Additionally, minimal discussion has been devoted to the electronic media's role during Los Angeles' civil unrest, with one exception being *Screening the Los Angeles "Riots"* (Hunt, 1997). In *Mediated Messages and African-American Culture: Contemporary Issues,* Ramaprasad (1996) examined the print media coverage of the 1992 Los Angeles riots. *The Los Angeles Times* published *Understanding the Riots: Los Angeles and the Aftermath of the Rodney King Verdict* (1992). Otherwise, the field is wide-open for discussion on the role of print and electronic news media coverage on the riots even among its journalistic practitioners. A number of scholarly books have been written on the political and social dynamics of the 1992 uprising and its impact on the increasingly nonwhite minority populations (Abelmann and Lie, 1995; Baldassare, 1994; Castuera, 1992; Chang and Diaz-Veizades, 1999; Gale, 1996, Gooding-Williams, 1993; Totten & Schockman, 1994; Wall, 1996; Yu, 1994). It was not the overall intention of this book to investigate the underlying causes of the riots, nor to make exhaustive comparisons to the civil unrest of the 1960s in Watts, Newark, and Detroit (see Horne, 1997; Thompson, 2000). In this book, some limited discussion exists on the Watts Riots of 1965 only in an effort to provide context to the 1992 events. This book is the story of one radio station's commitment to serving its community in times of celebration and crisis, with the latter being the primary consideration in this comprehensive review of KJLH's role among its audience.

The KJLH Story: Creating a Legacy

The station's legacy of community service and commitment is one that dates back before Stevie Wonder bought KJLH. It begins with the vision of its first owner, John Lamar Hill II, who very much embraced the tradition of Black radio to serve its community, a mission that ultimately translated into good business (Newman, 1988). KJLH's story is told mainly from the perspective of its staff and listeners, and also relies on station documentation as well as transcripts from FCC hearings and *Front Page*. KJLH is the oldest Black radio station in Los Angeles (Soul, 2001), and the only independent Black-owned radio station in the city.

Its story is also one of struggle against consolidation and deregulation within the radio industry. KJLH's story concludes with a look toward the future of independent Black ownership as it reaches toward the Internet to expand its community dialogue. Meanwhile, the FCC continues to investigate the status of minority broadcasters and the barriers that inhibit entry into radio station ownership. Among the key issues under study is localism. This book offers a case study of one station's commitment to its community during heightened consolidation and a shrinking pool of Black heritage stations, most of which were once independently-owned stations targeted to an identifiable audience. The KJLH news reporters did not have to imagine the audience, nor did they have to refer to a demographic profile or a marketing analysis to know who was listening and when. The reporters simply knew the listeners, met them at the coffee shop, ball game or school events. Black radio was all about being local, and that sense of mission is being increasingly overshadowed by the larger consolidated voice of corporate radio. This book offers the reader an opportunity to hear between the text, and to frame KJLH's story as a historical soundscape of the station's role during the riots, bringing together on-air dialogue between studio announcers, guests, and call-in listeners. This story is told through community voices as well as those of politicians, movie stars, governmental authorities, and other media representatives who found themselves captivated by the KJLH coverage of real people in a state of crisis. The KJLH story is the gospel of South Central within the context of Black radio's historical role: a message that cannot overstate the importance of preserving local Black voices in the commercial spectrum.

CHAPTER 2

KJLH's Sphere of Influence
Assessing Black Radio's Role in the Community

KJLH's mission of community service and commitment toward its audience is expressed through a willingness to discuss intelligent and often controversial topics across its airwaves. It also supplies an alternative voice in the marketplace that challenges mainstream opinion. What become obvious, when listening to callers, employees and community leaders, is that music is only one element of its programming mix. Community empowerment, community unity, and community service were represented by more than 800 references in station documents and transcripts. Other leading themes were economic empowerment and media's role and responsibility.

The KJLH mission toward community unity, service, and empowerment has been consistently articulated and exemplified through the words and actions of management, staff, and community leaders. Karen Slade, vice president and general manager of KJLH, spoke to the strong sense of community that weaves through the station's mission: "Our community is much more important than playing a few commercials, 'cause we say in our slogan that, 'We are you,' so whatever the pain that's going through our community goes through us too. And if we don't have a community, we don't have a radio station" (Slade, personal communication, 2002).

On one level, its music format caters to its audience; however, KJLH has a programmatic vision that identifies issues, discusses them, and uses the station as a vehicle to actualize solutions, when possible. That final element would be the defining ingredient in KJLH's ability to maintain its audience's loyalty as well as its station's credibility in journalistic and political circles: "There are a lot of stations playing similar or the same music, so we can't really differentiate our product very much by playing the music that we play. So it confirms the community involvement aspect of our business mission — because while others may play R&B or urban music, they don't necessarily go beyond that into the communities" (Slade, personal communication, 2001).

Los Angeles news veteran Larry Carroll noted *Front Page* represents one of a few programs in the U.S. "that exist, certainly in the [African-American] community at large, that is brave enough, that is committed enough to [engage in political dialogue]" (Carroll, cited in *Front Page*, 2002b). That statement was made during KJLH's 10th anniversary show. During that same show, a listener commented: "The only community leaders, the only community people who we have basically are the ones that [are] really kind of [politically] conscious and listen to KJLH (Listener, cited in *Front Page*, 2002b).

There is another aspect of KJLH's mission that appears intangible to those who work at the station. It is a sense that the staff and listeners are connected spiritually and have a commitment toward each other that cannot easily be defined. Marketing Director Greg Johnson spends a good portion of his job on the streets, talking to business leaders and listeners in the community. Seemingly out of left field, he states, "God lives inside of KJLH. I think the spirit of the Lord flows into this radio station through Stevie Wonder" (Johnson, personal communication, 2002). Such a statement, however, articulates the evangelistic undercurrent that runs through KJLH. The station's call letters stand for "kindness, joy, love, happiness," and the lyrics within Wonder's songs (many of which include references to God) appear to claim similar values.

This spiritually and electronically mediated call is reminiscent of Marshall McLuhan's idea that technology can serve as an extension to humanity. So you might say KJLHers are radio evangelists, spreading the message of community activism and responsibility across the airwaves and through the streets. Moreover, they are engaged in the national dialogue on the critical action that must be pursued to preserve and ensure minority representation and ownership in media.

In the series of more than a dozen interviews with KJLH staff as well as others directly tied to KJLH's programming and the 1992 events, the station's strong desire to serve the community and the public interest and to empower listeners through voter registration and information about the political process surfaced as critical threads among the discussions. Documentation of KJLH's efforts in newspaper articles seemed to confirm a strong track record of servicing its audience through issue forums and community events. In particular, an in-depth analysis of the *Front Page* transcripts (April 29, 1992, to May 2, 1992) indicated the presence of strong community-related themes in addition to other themes that specifically addressed listeners' immediate concerns during the 1992 civil uprising (Table 1).

KJLH file articles and other station documentation as well as an online search of relevant newspapers and periodicals revealed consistent community interaction with staff and the South Central audience. Newspaper articles discussed a number of topics related to KJLH's community initiatives: sponsorship of literacy efforts and town hall church meetings; activities that address physical and safety concerns; parenting; provision of information and assistance to listeners regarding personal finances and careers; dialogue on the violence among youth; promotion of voter registration and actual voting; creation of special funds for minority business loans to help rebuild Los Angeles; and others.

The transcripts of the 1992 *Front Page* broadcast also documented the need to come together as a community in an effort to strengthen social and political institutions. In virtually all of the documentation, the need to empower the African American community through information and service activity became evident as a theme.

In addition, two other themes — economic empowerment (211 occurrences) and the media's role and responsibility (159 occurrences) were also significant to this investigation. These themes were also very much community driven in that KJLH dedicated time and resources toward financial information and activities that would empower its listeners (and the larger community) to succeed in attaining educational goals and business opportunities. KJLH reiterated the need to rebuild South Central with more Black-owned businesses than existed prior to the 1992 unrest. The station provided information and perspectives not offered by non–Black media (with particular emphasis on the important role of stations like KJLH that are independently Black-owned and targeted toward an African American audience).

Information was indicated as key to political and economic empowerment ("Information is power"); and the role of Black radio to provide counter-information to that of governmental agencies and non-minority media was deemed essential toward serving in the public interest of the KJLH community. Moreover, specific discussion targeted the need for more Black talk, especially as a format, in Los Angeles and across the U.S. than presently exists over the airwaves. It became evident during the interview process that corporate radio, and to some extent Black corporate radio, is part of an economic and political system of power that traditionally and potentially limits solutions and information to its listeners. In essence, Black-owned businesses and media were viewed as critical elements toward the accomplishment of social and political objectives within the community.

Violence—Then and Now

Violence was the most frequent theme within the interview and 1992 program transcripts. It reoccurred as a significant issue during KJLH's latest ascertainment efforts as revealed through station documentation. This trend was consistent with a report in *Newsweek* which documented a rise in youth violence in South Central similar to the conditions that existed in the area before the 1992 uprising (Foote and Murr, 2002). Some interviewees mentioned that there was a possibility for another riot in the near future, and the likelihood of this happening was also reiterated through street reports (Foote and Murr, 2002).

References to the violence occurring on the streets and what had occurred during the King trial consumed a significant portion of interaction between KJLH hosts and listeners. This theme remained significant among discussions between KJLH moderators and listeners throughout the first three days of civil unrest, and then finally dropped off by Saturday, May 2, 1992. Interview statements on the theme of violence were also significantly discussed and point toward the reason that KJLH has regularly addressed the escalating rise in street crime among community youth since 1992 through activities and forums.

Very little news coverage about KJLH's efforts to address community violence was mentioned in the Black press and even less in the mainstream media. Nearly all the references to violence were related to the uprising. Interviewees revealed that violence had escalated among community youth since then. KJLH staff detected a rise in violence in 1992 after a series of instances continued to build anger and a sense of hopelessness within the community.

Various Themes

Several themes that surfaced in 1992 were relevant to the immediate situation as listeners, hosts, and guests attempted to cope with the crisis at hand. These issues were not strongly represented in KJLH file documentation or interview transcripts, but rather by the 1992 *Front Page* transcripts. Many of the transcript themes were concerned with the physical and emotional response (i.e., discussions centering on the Los Angeles Police Department, the King trial and other significant events leading to the violent street reaction) during the 1992 civil unrest. There had been a series of events prior to the verdict, including complaints of police brutality and strained relations between the African American community and Korean-American business owners. Other themes that emerged within the 1992 transcripts addressed community concerns for the welfare of youth and teens and evoked an occasional historical reference to Watts and similar events.

Another theme that emerged was related to KJLH's credibility as a source of information for its listeners and the larger African American community. There is a definite theme of mistrust that surfaces among KJLH listeners of the mainstream media, as well as of the socio-political infrastructure that has reinforced stereotypical images of African Americans; and this theme became evident across KJLH's airwaves from April 29 to May 2, 1992. During the civil unrest, some callers (and even the hosts) referred to a "master plan" and "conspiracy" by Police Chief Darryl Gates against African Americans. Moreover, mainstream media's portrayal of African Americans as looters, with minimal references to the Whites and Hispanics involved in the mayhem, may have only reinforced this feeling by KJLH listeners that they were alone in the community and perhaps hated by those living outside their neighborhoods (*Front Page*, 1992b). This sense of mistrust surfaced beginning the night of April 30, after listeners had an opportunity to analyze the events that were happening around them. Talk of a "master plan" beyond the media, one that involved public officials, is indicated in the following dialogue:

> *Caller*: I mean, if we cannot see as a people that there is a plan, long before this riot. They knew that there was going to be a riot; they knew that there was going to be an acquittal. And they could have had some sort of force [i.e., police] here before anything happened. But they want us to destroy each other; they want us to destroy our communities. We as a people must realize that we are alone [*Front Page*, 1992b].

That same night, KJLH listeners felt alienated from the mainstream media and its assumptions that African Americans were responsible for all the fires in Los Angeles:

> *Caller:* What's gotten me is the simple fact, to sit up and think that people are saying the Black folks is what's burning all these places down. But three fires every minute?
>
> *Rico Reed:* No, no. This is a plan. Somebody is out there with firebombs putting this together [*Front Page*, 1992b].

Community themes expressed through unity, empowerment, and service were cumulatively and consistently more representative of KJLH's responsiveness to its audience than other categories. Other issues, such as the media's role and responsibility, were significant toward defining KJLH as an independent source of information often alternative to the mainstream in its views — social, political and economic.

Social

KJLH's social mission is demonstrated by its promotion of community service activities and its plea for community unity through family and church. KJLH owner Stevie Wonder's desire to contribute to the social fabric of South Central specifically, and African Americans in general, is grounded in his mission to solidify his community through dialogue and action, namely through his station's programming and outreach. KJLH's target audience might be described as family-oriented listeners who are concerned with providing appropriate role models for youth and teens.

Political

KJLH's political mission is most evident through its push toward civic responsibility, including its success with listener turn-out at voter registration drives. Its staff strives to create awareness of the political and judicial process, and participation is encouraged through town hall meetings, rallies, and information. The key word in empowerment is power, which is a direct result of planned and purposed participation by KJLH staff and community leaders. "Change will result from participation in the system" is the plea from Slade (personal communication, 2001) and those words are echoed by her staff members. Political figures and civil rights activists, such as the Reverend Jesse Jackson and Dick Gregory, as well as a number of local and state representatives, have been guests on KJLH's public affairs programming.

Economic

Amid sweeping consolidation and convergence, KJLH has managed to survive as an integral member of the South Central community and the Greater Los Angeles market. Its economic mission will be revealed and elaborated upon in subsequent chapters. KJLH has sought proactive means to remain financially viable in a highly competitive marketplace, even given the economic roadblocks toward minority ownership set in place through governmental policy favoring mega corporate infrastructures. On another level, the Black church's role as a source of community revenue and small business loans for residents has been essential to the fulfillment of its economic objectives, notably, the station's advocacy of community empowerment through economic education.

Table 1:
Summary of KJLH-FM Themes —
Frequency and Rank of Occurrence

Category	Occurrence	Rank
Violence	436	1
LAPD	388	2
Community Empowerment	371	3
Community Unity	319	4
Economic Empowerment	211	5
Safety/Peace	175	6
Community Service	173	7
Media	159	8
Emotional Venting	134	9
Conspiracy	100	10
Concern for Youth	60	11
Education	58	12
Church Empowerment	57	13
Watts	13	14

Summary of Emergent Themes

Here are the descriptions of the major themes that were revealed in one or more of the three data sources (1992 transcripts, KJLH file materials, and interviews):

Church Empowerment: The church was viewed as a place of unification during the uprising and key to the political and economic rebuilding of South Central during the decade that followed. Town hall meetings were regularly held at churches.

Community Empowerment: This theme dealt with KJLH's efforts toward political and civic empowerment within the African-American community. This theme was actualized through KJLH sponsored voter registration drives and the station's efforts to provide information to its listeners on the political and judicial process.

Community Service: KJLH has historically been involved in a number of community service activities (i.e., literacy programs and fund-raising efforts). This particular theme also refers to KJLH's community service activities during the 1992 uprising, such as assisting residents with specific needs: food, shelter, medical care, electricity, clean water, (the need to cash) checks, and school closures. The hosts and guests, rather than the listeners, primarily raised these issues.

Community Unity: A consistent theme was the necessity of unity within the African-American community as well as all the cultural groups within South Central. Strong family units and churches were perceived as integral to the larger issue of community unification.

Concern For Youth/Teens: This theme was concerned with the welfare of children and teens during the Los Angeles uprising as well as in the future. It specifically addressed the need for parents and community members to serve as positive role models for youth.

Conspiracy/Mistrust: This theme is concerned with a mistrust of the political, judicial, and economic systems (as well as mainstream media) within the U.S. by many members of the African-American community.

Economic Empowerment: A number of station activities and discussions have dealt specifically with personal finances and the larger issues of rebuilding Los Angeles, Black ownership, and particularly the importance of recycling Black dollars within area neighborhoods. This category has also been ascertained as a major theme by KJLH ownership and staff.

Emotional Venting: During the civil unrest, hosts encouraged listeners to discuss their frustration with the verdict over the KJLH airwaves instead of letting anger build within themselves or taking it to the streets.

LAPD/Trial/Other Events: This category was concerned with the reaction of listeners, hosts, and interviewees to the verdict in the Rodney King trial, as well as their perception of the LAPD's attitude toward the African-American community. A number of issues addressed allegations of racism and police brutality by the LAPD.

Media Role & Responsibility: This category pertained to the perception of KJLH staff, listeners, and guests regarding what was believed to be the mainstream media's failure to accurately report on and provide perspective to the 1992 Los Angeles uprising. In addition, KJLH, as an independent Black-owned medium, was viewed as a significant and necessary force within South Central by listeners and guests, especially in the presentation and representation of issues relevant to the African-American community.

Safety/Peace: The need to stay safe and increase the peace on the streets was a consistent theme relevant to the civil unrest. The hosts and callers warned listeners, especially young people, to stay off the streets and keep within curfew. A number of callers expressed fear regarding the events that were occurring on the streets and near their homes.

Violence: This category was primarily revealed through the eyewitness reports of listeners, guests, and KJLH staff with regards to the violence occurring in the South Central neighborhoods of Los Angeles during the 1992 civil unrest. Reports of violence, as in looting, fires, vandalism, and destruction, were documented by program transcriptions and then referenced within context. Violence especially among youth continued as a theme in interviews and other *Front Page* programs weeks after the 1992 uprising.

Watts Riots/Historical Context: A handful of references to the historical Watts uprising and related occurrences emerged from the data. This category did not emerge as a significant theme. The lack of its occurrence was deemed as a significant finding in and of itself, in that the location of the 1965 riots was in close proximity to neighborhoods impacted by the 1992 civil unrest.

KJLH's Sphere of Influence

The idea that KJLH has established a means for listeners to vent their frustrations in a safe and secure place with a sense of release and empowerment in an environment that openly honors and values their disappointments and dreams among a community of peers is heard on a daily basis and is what radio in general has the ability to do (provided the right commitment by the right station owner exists within a community). The Black press, in particular the *Los Angeles Sentinel*, has continually underscored the significance of KJLH's community service efforts in its coverage of station events. It is likely that the *Los Angeles Sentinel* understands the need to address certain issues and events that the mainstream press (as well as the electronic mass media) often narrowly perceives as serving only a specific interest population:

> Creating oppositional frameworks for African Americans and rearticulating black identity, the Black press has served as a site for grievance to be aired when even letters to the editor were segregated, spread the word for activists and scholars, and allowed blacks to use their expertise and modes of expression without much censure from the dominant public [Squires, 2000, p. 77].

What I propose is the existence of various levels of influence among community institutions within the KJLH public sphere. Applying the work of Dawson (1994a) and Squires (2000), KJLH appears to be an alternative and oppositional voice to the mainstream in Los Angeles that engages its community of listeners and representatives from culturally specific institutions (i.e., Black church, Black press, Black business) in dialogue. However, its level of influence radiates beyond its immediate listening area to often set the agenda for mainstream media. Its discussions cross its community borders via the Internet to inform, engage, and perhaps motivate the larger African American community as well as those seeking alternative views to the mainstream media.

The station's public sphere, as defined by Squires (2000) and Dawson (1994b), is evident in KJLH's ability to connect with the listener and its community of listeners as expressed within the *Front Page* transcripts of the 1992 civil unrest as well as through its events and daily discussions. KJLH is a safe haven. Its connection to listeners and its historical link to area Black churches and neighborhoods initiates public dialogue, actualizing Dawson's ideal of a Black counter-public. Dialogue flows through its airwaves to engage local leaders, celebrities, and governmental officials from both inside and outside South Central and the larger African American community.

Perhaps unique to this KJLH study is fact that the prominence of these discussions has drawn business owners, and even state and national leaders, into community activism. The immediacy of response to KJLH's coverage of the 1992 civil uprising from various actors (e.g., station employees, church leaders, celebrities, and attorneys) and the level of interaction and involvement with the station from those people during the crisis determined their placement on KJLH-FM's Sphere of Influence (Figure 1). In addition, the historical network among the personalities, programmers, and management of Black-targeted radio stations — some of which were formerly Black-owned — became evident when KJLH's programming aired across the nation to African American and other audiences.

Three factors — proximity, prominence, and participation — seemed to determine KJLH's ability to rally the community to social and political action as employees and listeners worked collaboratively to meet the physical, social, and emotional needs of its listeners and to provide some hope, a sense of renewal, and recommendations toward restructuring the socio-political and economic base of South Central Los Angeles.

Proximity

KJLH made a decision to stop the music and spread a message of peace to listeners and the community. It became a focal point of dialogue and community responsiveness. The station worked with local churches and community organizations to find help for the displaced and the homeless. KJLH was located in the Crenshaw district, and it was literally in the middle of the civil uprising. When celebrities and local leaders wanted to talk on the air, they knocked on the door of KJLH and asked to come into the studio. Congresswoman Diane Watson was a few doors down the street and thus was readily available for comment and discussion.

Proximity is best demonstrated by events happening just outside KJLH's studio in 1992. KJLH was the neighborhood station, a trusted voice in the community that elevated the concerns of listeners and residents through station-sponsored community benefits and discussion forums. Later discussion will demonstrate the overall significance of the station's location within southern Los Angeles and its consistent role as a community resource.

Prominence

KJLH's ongoing participation in political dialogue over the airwaves and on the streets of South Central is indicative of the station's long-term commitment to the area. The concept of localism becomes relevant when discussions move beyond physical location to a community-centric activism that connects listeners to information and political change agents. For example, local mentions of weather conditions several times an hour, an announcement of a band performing in the community arena, or the airing of a local remote for a community business is not on the same level as what KJLH considers its ultimate service mission in South Central. Napoli (2001, p. 383) provides this definition of localism to help clarify policy discussions such as this one: "In an effort to bring greater precision and rigor to the localism principle ... policymakers and policy analysts need to take a two-tiered approach to the concept of 'local programming.'" On a very general level, localism is based on the "point of origin of the programming." Napoli elaborates (p. 383): "The point of origin of programming may alone be the relevant objective in those instances in which policymakers' primary concern is facilitating the decentralization and localization of decision making that are prominent components of the political and cultural rationales for localism." The second tier, more importantly, "focuses on the nature of program content, in terms of whether or not the content addresses local interests and concerns. Those policies more directly concerned with promoting cultural diversity or political knowledge within communities must have this content-based definition incorporated into their assessment plans" (p. 383).

KJLH had been already established as an influential and credible voice within the community before the civil uprising. When other media organizations from outside South Central entered the community, their reporters and vans were often greeted with rocks and violence. KJLH's reporters, on the other hand, were applauded as they drove through the community.

PARTICIPATION

KJLH is politically involved in South Central Los Angeles. However, its neighborhood struggles economically as businesses move into the suburbs. Stevie Wonder's station membership in the National Association of Black-Owned Broadcasters (NABOB) is indicative of his commitment to Black-owned radio. And yes, the station has been fortunate to have Wonder as its financial benefactor, while other radio corporations have purchased a number of formerly Black-owned radio stations. Economic capital often determines political participation in the consolidation debate over ownership of the airwaves.

Purchasing a radio station today is cost prohibitive, with price tags in the millions. Moreover, massive consolidation since the passage of the 1996 Telecommunications Act continues to raise the stakes for playing in the radio arena. Independent radio is virtually non-existent in Los Angeles. Goliath-type media corporations determine revenue and shares for the regional and national markets. In 1999, KJLH's station owner and general manager were invited to appear before the Federal Communications Commission (FCC) to testify on broadcast issues related to consolidation and the loss of localism in the U.S.

Even with its recent upgrade in terrestrial transmission, KJLH's relatively weak radio signal outside of its community of interest has limited its potential advertising dollars and audience in the greater Los Angeles market. On the other hand, the station is communicating with the larger African American community via the Internet. It has tapped into a national under-served audience. KJLH provides access to change agents and policymakers across a local, national, and global spectrum. That is why the dwindling population of similar independent Black-owned stations is such a major concern to NABOB members.

Radio Is Community

In essence, it was a video that ignited the world with powerful visuals, but it would be a small, independent Black-owned radio station that would calm down the city through dialogue. By the very fact that the owner has refused to sell his property to mainstream competitors, the KJLH staff and management are reminded of their significant role in empowering listeners to embrace their cultural heritage as well as the importance of working together to expose the stereotypical depiction of African Americans to those within and outside the community.

The primary themes of community empowerment, unity, and service that emerged from this investigation were central toward understanding KJLH's role in preserving and serving the multitude of voices that comprise its audience. Moreover, the themes of unification and empowerment seem to extend beyond KJLH's listeners to benefit the larger community of South Central. Other themes, such as economic empowerment and the role of Black-owned media, appeared to be integral to KJLH's call for discussion of issues and concerns within its community prior, during, and subsequent to the 1992 Los Angeles Riots. Discussions surrounding the residents' attitudes toward violence on the streets and among youth, as well as their perceptions of the Los Angeles Police Department's behavior toward the African American community, appeared to provide an opportunity for some residents to vent their frustrations and concerns not otherwise voiced outside their neighborhoods.

The world listened to KJLH's residents and civic leaders as they cried out for peace on the South Central streets and social and economic justice across the nation. Moreover, three factors that emerged and appear central to KJLH's ability to connect and communicate with its audience have been identified as:

- its proximity to African-American listeners (and to the events of 1992)
- its prominence as a community activist (and its proclivity to attract political and civic leaders into the discussion)
- and its ability to participate as a viable player (albeit for a small

piece of the pie) in the nation's second largest radio market, even prior to its current ownership

The ability to identify community issues and service activities that are locally-relevant (proximity), and to give them prominence within and beyond the station's licensed coverage area, is very much dependent on KJLH's financial viability in the Los Angeles marketplace as a Black-owned entity (and its future positioning on the Internet). KJLH has provided relevant dialogue between on-air staff and listeners, as well as continuous outreach to nearby neighborhoods, such as when the station raises money and resources for community organizations or localizes national issues through *Front Page*. What has made KJLH so unique to any investigation of the community role of Black-owned and -formatted radio, as well as to observers of today's consolidated and competitive marketplace, is that it has captured the trust of its listeners. The next chapter explores KJLH's early history, and how Wonder's station exemplifies the larger social goals of Black radio.

CHAPTER 3

Lighting the Torch
KJLH and Its Black Radio Roots

> "[William Seymour] affirmed his black heritage by introducing Negro spirituals and Negro music into his liturgy at a time when this music was considered inferior and unfit for Christian worship." — Walter Hollenweger, p. 20.

American media have a unique relationship to African American culture. On one level, African American culture has become branded and increasingly sought after for its economic viability as a pop culture commodity. With its context stripped away, media merely perpetuates myths and misleading cultural conceptions of a group of people that span a diversity of interests in popular culture, politics, and spirituality, more so than what is presented in music and image within the mainstream fare. The African American culture has often been reduced to absolutes and then mass (re)produced as entertainment (Postman, 1986). Radio, in its local format and when programmed to its audience's needs and interests, has until recently provided a mouthpiece for participation and presenting issues on the air, alongside targeted entertainment and information. In early radio, religious programming fed into interests of African American audiences and formed a sense of community for its listeners. Local radio, much like the telephone, provided immediacy and connection to users. Listeners could speak directly with the deejay, typically someone familiar with the community. Radio had become a *religion* to many listeners as they had become accustomed to certain voices on the air.

Best described as a medium that thrives on voices, sounds, and stories, radio was unfortunately born into the bleakness of the industrial era. Machines and moguls, not listeners, ruled the land. Italian futurists

48

Tomasso Marinetti and Pino Masnata (1933) in *La Radia* would argue that early radio had moved away from its potential to settle for a community jukebox devoid of imagination. And that was already in the emerging decades of radio. Large corporations such as RCA and Westinghouse had readily identified the economic value of the airwaves. After a brief stint of experimentation, here and there, the formula for financial success was viewed the same for most stations, and voices, songs, and news became transactions. The question remained: how to efficiently operate a station with minimal cost while presenting the semblance of listener involvement. To date, owners have argued endlessly regarding the significance of radio's local roots.

Black radio in its heyday, before today's corporate radio, did well by capitalizing on the experiences and stories within neighborhoods of listeners. All of a sudden, broadcasting itself had become an industry, not an experiment, not an educational tool, but a business. To many like Mark Newman (1988), Black radio owners knew that to make a profit, they had to relate to their listeners in significant ways that touched lives through meaningful local events and experiences. These stations are known as heritage stations, and only a handful exist in the U.S. For others, it was always about the money, with programming aspirations geared toward the manufacture of a format at the forefront of the station's mission, with the semblance of *caring* and *responsive* radio as part of the branding.

To understand radio and its relationship with the American culture, one must seek the context into which it was born and shaped. In the case of Black radio, that culture is rooted in the church. E. Steven Collins, a longtime Black radio executive, insightfully illustrates the role of the gospel announcer as a "shaper of public opinion":

> Why would Yolanda Adams singing a song that talks about inspiration and faith and Jesus having a plan for us, as in the smash hit: *The Battle Is Not Yours* or Kirk Franklin's *Why We Sing*, or Donny McClurkin's *We Fall Down* or so many of these artists that are purely gospel artists, why would their songs be interspersed in Urban Contemporary formatted radio stations? It's because African Americans expect and require a different approach. So I believe if African Americans are expecting and are requiring something more than just hit songs, then they're going to expect something more in their morning radio music show that talks about substance over merely jokes and games [Collins, personal communication, 2002].

Collins was the lead organizer for Philadelphia's largest promotional event called Unity Day, which grew to more than one million in attendance in the 1990s. His background in public affairs and marketing helped to not only identify critical issues in his community, but also to seek ways to engage the community in discussion at public venues. Live music, motivational speakers, and family entertainment helped to define the Unity celebrations over the years. Comparable events such as city-wide African American expositions executed by Black radio stations across the U.S. had been signatures of long-time heritage stations like WDAS-AM/FM. Many of these stations are no longer Black-owned; some have carried on the commitment, while others have not in recent years. The issues drive the events, and the community responds to radio's on- and off-air call to gather together as a family and community. Collins continues,

> Whether it is police brutality, AIDS awareness, corporate racism ... it's going to be something; somebody is going to call up, or some commentator is going to present a view of a serious issue that's not light, it's a serious commentary or dialogue. That's what I think the genuine role Urban radio has played and will continue to play as long as it is a valid mass form of communication for Black America. And you can compare local Urban radio's presentation, with the syndicated Tom Joyner Morning Show, and find the exact same elements. Great music, relevant news, and meaningful and varied discussions and appropriate Black humor. Those are the elements that I think Urban audiences are always going to expect and require from the source of information and entertainment that they choose over all else. More African Americans listen to the radio and listen longer than watch television, than read newspapers, than read magazines, or go to the movies. So, that needs to be considered. And then I think there is still an important relationship between the individual announcer and the audience. The Urban contemporary DJ, the news announcer or Gospel Queen still is a major, major influencer or shaper of public opinion in Black media [ibid.].

The challenge of creating a marketplace of ideas within a commercial industry is not necessarily viewed by the government or mainstream broadcasters as a cultural mandate, or even a wake-up call for assuring diversity across the American airwaves. The rise of hate radio and racial epithets on the dial during the Howard Stern era of the 1990s and his emulators since then, as well as the lack of minority representation within the industry, move to alienate rather than to encourage Black audience participation in mainstream radio. Culturally specific media struggle to serve neighborhoods of license in efforts to keep the legacy alive.

The message and music cannot be readily separated in Black radio. Singer and activist Mahalia Jackson unified blues, gospel, and choir music into powerful inspirational ballads. She developed her singing ability as a child in her Baptist church in New Orleans, and would eventually move to Chicago in the late twenties to sing with the Johnson Brothers, one of the first gospel groups (albeit short-lived). She viewed the Black church as the true birthplace of rock and roll, which was originally intended for sanctification and prophetic worship, not crass commercialism (Schwerin, 1992). Jackson would acknowledge the need for community in communication similar to African American radio founders like Jackie L. Cooper.

Chicago, in the view of many historians, is the birthplace of modern Black radio, and it was here, under the guidance of Cooper, that it grew into a mature and responsible medium. Cooper, the father of Black radio, helped Chicago radio flourish as an outlet for African American programming, according to historian Mark Newman (1988) in *Entrepreneurs of Profit and Pride: From Black-Appeal to Radio Soul*. Newman speculates that the story of Black radio in Chicago, and perhaps all Black radio, began in 1929, when Cooper's *The All-Negro Hour* was aired on Chicago's WSBC-AM. Cooper, as the host, exclusively targeted the Black community. He envisioned the role of his Black talk show as one extending beyond entertainment "to gain as much black control and participation as possible" (p. 57). His struggle to overcome racism in broadcasting would continue over the next two decades, and because of his efforts "Chicago radio became a fertile ground for African-American programming prior to World War II, setting an example for many other metropolitan areas" (p. 68).

Cooper's *pioneer* role is significantly noteworthy in the area of community service promotions, in which he developed a strong relationship with area churches, social agencies, Black-owned businesses (reporting on the first Black business exposition in Chicago), and the African American community in Chicago (Newman, 1988). He broadcast missing persons' shows (reuniting 20,000 people with their families by 1950), instituted an on-air job placement service, provided legal advice and aired civil rights programs (Newman, 1988) in those first decades of radio. The tradition of community outreach was established early in the history of Black radio — it became gospel to many early African American programmers and personalities. Cooper's philosophy would become foundational to the success of KJLH in South Central Los Angeles in years to come.

Spreading the Black Gospel

Gospel has remained relevant today as a style of listening and church worship, although many religious radio stations in the U.S. have segregated this genre into formats that target predominantly White and Black audiences, respectively. Its history reaches far beyond the inception of radio broadcasting. Jon Michael Spencer (2004) traces gospel music's genealogy from its transitional period that began in 1900 to the gospel hip-hop of Contemporary Christian radio. In retrospect, it was the early black church experience — one that encouraged community through worship and activism — that would shape the identity of many of the first Black radio deejays and stations through the 1970s.

Early worship might be displayed through prayer, clapping, circle dancing, singing, and any number of other forms of expressive worship, often prompted by emotionally charged call-and-response spirituals. The call liberated the singer toward an impromptu and perhaps prophetic composition of words and melody which was received by the community of worshipers with chorus or refrain.

By the close of the 19th century, African American ministers Charles Albert Tindley and Charles Price Jones emerged as outspoken political and worship leaders. Tindley, an African American Episcopal minister in Berlin, Maryland, wrote nearly 50 hymns in the latter 1800s. Jones, one of the prominent leaders of the Holiness Movement, composed more than 1,000 hymns that became the musical backbone of the Black church for decades thereafter.

As the 20th century approached, ragtime had introduced America to Scott Joplin, and his blend of blues, spirituals and the European classics. The seemingly chaotic mix of genres, complete with vocal shouts, found residence within the Holiness-Pentecostal movement, which was inspired by African American pastor William Seymour and other emerging evangelistic pastors around this time. Seymour led the Azusa Street Revival, one of the largest evangelical movements in America that began at a private home in South Los Angeles in 1906, and then moved to the first floor of a tenement building, formerly a Methodist church, on 312 Azusa Street.

The congregation — a mix of White and Black believers — sat on planks held up by nail kegs. More than curious to check out reports of healings and miracles, visitors and reporters from all over the world crowded into the building. A new generation of religious leaders was encouraged by this movement to take the gospel — in music, word, and deed — to the world. In this way, the Azusa Street Revival was pivotal to the rise of gospel music in Los Angeles (Boyer, 1995). Spirituality, varied music styles, and African American culture began to define Los Angeles and highlight the need for culturally specific media; this convergence would ultimately shape Black radio's community mission, especially in South Central. The revival lasted only three years, yet that was enough time for gospel music to sweep through Los Angeles.

Pentecostal fervor continued to spread across the West for the next two decades. In the 1920s, Aimee Semple McPherson and Charles E. Fuller of the Bible Institute of Los Angeles became powerful radio evangelists (Sitton and Deverell, 2001; Hangen, 2002). It is not definitively known whether McPherson or Fuller first ignited the early religious broadcast movement in Los Angeles. Most likely, KJS-AM (King Jesus Saves) was the first station to play religious programming in L.A. The station was housed within the Bible Institute on the corner of Hope and 6th Streets. It began by airing church services on Sundays in 1922, and then began to broadcast an all-religious format. In 1925, its call letters were changed to KTBI-AM, and the station stayed on the air until 1931 (when it was sold and renamed KFAC-AM in 1931, and again as KWKW-AM in 1989). KTBI was soon forgotten, and KFSG would become remembered as the first religious station in Los Angeles.

McPherson arrived in Los Angeles in 1918 with a passion for God, a talent for theatrics, and her mother and two children. By the Summer of 1923, she had more than one-half million followers and opened the 5,300 seat Angelus Temple in Los Angeles. She established more than 400 branch churches and 178 mission stations throughout the world (Blumhofer, 1993).

It was radio that made McPherson a household word in the 1920s and 1930s. She was known to present her sermon within the context of a worship service filled with jazz and rhythm and blues. McPherson brought together Hollywood celebrities, musicians and pastors in the same venue. Her radio show popularized gospel, jazz, and rhythm and blues and fueled a hunger for soul music. In 1924, KGFJ 1230 AM became the vehicle for McPherson to broadcast her sermons across the airwaves. She founded the International Church of the Foursquare Gospel, which evangelized a strong message centered on salvation, divine healing, baptism in the Holy Spirit, and preparation for the Second Coming. Her extravagant services broadcast live across the airwaves drew an audience of White and Black believers — and the music challenged the conventional doctrines of the traditional church. Los Angeles was in a period of transformation in the churches and on the streets, and this radical female radio evangelist was unapologetically crossing racial boundaries.

The Birth of the Los Angeles Disc Jockey

Los Angeles was a fertile area for Black radio. By the mid–1920s, musician Isaac "Satchel" McVea became the first African American on-air host on Los Angeles radio, and possibly the first in the U.S. (Dawson and Guizar, 2000). His show, *The Optimistic Doughnut,* aired on KNX-AM in the early 1920s. In 1927, KGFJ-AM made its debut on the air, but it did not play a Black format until the late 1940s or early 1950s (Love, 1992a). Musicians would readily grasp the power of radio to reach the people who could buy their records. In the 1930s, radio in general was not yet playing rhythm and blues; however, that was about to change: Joe Adams had not yet begun broadcasting in Santa Monica. By the mid–1940s, he would become one of the first, if not the first, Black disc jockeys in Los Angeles — and at KGFJ (Bryant, Collette, and Green, et al., 1998).

In Brian Ward's (1998) *Just My Soul Responding,* he describes a new surge in the music scene from independent record labels that surfaced in the 1940s. The top companies had secured the popular market, or they thought they had; however, a revolution had been taking place on the ground level. They had not monitored the local music that was gaining interest at nightclubs and record stores in the African American community. It was then, in 1948, rhythm and blues emerged on the airwaves and captivated the youth, according to Ward (1998), in what would launch a movement across the nation. Five years later, White teenagers would flock to all-night radio remotes at one of the Black-owned local record stores on Central and Vernon. From 1910 through the early 1950s, Central Avenue became the soul of Los Angeles as its creators and observers alike perpetuated a unique rhythm, as well as a fiery evangelism, of spirited-filled preachers and patrons. By the late 1940s, rhythm and blues could be heard on a number of Los Angeles stations, as well as in clubs and ballrooms (Bryant, Collette and Green, et al., 1998). About this time, Santa Monica's KOWL-AM, a station owned by Gene Autry, switched to a format that also targeted the Los Angeles African American community (Marion, 2001).

Many record stores quickly emerged as outlets for rhythm and blues programming in African American neighborhoods in the 1950s (Marion, 2001). By mid–1951, the Mutual Broadcasting System had aired the first all Black program on network radio (Marion, 2001). Beyond jazz and rhythm and blues, young South Central Black musicians were instrumental in bringing rock 'n' roll not only to the city, but also to the nation. The Penguins (*Earth Angel*), Jesse Belvin (*Goodnight My Love*), Gene & Eunice (*Ko Ko Mo*), The Cadets (*Stranded in the Jungle*), The Jewels (*Hearts of Stone*), The Platters (*Only You*), The Coasters (*Charlie Brown*), and Bobby Day (*Rockin' Robin*) and other musicians drew crowds of African American, Chicano and White teenagers in 1950, alas creating a melting pot among the nation's youth (Dawson and Guizar, 2000). Black radio rocked its way into American culture, while its underlying message for social justice was often lost among its White audience. The message came strongest mainly from Black deejays and performers employed by independent Black-owned companies.

Convergence Along Central Avenue

Styles merged as musicians, tourists, and residents seemed to appreciate the diversity and energy on the streets and on the air. Jelly Roll Morton had already helped to transform ragtime into the emergent fresh genre, jazz. He arrived in Los Angeles to introduce this new blend along Central Avenue. What began as a neighborhood performance attracted people from all over the city and the United States. Around Christmas 1919, the first Black music store and record label opened for business in the area. Los Angeles attracted numerous Black musicians, including Morton, Charlie Parker, and Louis Armstrong, who made some of his first recordings there. Even late night after the city curfew, African American residents and musicians and White tourists moved the beat along Central Avenue to the Watts nightclubs. The Depression slowed down some of the business, but it quickly resumed as locals, celebrities, and musicians alike sought entertainment venues. Parker, B. B. King, Nat "King" Cole, and Big Joe Turner would play and record their music on that avenue. College educated African Americans, who were excluded from White-collar workplaces, appreciated (and contributed to) the cultural renaissance of the area.

In the early 1930s, Central Avenue became home to independent Black-owned record labels and music stores, recording studios, nightclubs, and a funeral home. John Lamar Hill, Sr., built his funeral parlor in the early 1930s at Jefferson and Central Avenue. By 1936, the first African American owned funeral home, under the management of Hill, Sr., sponsored the commercial religious services of the Peoples Independent Church of Christ on KFOX-AM radio. The station was located in Mottell's Mortuary in Long Beach. Early radio regulation wreaked havoc on the first stations in the U.S., and by the 1940s Long Beach station KFOX's weak signal was upgraded to extend its reach. The early KFOX survived by selling airtime to commercial sponsors, so the programming would be varied at times but always locally originated. In 1939, actor Herb Jeffries, America's number one singing African American cowboy, would be cast in the first all Black produced and directed radio show aired on KFOX (Halper, 2004). The call letters KFOX became legendary, and synonymous with the legacy of country music, of course mixed with religious programming.

In the 1950s, KFOX aired rhythm and blues and included in its personality roster Hunter Hancock, a White deejay credited with popularizing rhythm and blues across racial lines in Los Angeles. The early history of KFOX is sketchy, with programming targeted to African Americans by the 1940s for a period of time, for how long, whether on the AM or FM or both, and beginning when is unclear. John Lamar Hill, Jr., eventually bought the FM station around 1965, owning it for 14½ years. The format then was country, and the AM and FM were simulcast. The sellers kept the KFOX calls, and the letters were changed to KILB (In Long Beach). Hill, Jr., soon changed the calls to his initials, J-L-H. Later, he told his employees that the station letters represented kindness, joy, love, and happiness. Stevie Wonder would also be credited for that meaning of the letters upon his purchase of the station. KJLH, under Hill's ownership, would broadcast services on Sunday mornings, especially for shut-ins who were unable to attend church: "Understanding the impact of radio, and working with local church leaders, [John] Lamar [Hill] purchased KFOX radio.... Eventually he changed the call letters to KJLH, and a community institution was born. This was the first black-owned radio station on the West Coast" (John L. Hill, Jr., 1998).

Hill was definitely influenced by radio's ability to touch the lives of African American listeners in his decision to purchase the FM station. Hill and his family business would underwrite a number of church programs for more than 40 years. When Hill bought KJLH-FM in 1965, it ran originally out of the Long Beach studios, but he remained committed to serving his African American listeners. Stan Kelton reflected on his radio experiences at KJLH when the station was located inside the funeral home, a fairly intimidating site for a 16-year-old board operator:

> We would pay the rent by saying, "From the Garden Room at Mottell's Mortuary, this is KJLH, Long Beach.... Never wanting to be a mortician, it was kind of a spooky place for me to work; however, I must admit that I was *never* vis-

ited by any of the inhabitants of the place. I later worked at the transmitter when it was moved to Dominguez Hills, and at the studios when they were moved to Crenshaw Boulevard next to Mr. Hill's Angelus Funeral Home" [Barrett, 1999].

Hill, Jr., would eventually move the family business westward to 3875 South Crenshaw in Compton. That would also be the location for KJLH for a number of years under Wonder's reign. In those early days, KJLH-FM was promoted as "the only Negro-owned station in the West" (*Black Radio*, 1970, p. 45). It would become known as the first Black station in Compton at the same time Compton was dubbed the first Black city of greater Los Angeles. The station through the years aired rhythm and blues, gospel and jazz, and a variety of music and news-public affairs programming targeting the African American community, as well as a plethora of religious services on Sundays. In the early 1970s, Hill leased the station to KJLH general manager Chuck Johnson, who had already gained quite a bit of radio experience in the 1960s, having worked in Los Angeles as a general manager and becoming the first African American owner of a station in San Diego, where he was also the president of the local chapter of the NAACP (Tanter, 2004). The point being that Hill was looking for a strong African American manager to run his station and maintain its community commitment while he tended to his mortuary. Hill, Jr., died in 1998.

Learn, Baby, Learn

Born in 1897 in Fallis, Oklahoma, Jesse B. Blayton, Sr., was the first African American to own and operate a radio station in the U. S. He studied at the University of Chicago and moved to Atlanta in 1922. He became a bank president and a professor at Atlanta University by the 1940s, and in 1949, he had purchased WERD-AM. He hired his son to run the 1,000 watt station, and one of his first decrees was to hire Jack "The Rapper" Gibson as the program director. The station set in motion the popularity of the Black radio deejay as an entertainer and activist. The studios were located in the same building as the Southern Christian Leadership organization later would be in the 1960s. Gibson "ran a long line and microphone out the window to the street below, where Martin Luther King, Jr., as a young preacher, delivered "a stirring speech heard all over the city" (Koch, 2000, p. 1).

That was the first time King's voice was heard across the airwaves thanks to "The Rapper," who became known as one of America's early Black radio pioneers; Joseph Deighton Gibson Jr. "popularized what is now called urban radio and later, as a record executive, helped launch the singing careers of Smokey Robinson, Stevie Wonder and Michael Jackson" due to his friendship with Motown founder Berry Gordy (Koch, 2001, p. 1). Black radio was coming into its own identity. The music was only one component of the programming mix. Listeners were hungry for a station that could relate to their needs and interests.

Another deejay, Magnificent Montague, had already begun his radio career in 1949 when WERD-AM, Atlanta, went on the air. He became popular among his young listeners for saying, "Burn, baby! Burn." He had been screaming those words over the climax of his favorite soul hits since 1963, first in New York and then one year later in Chicago. Teenagers would call him at the station, and scream back the words. He would take his show to Black-oriented rhythm and blues station KGFJ-AM of South Central in February 1965. About the time of his arrival, his friend Malcolm X was assassinated. The date was February 21 (Maycock, 2002). Months later, in August, he would hear his own words — "burn, baby, burn" — on television, as cameras caught rioters in Watts chanting the words, words that echoed from the airwaves of KGJF (Montague and Baker, 2003). KGJF was located on Melrose Avenue, but Montague's words immediately transcended his station's audience and were broadcast across the nation. In his book *Burn, Baby! Burn*, he reconsiders what might have happened if he had had the foresight during those days to tell the rioters, "Learn, baby":

> Learn about the forces that are controlling you. Learn to dominate them. Learn that your people in America have always struggled against oppression and always will. Learn, in ways that will astonish and inspire you, that they have often won despite odds much greater than those you face [p. 5].

Montague remembers the era as "a time when music and society and race and technology all exploded like a bomb, a time when black deejays made rhythm & blues erupt from that old marketing niche of 'race music'" (Montague and Baker, 2003, p. 4). It was a time that offered change to "the way young Americans — white as well as black — saw their world. To live in that vortex was to touch America's soul and be touched by it" (p. 4).

The Night That King Died

Black radio's power to inform and unify the community, especially during times of crisis, has been documented (Alston, 1978; "Black Radio," 1970; Fornatale and Mills, 1980; George, 1988; Jeter, 1981; MacDonald, 1979; Newman, 1988). In 1968, Black radio came of age the night that King died, and African American disc jockeys across the country interrupted the music to tell people "to cool it" (George, 1988, p. 111). On their own initiative and often against the wishes of the station owners, they halted programming. They stopped and talked to Black America, trying to ease the anger building up within the African American community. WLIB-AM, in fact, was awarded the George Foster Peabody Award for its decision to stay on the air (George, 1988).

King's death, in a sense, liberated Black radio from its White owners, if only for a night in some cases. The "genesis for this change" in Black radio occurred, according to WLIB's former personality Del Shields, "the night Dr. King was killed" (George, 1988, p. 111). Many Black radio personalities across the nation made the decision to stay on air all night, and did so against the wishes of the station owners. They attempted to assuage the grief and anger of the African American people. Shields explains, "We tried to do everything possible to keep the Black people from exploding even more than they were" (George, 1988, pp. 111–112). WLIB, a day-timer, remained on the air until 1 A.M., and Shields added that broadcasters "had to answer to the FCC later with reports about why we stayed on. The oddity was that we, the Black disc jockeys, made the decision to stay on; as a result, the station got the Peabody Award" (p. 111). The owner called Shields and told him that he had no authority to remain on the air. Shields rebutted that he did not have time to talk to him, and went back to his microphone: "When America looked at Black radio in that particular period, it suddenly hit them that this was a potent force. If, in every major city, a Black disc jockey had said, 'Rise up,' there would have been pandemonium" (George, 1988, p. 112).

Phone calls flooded the Atlanta studio lines of Black-formatted WIGO-AM, and media outlets nationwide requested news feeds on the assassination of King and the unrest that followed. African American radio personality Rudy Runnels was inspired to join forces with rival station WAOK-AM to create the American Freedom Network, a "temporary national pool of reporters ... provid[ing] coverage for some 200 stations" during those critical hours (Ferretti, 1970, p. 38; also "Black Radio," 1970).

In Memphis, WDIA-AM's 50,000 watts transmitted the news of King's death, and the station, well-known for its community service to the African American community, departed from its regular programming: "The station helped cool tension in the riot-torn city by continuously cautioning the Black community to stay calm. It also carried messages from local, state, and even federal officials, reassuring Memphians that law and order would prevail and that King's murderer would be brought to justice" (Cantor, 1992, p. 227). WDIA reported on the stream of events that followed the assassination, including Coretta Scott King's decision to "stand in her slain husband's place during a mass civil rights march in Memphis.... [H]er only concern since her husband's assassination was that his work would not die" (Caldwell, 1968, p. 1).

According to Louis Cantor (1992) in his book *Wheelin' on Beale*, King's death changed the history of Black radio "more than any other single event": "[It] galvanized Memphis' and the nation's resolve to work harder than ever to achieve the martyred leader's dream of complete desegregation" (p. 227). Cantor noted the evolution of Black radio. An era had ended for WDIA and for the nation: "First to go were the euphemistic names originally employed in order to avoid the word Black.... The first Black program directors came in the late sixties about the same time that one of the most important remnants of the old order — white control-board operators — finally died off" (p. 227). Over the course of time, Black radio has withstood many changes in musical styles, from the church choir renditions of traditional gospel and rhythm and blues to the more contemporary influences of dance and rap. Its intent to politically empower listeners appeared to be the consistent thread that had connected African American audiences with each other throughout the U.S., especially for many of those who continued to tune into the nation's Black heritage stations.

Hearing the Gospel Message

Black radio has regularly promoted political activism to its listeners as an extension of its community service mission. An artery connecting music and politics pulses in the heart of heritage Black radio. Call it the gospel of Black radio: a message that encourages and inspires community activism and a sincere hope for transformation in urban areas often neglected by the political elite. The church has been central to this mission.

The African American church had a direct influence on African American radio, according to Norman W. Spaulding (1981) in its early days; for instance, "choral groups and church choirs appeared more frequently on Chicago radio than any other form of Black/urban programming from the 1920s until World War II" (p. 34). WDIA and KWEM (later KWAM) would become instrumental in programming Black gospel music and other Black-oriented programming on Memphis radio after World War II (Lornell, 1988).

The African American church, beyond its musical contributions, has been a strong political and social institution in the urban community; historically it has encouraged liberation from racism, illiteracy, and poverty.As early as the mid–1950s, Alex Haley recognized Black radio as an outlet for community service promotions and church groups (George, 1988). Black radio found its direction initially from the African American church, which served as a spiritual and inspirational force and later from the preaching of the Reverend King, Jr., during the civil rights movement.

In a public statement on Martin Luther King, Jr., Day, FCC chairman William E. Kennard acknowledged the role of African American radio personalities during the early days of the civil rights movement in America:

> On December 5, 1955, at the height of the bus boycotts in Montgomery, Alabama, five thousand African Americans flocked to the city's Holt Street Baptist church to show their support for the struggle against Jim Crow. One thousand people stood in the church's pews and aisles while four thousand others lined the streets surrounding it. Around 7 that night, the Reverend Martin Luther King, Jr., made his way past the throng and spoke words that would make him a national leader. As his words echoed off church walls and over loudspeakers, it became clear that Dr. King was not only a man of vision but that the churches would play a critical role in the civil rights movement [Kennard, 2000, pp. 1–2].

Kennard also espoused the courage of visionary African American radio personalities, who sensed the timing, the beginning, of a movement that would give voice to their listeners in the midst of confusion and disillusionment:

> Black DJs kept listeners informed and inspired people to work in their communities; DJs, of all people, challenged the country to do more, be better, and fulfill the promise of equal opportunity for all. In Columbia and Cincinnati, Ohio, the DJs Eddie Castenberry and Jack Gibson urged listeners to take part in community marches and rallies. Without Black radio, Gibson said years later, "there would have never been a movement" [Ibid.].

This cry aloud for unity, locally and nationally, was not one unfamiliar to African American audiences. Black radio, as an institution, knew early on that personalities and listeners had to work together on community issues, for much of their concerns were addressed sensationally in the mainstream press which did little to offer solutions. In the 1950s and 1960s, community service efforts like raising money for Goodwill through WDIA's *Star-lite Revue* (which featured musicians such as Aretha Franklin, The O'Jays and The Delphonics) set the stage for political struggles to come in the years that followed: "The DIA story starts before Martin Luther King, Jr., and Rosa Parks ... before [Birmingham commissioner Eugene] Bull Conner and the police dogs, before sit-ins and voting-rights drives, civil rights marches and busing bills, before Stokley Carmichael and H. Rapp Brown, Malcolm X and Elijah Mohammed, Black power and white backlash, political assassinations and riots in the ghetto" (Cantor, 1992, p. 227).

Black radio became an agent of change, creating partnerships and alliances with social institutions. Black radio, serving as the voice of African Americans nationwide, became a unifying force on the night that King was assassinated. During the late 1960s and early 1970s, a number of researchers, as well as the national press, criticized Black radio for its failure to address the needs of the African American community (Fedler, 1973; Ferretti, 1970; Meyer, 1970; Meyer, 1971; O'Connor and Cook, 1975). Louis Cantor (1992, p. 172) dismissed these complaints in *Wheelin' on Beale* when he wrote, "There were very few people who found fault with Black radio. Almost everyone, from entertainment critics to entrepreneurial leaders, Black and White, rejoiced that more Black voices were being heard on the air." Black radio stations were instrumental in vocalizing the concerns of the civil rights movement. For instance, at that time, the activism of the Black Panthers impacted the direction and programming of Black-owned KDIA in San Francisco (Buffa, 2000). In essence, the civil rights movement provided inspiration and frustration for African American broadcasters.

Although Black radio had become a force in urban communities, there were only a handful of stations owned by African Americans at the time of King's death:

> The surge of Black consciousness (the Dr. King era, Elijah Mohammed era), and all those things that prompted the Black community to seek political empowerment, economic empowerment, needed a place to be aired.... [There was a] recognition on the part of the Black community that Black radio was

its best media friend.... We still play a lot of Dr. King. A lot of that is a response to what we perceive as Black leadership, and White America would never recognize [Louis] Farrakhan or view him the way Black America does. The same [with] Nelson Mandela [Collins, personal communication, 1993].

E. Steven Collins (1993), when interviewed, already had a long history in Black radio, and pointed out the importance of crediting Black radio for having "generally ... a different viewpoint" and that its personalities "bring that perspective to life on-air." Drawing from his experiences, he reflected on how this theme evolved throughout his career: "While I was in college, I was at WBLS for a couple of weekends, and at the time B.L.S. stood for New York's Black Liberation Station." In the 1990s, it became known as "New York's Best Looking Sound." Collins added, "So there is an alteration. But their AM station, WLIB, continue[d] to be the community active station" (Collins, personal communication, 1993). WLIB's banner statement today, "Your Praise and Inspiration Station," is a reminder that Black radio began as a means to inspire listeners to come together as a community of hope and faith through music and message — a message of transformation and empowerment.

A Legacy of Black Radio

Among the first powerhouse radio stations for African Americans was White-owned WDIA in Memphis with 250 watts (50,000 watts in 1954) blasting throughout the South in the 1940s. In October 1948, a former high school history teacher named Nat D. Williams became the first African American on-air personality in the South, broadcasting from WDIA's studio on Beale Street. His popularity was one of the reasons for the station's switch to an all–Black format. During Williams' first week on air at WIDA, he received 5,000 letters (Newman, 1988). His radio career had begun a few years earlier at WHBQ-AM, a small, independent 100-watt station that aired Black-oriented programming into Memphis as early as the 1930s (ibid.).

WDIA's Black-oriented programming was inspired by the marketing ingenuity of its management and evolved into a genuine concern for its African American listeners: the station encouraged audience participation and community involvement and was promoted through a number of community events (Cantor, 1992; Love, 1999f; Newman, 1988). WDIA soon assumed a leadership role in organizing a number of fund-raising community service events in the South, some of which included sending African Americans to college, establishing a school for physically challenged African American children and saving a town from bankruptcy (Cantor, 1992). WDIA's impact in Memphis and the surrounding region was astounding, and it attracted large crowds to religious and popular music concerts and other events such as the *Hallelujah Jubilee Caravan*, *Star-lite Revue* and *Goodwill Revue* (Lornell, 1988).

WDIA was known for its Goodwill Announcements, which went far beyond the role of traditional public service messages, for example: "announcements about missing persons, lost personal property, church meetings, and socials; it answered appeals for blood donors, helped reunite families, assisted listeners in getting jobs, and even found occasional lost animals" (Cantor, 1992, p. 197). While some of its public service programming (such as missing person announcements and job openings) sounded similar to what Cooper first aired in Chicago, WDIA developed its own niche in the South:

> The Goodwill Station, as it came to be known, spoke directly to the need of the Black community, and was an unprecedented pioneer in community affairs involvement, setting new standards for civic-minded responsibility for the electronic media.... By the 1960s, the station boasted that it had spent a quarter of a million dollars annually "in cash, time and talent to carry out a program of personal service to its audience" ["Southern Folklore," 1992, p. 11].

Black-formatted radio springing up in urban areas across the country in the late 1940s and 1950s focused on developing a Black image through aggressive community service activity and promotion (George, 1988). WDIA's John Pepper and other station owners soon realized "listener response in the Black community [was] higher than it [was] in the white community, not only to advertising, but also to programming" (Newman, 1988, p. 112). In 1949, WDIA-AM became the first all Black-formatted station in the U.S. WEDR-AM in Birmingham was the first station with all African American personalities. WMRY-AM, New Orleans, soon boasted of an all African American on-air staff (Marion, 2001). That same year, WERD-AM in Atlanta became the first Black-owned station in the nation, and was purchased by Jesse B. Blayton, the only African American certified public accountant in Georgia at the time (Alston, 1978); KPRS-FM in Kansas City, Missouri, became the second in 1950 (Cantor, 1992; Marion, 2001; Schuyler, 1990; "Southern Folklore," 1992). Mildred Carter helped her husband, Andrew R. Carter, build KPRS into a community-minded commercial station: "We have built a legacy, one I intend to keep in the family and my race ... you're going to have struggles and trials, but this can be done" (Schuyler, 1990, p. 14).

In 1949, WDAS-AM and WHAT-AM aired live broadcasts from the bandstand at the Showboat in Philadelphia (Marion, 2001). African American radio deejays could also be heard on Winston-Salem's WAAA-AM in 1951, and by late 1953, rhythm and blues station WNJR-AM, Newark, featured an all Black staff (Marion, 2001). During this period, African American radio "grew from 56 hours weekly (including religious programming) to more than 400 hours a week" (Spaulding, 1981, p. 47). Early community promotions generated participation in educational and civil rights activities, such as keeping students in school, sending African American reporters to Vietnam, and raising money for Martin Luther King, Jr. (Settel, 1967).

By the mid–1990s, WDIA had shifted much of its promotional activity to its sister station WHRK-FM. However, WDIA has launched a promotional effort to reaffirm its position as the community voice for Memphis; its logo is "America's Original Black Station." The WDIA Web banner flashes "60 Years of Goodwill and Good Times." WHRK is a hip-hop and rhythm and blues station that is highly targeted toward African American pop culture with programming geared to the needs of the community in its message and contests (i.e., Win Gas for Life). Both stations are now owned by Clear Channel Communications, Inc. Some of the other original players such as KFFA-AM in Helena, Arkansas, and WSBC-AM in Chicago that aired only a few hours of African American programming weekly in the early days of Black radio nevertheless had made an impact in the communities that they served. KFFA-AM still airs the *King Biscuit Time Radio Show*, which is the longest running daily radio show in the U.S., airing for more than 60 years. WSBC-AM now airs primarily Russian language programming, along with Spanish, Greek, Romanian, and Ukrainian. A handful of the original Black-formatted stations of the forties and fifties remain true to their African American heritage today; the falling away for many occurred after ownership changes.

The Community in Black Radio

For more than a half century, programmers at landmark Black-urban radio stations, such as WDIA-AM/FM in Memphis, KPRS-FM in Kansas City, WDAS-AM/FM in Philadelphia, WLIB-AM/WBLS-FM in New

York City, WJLB-AM/FM in Detroit, WBEE-AM, WVON-AM and WGCI-AM/FM in Chicago, and WLYD-AM/FM in New Orleans had espoused the virtues of community service and had demonstrated a strong commitment to their core audience (Johnson, 1992; Love, 1991d; Love, 1998). In 2006, nearly all of these stations were operated by Clear Channel Communications Inc. (the largest radio chain in the U.S.). The WLIB/WBLS stations are owned by Inner City Broadcasting Corporation, a corporate Black radio chain. WVON is owned by Midway Broadcasting, an African American company that made a shared broadcast agreement with Clear Channel in 2006, yet it operates independently from the corporation. KPRS remains Black-owned and operated by the Carter family, and according to the FCC, it is the longest operating African American owned station.

Over the years, a number of Black and urban radio stations, with secular formats but Christian messages, attracted from 5,000 to over a half million listeners to their promotions, such as Juneteenth celebrations by WFXE-FM, Columbus, Georgia, WQUE-FM, New Orleans, and KJMS-FM, Memphis, and family unification days sponsored by WJLB-FM, Detroit and WDAS-FM, Philadelphia. Now all of those stations except for WFXE-FM are owned by Clear Channel. WFXE-FM, a NABOB member station, is still operated by Davis Broadcasting. Unity Day in Philadelphia, at its height a five day event with an estimated attendance of one million people, has annually drawn national attention for many of its African American political and celebrity speakers and its community events centered on the family.

Black radio has historically facilitated community alliances when they are committed toward tackling difficult social problems, with stations providing airtime and resources to help fight street crime associated with drugs and to generate money and supplies for a number of non-profit organizations.. They have sponsored fund-raising promotions for Big Brother, Big Sister, United Negro College Fund, March of Dimes, American Cancer Society, and The National Civil Rights Museum, as well as local police departments, social agencies, schools, and a host of other organizations. Black expositions sponsored by stations in Oakland, Indianapolis, St. Louis, and other cities have inspired civic pride, promoted minority-owned businesses, and have provided a context for civil rights issues.

Black radio has been a social and political force nationwide for over a half century, encouraging community participation in education, demonstrating citizenship through ongoing voter registration efforts and civic pride, promoting cultural and religious events, and providing activities that encourage family unification (Barlow, 1999; Cantor, 1992; Newman, 1988). In an effort to help urban youth, the bonding of families, businesses, social agencies and media into inner-city community partnerships was the focus of education research, particularly in the eighties (Hale-Benson, 1986). The National Urban League called for participation in elementary and secondary education through "intensive mobilization and coalition-building activity" (Jacob, 1987–1988, p. 16) within the Black community. In the past, a number of researchers have suggested an alliance between Black parents, civic groups, business leaders, politicians, inner city churches, and schools would provide the socializing forces necessary to help African American youth overcome educational inequities (Chapman, 1991; Hare, 1988–1989; Hilliard III, 1987–1988; Slaughter and Kuehne, 1987–1988; Thompson and Cusella, 1991).

As early as 1970, WWRL-AM won the *Billboard* Community Service Award for its Bust a Pusher campaign ("Black Radio," 1970, p. 49). WWRL waged war on drugs and violence across the New York airwaves. Twenty years later, Robin Breedon, morning host for WPGC-FM, waged a war on drugs and violence in Washington, D.C., as one of the highest paid and highly rated personalities in the market (Rosenfeld, 1991).

> She has helped the station with its latest, most ambitious campaign: trying to get all the thugs in the Washington area to stop killing people for a 24-hour period.... Last year, the station set Thanksgiving as its murder-free day. There were, indeed, no homicides on that day.

The article continues,

> Breedon has been soliciting calls from drug addicts, dealers, their relatives, prisoners, relatives of homicide victims, kids — whoever has something to say in 30 seconds or so. In seconds, their thoughts have been heard by 650,000 people, according to the ratings services. And she, and the other announcers, repeat the slogan every few minutes. "Stop the Violence: Increase the Peace," is what they say [Rosenfeld, 1991, F1, F4].

In the 1990s, her youth summits attracted 3,000 youths and giveaways included T-shirts and contraceptives. Discussions centered on violence, drug abuse, AIDS, dropping out of school, teen suicides, and employment opportunities for youth. Radio promotional events, such as teen concerts and guest lectures from on-air personalities at area schools, were organized to send strong anti-drug and anti-violence messages to urban youth. Some Black radio stations targeted young adults in the inner city and, in some cases, attracted the attention of gang members by airing rap music and street news. In Dallas, KJMZ-FM sponsored a Stop the Violence movement, with the idea of stopping the music, getting its staff on the streets, and "asking its listeners for solutions to street violence" (Love, 1992b, p. 41). KPRS-FM's show *Generation Rap* in Kansas City inspired area youth to become involved in career preparation while still in secondary school, encouraging them to succeed through educational advancement and cultural literacy (*Generation Rap*, 1993). Baltimore's WXYV-FM established rapport with urban youth by asking that its on-air personalities become involved in community organizations (Love, 1991c, p. 42). This type of commitment is becoming the exception rather than the practice.

KJLH: Keeping the Heritage

Close to 30 years after Black radio's coverage of the Watts riots, KJLH-FM would be in the front seat. Black radio could not help but learn from KGFJ's experience and consequently respond effectively to its community needs, especially in a time of crisis. As KJLH matured under Stevie Wonder's ownership, it would become the clearinghouse for listeners seeking assistance and reassurance in 1992, as did KGJF in the 1960s. By 1979, KJLH sponsored 21 different church services. That same year, Hill, Jr., decided to sell KJLH "only to a black buyer" (Barlow, 1999, p. 269). Stevie Wonder (under the company name of Taxi Productions, Inc.) purchased KJLH for $2.2 million. Wonder was a strong advocate of the civil rights movement, and recognized the power of radio even as a boy. Years later when he was invited to speak before the Federal Communications Commission, he testified on behalf of KJLH — and locally owned and operated stations like KJLH:

> I am Steven Morris, professionally known as Stevie Wonder. I am an artist. I bought a radio station in 1979 because I understood and valued the power of radio. As an artist, I appreciated the marketing power of the airwaves. As a student of social justice, I witnessed the power of and the reliance of mass communications.... The reality is that the very reason that I'm able to be here today as Stevie Wonder, born as Steven Morris, is because of the radio station that was a minority-owned station in Inkster, Michigan, WCHB, which is a daytime station. And it was through me listening to the music and listening to the news and information that inspired me to as a little kid, far against my mother's rules — I went and I took one of the radios she had and kind of put some plugs in different places and tried to broadcast through the house and got a whip-

ping. But the point I'm making is never did I imagine that I was going to be the owner of a radio station. But I — when coming to Los Angeles and hearing the station that was licensed by the city of Compton, KJLH — was so inspired by how much it sounded similar to the format of music and information as did the station that was an AM station in Inkster, Michigan.

The truth of the matter is that I, a few years ago, was approached to sell that station, to give it up. And I could have gotten myself forty or fifty million dollars. I love playing with money. It's okay. But the — the real important thing for me is that I wanted to — far more important than — than getting some money, I wanted to make sure that the voice of a community would be consistently heard and that it would open up a place of communication so that not that — not just that minority community, but all various peoples of this melting pot that is to be called the United States, various cultures could be heard and united. I just wanted to make that point [*FCC Proceeding*, 1999, p. 97, 98].

WCHB-AM was the first Black-owned station in Michigan and the third in the nation. Wendell Cox and Haley Bell (Bell Broadcasting) were the original owners of that Inkster station in Michigan, and the first African Americans to receive a construction permit from the FCC in the early 1950s to build a station from the ground level. The call letters actually represented the names of the owners. Wonder, when he purchased KJLH, thought about the significance of his call letters, and what each letter would mean to his audience. He would decide not to change the call letters K-J-L-H, and instead each letter would remain symbolic of his desire to bring the community together through "kindness, joy, love, and happiness" (Gronau, 2001, p. 1). As a side note, KHJ-AM of Mutual Network was one of the top Los Angeles stations of the 1940s, and its call letters signified kindness, happiness, and joy.

In its early days on Detroit's airwaves, WCHB-AM aired rhythm and blues, and was a street smart station, tapping into the needs of its community. Bell Broadcasting added an FM station in 1960. WCHB-FM separated from its sister station in the late 1960s and began playing jazz. Bell Broadcasting, the original owners, changed the call letters to WJZZ, and that format run ended in 1996 when the station flipped to urban contemporary. Two years later, Radio One bought the AM and FM and changed the FM to WDTJ. Radio One is one of the nation's largest radio broadcasting companies — and the largest Black radio conglomerate. The Russ Parr morning show was picked up by the new owner from its company sister station WKYS-FM in Washington, D.C., Parr would be a guest on KJLH during the critical hours of the Los Angeles unrest in 1992. He would be calling for peace on the streets.

In 2005, the WDTJ-FM programming was flipped with another Radio One station in the market, and it became WDMK, Kiss-FM, playing classic urban adult contemporary music and adding the Tom Joyner morning show to its program schedule. WCHB-AM, known for many years as the People's Station, went through some format changes as well over the years; in the 1960s, it was all about the Motown sound. It dabbled with disco through the 1980s. By the 1990s, the station had positioned itself as a community leader once again for African Americans, and Radio One upgraded its signal near the end of the decade. In 2005, the AM downsized its gospel music to nights and aired mostly news and talk in the daytime. In June 2008, it converted back to a gospel music station. Regardless, the core of listeners is urban African Americans for both stations.

WCHB-AM signed on November 1956 when Wonder was six-years-old, and listening and living in Inkster, which is now part of the Detroit metropolitan area. It was a neighborhood station, where everybody knew the owners and radio personalities, and they worked together to make a difference in the community. The impact of this station on his political and social views clearly influenced his decision to buy KJLH, as well as how to program it. The legacy of WCHB reaches into Detroit, beyond being that small community station that Wonder grew up listening to as a child. Mildred Gaddis is one of the top morning personalities in Detroit, and hosts *Inside Detroit* on WCHB-AM weekdays. Known for her ability to handle tough issues and tight-lipped interviewees, she offers a political edge to her show's content. She's a 30-year radio veteran who has been named Professional Woman of the Year by the National Association of Negro Business Women's Organization and a Living Legend by the City of Detroit. The station continues to make a difference to its African American audience, inspiring them through music and message. The station airs what it calls inspiration music daily, basically a strong mix of Black gospel, contemporary and classic. Wonder's station devotes at least 10 percent of its music programming to gospel music as well. Unfortunately, the gospel music at WCHB is now automated, but Gaddis is very much a radio legend, airing her program live every weekday morning.

The philosophy behind Black radio is one of appreciation for its community leaders, and it attempts to impart its African American legacy and history on social, political, and economic issues to its listeners. As a testimony of KJLH's historical link with area churches, it continues to broadcast church and gospel programming on Sundays. Listeners can tune into not only traditional church services and related discussions, but the station hosts one of the largest gospel music concerts on the West Coast. The annual Gospel Showcase at Knott's Berry Farm in Los Angeles features musicians, theme park rides, and family events for the approximately 20,000 people in attendance; through such activities KJLH reaffirms its historical roots (CAAM, 2007).

William Barlow (1999, p. 270) reminds us that Wonder was "an early proponent of establishing the [Reverend] Martin Luther King's birthday as a national holiday and an outspoken opponent of apartheid in South Africa, where his music was banned." His song *Happy Birthday* became the theme of the King campaign: "I just never understood/How a man who died for good/Could not have a day that would/Be set aside for his recognition" are among the lyrics. Barlow (1999) sees Wonder's music as an extension of his political outreach — actualized through his radio station, KJLH: "His song, 'It's Wrong,' says it all about his feelings on apartheid. His concerns toward social issues and commitment to the local Black populace became the centerpiece of the station's new format" (p. 270).

CHAPTER 4

Fueling the Passion
The Wonderful Black Community Mission

Quincy McCoy warned the radio industry at the turn of the 21st century: "Born only 50 years ago, Black-owned, independently run stations are facing extinction, suffocating under the heavy weight of consolidation" (2000, p. 1). Slowly, Black radio stations are being replaced with corporate counterfeits. The stations sound the same. Sometimes the radio personalities and station employees continue on with the new companies. But the soul — the very essence of the station — is somewhat different, perhaps barely noticeable at first until an event reveals otherwise. Take for example, the case of New York's Hot 97's reaction to a February 2000 event, in which young Black and Latino New Yorkers tuned to the station for news and analysis after a jury acquitted the four New York City police officers who shot and killed Amadou Diallo with 41 bullets: "They were stunned by what they heard; the one person interviewed on the station's public-affairs show, 'Street Soldiers,' was a police officer" (Buffa, 2000, p. 1). Demonstrators picketed the station.

Hot 97 is an urban commercial station that is not minority owned. There is the swelling desire to target music and advertisements toward African Americans, but very few non-minority companies offer anything of significance in the way of community service and perspective. In another example, when Chancellor Media consolidated interests with radio giant AMFM (which would eventually become part of Clear Channel Communications), one of KMEL's highly rated public affairs shows that targeted San Francisco youth with programs on violence, drugs, and teen pregnancy was canceled. Host Joe Marshall blames corporate radio, which "tries to pump more and more dollars out of the community that it programs to but does not attempt to serve that community in any meaningful way by giving something back to them" (Buffa, 2000, p. 1). Sparked by the elimination of the Fairness Doctrine to the rubber stamping of the Telecommunications Act of 1996, deregulation has created a new corporate breed of radio that has "all but eliminated minority-owned radio and community-based programs geared to people of color" (p. 1).

In late spring 2007, recording industry executives had closed door meetings with the Reverend Al Sharpton in response to his criticism toward promotion of controversial lyrics in the hip hop industry. Sharpton, a nationally syndicated radio talk show host, was one of many African American political activists who called for reform in the music and radio industry. Sharpton worked alongside the National Action Network (NAN), which organized a march against the record industry's promotion of racism, sexism, and homophobia in May 2008. The group of protestors marched down New York's Music Row, moving from the Sony Music Building, to the Warner Music Group building, then Universal Music Group building, and the Time Warner Building. Radio stations owned by large corporate groups were also under fire for their airplay of these controversial songs. Reports of gang violence outside the top hip hop New York stations were blamed by critics on the airplay of these songs.

Raising the Standard

As consolidation escalated in the 1990s, KJLH would position itself stronger as a community station with international outreach. It became evident in 1992 that KJLH had the pulse of the community running through its airwaves when it fed into the needs of its listeners and South Central residents in a responsible way that engaged the citizenry. One decision back then, the creation of *Front Page*, KJLH's flagship broadcast program, would earmark the station as a leading alternative voice in Los Angeles and across the U.S. A significant factor that led to the station's grasp of community issues in 1992 was its location, or proximity to its listeners, during the Los Angeles Riots. KJLH staff and management had regularly ascertained issues and concerns that plagued its community even before the 1992 events.

KJLH's role as a mediator, community activist, and change agent within the community and how its social role compares to other Black (and urban) radio stations in the U.S. are both critical factors that have contributed toward the station's longevity. Even its day to day community service activities demonstrate the station's mission is more than talk; it is action. It acted upon the residents' needs during the 1992 civil unrest and has subsequently remained responsive to its audience. During the unrest, the station turned into a community network of information on places to go in the city for food and shelter, places to cash checks, and ways to discuss with children what was going on in the streets. By its very service to the community, KJLH countered some of the negative images strewn across television. But, more importantly, the radio station became the focal point for discussion and implementation of non-violent solutions to the social ills of Southern Los Angeles and to the larger Black community across the nation.

The Black Press as a Mentor

KJLH's story actually began before radio. Its legacy was built on the foundation of the Black press. With more than 100 channels beaming across satellite dishes today, and streaming video and audio across the Web, it is sometimes easy to forget that some of the more traditional forms of media have created precedent in positive and negative ways. The media, like other institutions, have the power to unify or alienate a community or nation of people. The desire to create unity within the African American community is not unique to Black radio. Culturally specific entities such as Black-owned churches, minority-owned businesses, urban schools, and the Black media (especially the Black-owned press) have been identified as essential toward establishing urban partnerships (Allen, Dawson, and Brown, 1989; Garland, 1988; Sherard, 1988). These social institutions have been influential in strengthening what Richard L. Allen et al. (1989, p. 426) referred to as a community's "racial belief system," which creates a social bond among the masses and provides positive role models.

The Black press and Black radio should be viewed as working together toward the same goal of establishing strong community partnerships within urban neighborhoods. The early success of "Black-oriented radio" in Chicago, for instance, was fueled somewhat by "Black illiteracy" as well as the failure of print media to appeal to many African Americans seeking alternative sources of information and entertainment (Spaulding, 1981, p. 43). From its early origins, the role of the Black-owned press has been to create a sense of communal identity dating back to the first anti-slavery efforts in America (Garland, 1988; Hutton, 1992; Sherard, 1988). *The California Eagle*, founded in 1879, was instrumental in promoting the cause of equity and justice in the life of the African American in Los Angeles. Although its last paper was published in the early 1970s, it had paved the way for the *Los Angeles Sentinel* (first published in 1933) and other Black-owned newspapers such as the *L.A. Watts Times* and *The Wave* in Southern California (Burroughs, 2002).

KJLH's role during the civil unrest was published by the local Black press (i.e., *Los Angeles Sentinel* and *L.A. Watts Times*) in the early 1990s. On the other hand, mainstream media coverage of KJLH's activist role in the 1992 Los Angeles riots was virtually non-existent, except for a few lines in *USA Today* ("Celebs Pitch," 1992) during the unrest, a few articles a year later about the 1993 George Foster Peabody Award winners (they mentioned KJLH), and a feature story in the *Los Angeles Times* (Hawkins, 2000) several years later. One newspaper article in the *Times* stated that KJLH was awarded a Peabody for "timely, exhaustive and important coverage" (Weinstein, 1993, p. 13) of the 1992 Los Angeles Riots. KJLH also won the NAACP Humanitarian Award, as well as a number of community awards from the L.A. Press Club, *Los Angeles Sentinel*, New Frontier Democratic Club, Brotherhood Crusade, and the City of Los Angeles.

W. Phillips Davison, in his study on *How Communication Affects the Quality of Life in an Urban Neighborhood*, points out that community media, namely the local press, have the potential to promote community events and provide links to businesses or the government, especially if the coverage "leads to stories in the city-wide press or on television, or if the local reports are forwarded through interpersonal channels" (Davison, 1988, p. 25). Community leaders in one urban neighborhood, for instance, described their local paper as "responsive [and] an active participant in community enterprises" (ibid., p. 22). The small press was also acknowledged by Morris Janowitz (1952) as a significant force in the social fabric of the urban community through its support of area businesses and its shaping of positive attitudes toward civic organizations. The Black press particularly has supported the efforts of Black radio in its desire to promote community unification. The Black press and Black radio, as culturally specific media, struggle to maintain their financial independence (and thus their unique identity) in an era of consolidation.

Knowing the Listener

Unemployment, gang-related violence, poverty, racism, and school absenteeism are issues that have plagued the health of urban youth in general, with homicide as one of the leading historical causes of death for teenage African American males (Anderson, Kochanek, and Murphy, 1997; "Facts," 2002; Fingerhut et al., 1992; Smith, 1985–1986; Thomas, 1990). Slade (personal communication, 2002) noted that the numbers on youth violence released a decade after the riots were "horrendous" and appeared on the rise comparably to other years:

> We got the numbers from Los Angeles Police Chief Bernard Parks ... and the numbers are just frightening and will reach a crescendo by the summer. So we are going to head them off at the pass ... and we'll work that into our Black History month campaign.

KJLH's ascertainment efforts not only provide a means to identify community issues, but they also afford management the data to prioritize them. Slade said: "We do ascertainment forms or assessment forms throughout the year to try to find out, well what's the hot topic, what issues are concerning you and they're usually education, violence, you know; there's usually a top three, four, or five and I try to do some type of either town hall meeting or extended coverage in our public affairs programs to make sure that they get the information they need."

She continued,

> Usually about March or April of every year our youth violence goes up, and we anticipate it's because of impending summer and spring vacations and the kids just really start killing each other; so it's something we know happens every spring/summer — we try to prepare for it, we try to get the parents geared up; we've had [the sheriff] come in.... Even though we don't air a lot of politicians, we've had a lot of politicians and people step forward and come to the table and communicate with our audience to try to give them the information that they need. And that's probably been an outgrowth of the civil unrest that [this approach] has worked well" [ibid.].

Slade also underscored the reasons behind the station's longstanding commitment toward community service and its ascertainment of audience needs, regardless of governmental deregulation on mandates of public service, as matters of principle, ethics, and good news sense:

> We also do news, which is, you know, a rarity in a music-formatted station. But our public affairs keep us in tune with what the community is thinking. I mean it really does — I can't say that enough, because people will call in and

they'll tell you what they think about any given topic and you know, when the phones are lit, it's a hot topic — if they call in and ask for tapes of the show or information about the interviewer or guest, and then the website, how much they talk about it in the chat room. So you know, this is hot, guests can come back; maybe we should build something around this guest, that type of thing. So, it really does help you. The information is there; you just have to know how to retrieve it and what to do with it once you've gotten it and I think ... they've taught us, pretty much our audience has taught us what they need and we've listened [ibid.].

The station projects more than simply a positive image to its audience. Rather, KJLH identifies with the needs and concerns of its listeners, many of whom are parents, and it has a special concern for African American youth (Johnson, personal communication, 2002; Nelson, personal communication, 2001; Slade, personal communication, 2002). The "We are You" positioning statement can be heard on the air and seen on the Web, and what it conveys at first glance is a desire to move beyond its station image toward identification with the larger African American community.

Racial identify, as defined by Davis and Gandy (1999), is both an individual and social phenomena that likely impacts one's view of, as well as response to, the world and media and is both "situationally emergent" and contextually-driven by "cumulative" social modeling: "Cognitive schema are influenced by who we are (our background), what we do (our direct, personal experiences), and what we see, hear, and learn through our exposure to mass media" (p. 1). "Media representations," according to Davis and Gandy (1999, p. 1), "play an important role in informing the ways in which we understand social, cultural, ethnic, and racial differences. Racial identity may play an especially powerful role in shaping our responses to mass media." It should be considered "a powerful determinant of individual behavior. It affects the individual choices we make with regard to mass media and our role as audiences and consumers" (ibid.).

Consequently KJLH's decision to empower listeners and staff members could have very well contributed toward community participation in political and civic activities and organizations (Davis and Gandy, 1999; also see, Dawson, 1994a and 1994b; Shingles, 1981; Thompson-Sanders, 1990). KJLH created a shared identity among its listeners as they called into the station to voice their outrage to the verdict. Slade, Nelson and others describe their listeners and the residents of South Central as ordinary people faced with extraordinary circumstances that were far beyond their control. Black radio, likewise, with its powerful community message, has the potential to unify, rather than alienate, its audience (Legette, 1994;

Johnson, 1992). KJLH is an institutional member of the Black community and, as such, it attempted to empower its listeners in South Central Los Angeles as well as across the nation. In contrast, Davis and Gandy (1999, p. 13) point out that "mass media images of Black males as violent and threatening" forces both challenge and contradict racial identities embedded in personal and social experiences within the African American community. These negative images are "internalized" (ibid.) by African Americans and accelerated during times of crisis, like when television producers stereotypically depicted Black youth as villains during the 1992 civil unrest. Moreover, it is likely that regular listeners prior to the King verdict had already anticipated outrage on the streets, as suggested by Nelson (2001) and Slade (2002). Alcalay and Taplin (1989, p. 106) criticize mass media, in general, for its failure to connect to community issues and its neglect of "cultural, economic, demographic and health priorities."

In the mid–1980s, a national study of African American and minority health concerns indicated that the success of campaigns dealing with drug abuse and homicide was dependent on the delivery system's ability to change the social and political environment in the community (Heckler, 1985, 1986). Other minority health issues "most likely to be affected by health education interventions" were smoking, teenage pregnancy, sexually transmitted diseases, child abuse, stress management, diet and exercise (Heckler, 1986, p. 194). Reagan and Collins (1987) claim mainstream media have been less effective for providing usable information to listeners than interpersonal sources such as families, friends, and schools. National media networks often at the exclusion of smaller media organizations have typically set the agenda for discussion, but they have had little impact on public policy (other than mobilization) that would assist African American audiences (Shaw and McCombs, 1989).

Awareness campaigns targeting substance abuse, for example, have not been as effective as those that allow members of the neighborhood to participate or intervene in the actual prevention programs (Alcalay and Taplin, 1989). Spergel and Curry (1990, p. 295), in a comprehensive survey of 45 cities, found that community organizations working with youth have focused on "involving the schools, mobilizing the community, building community trust, involving parent groups in community programs, educating the community [and] changing the community." Along this line, mass media has sent mixed messages to African American youth. This is especially significant when one considers that African American youth, male and female, are heavier users of radio and television than other populations (Brown, Childers, Bauman, and Koch, 1990; Davis and Gandy, 1999). Public service announcements warn teens to "Just Say No" to alcohol and cigarettes, yet advertising for these products are plastered across inner city billboards and often directed toward African American youth (Thomas, 1990).

On April 24, 2002, MTV aired *Back to the Hood*, a one-hour documentary that asked a number of musicians and young people to reflect on the violence that they had witnessed during the Los Angeles riots while living — many as children — in South Central or the neighboring communities of Watts, Crenshaw, and Koreatown. One rap artist, Jurrassic Five, who lived a block from Florence and Normandy, recalled the Denny beating. Others interviewed for the MTV special admitted to looting and participating in the destruction. Mass media's perception and portrayal, however, of urban teens is not a new problem, notes Rubel (1980, pp. 18–19): "[What] sources put forward as an 'objective portrayal of vandalism and violence' ... in general [is] actually a presentation of rare and bizarre incidents." For the most part, mainstream media's coverage of the civil unrest played out like a bad Hollywood movie, with all the African American actors typecast as the Black hats.

On May 1, 1992, one listener — audibly frightened, yet articulate — intuitively knew that the South Central residents, especially the young adults, needed to seek ways to pull together and solidify the community:

> There also needs to be some type of planning for the aftermath, because when this is over and when this is ended, then our people need to be able to turn somewhere to look for some type of an answer and some type of a solution, and I don't know how it will come or how it will happen, but like the churches need to develop some type of community caravan to try to find our elderly citizens and try to find transportation for them to get medicine and to get food and to make sure that they're okay, because they're the ones that are stranded in their homes and cannot go anywhere. There are other people who are still mobile, but our elderly people, they have nothing. They need to have some type of transportation, and some way for them to get food. I think it is time right now for our young people, and I'm talking about people between the ages of 20 and 27, our young leadership to come to the forefront now, not only to make a statement but to show some type of a sign of solidarity, to come out and to show people that, "No, we are not going to stand for this, and that some type of way we are going to try to provide some solutions, some resolutions, because that's all people are looking for. People are looking for answers and they haven't found anything. Unfortunately, they're looking for the answers in the wrong place. But they are looking for an answer; they're looking for a solution

to their problems and to what's going on and I'm angered by it as well [*Front Page*, 1992c].

"Increasing the Peace"

Black-owned mass media (e.g., Black press, Black television) and the African American religious infrastructure have been identified as powerful forces for positive change in the African American experience (Garland, 1988; Sherard, 1988). In the early 1990s, WPGC-FM's Robin Breedon emerged as the number one Arbitron-ranked morning host in Washington, D.C., at a time when her competitors like shock jock Howard Stern relied on pranks and crude jokes to attract their audiences. "I need a death toll," announced Breedon to her intern as her urban audience listened to her call for the murder count from the previous night, in response to the alarming rise of violence in DC (Rosenfeld, 1991, p. F1).

Black-owned and Black-oriented radio have the potential to target audiences often neglected by mainstream media, especially when it comes to achieving equity and social justice on and off the airwaves. Similar to the actions of other Black radio stations across the U.S., KJLH has created partnerships and alliances within the African American community and subsequently has served as a change agent (Erskine, 1991–1992). In 1992, KJLH became a unifying force among listeners and residents during the Los Angeles riots just as a number of Black radio stations did on the night that King, Jr., was assassinated. Black radio became the voice of African Americans nationwide then, and again in 1992 when KJLH interrupted its regular programming to report on and to discuss the events that transpired for nearly a week in the heart of southern Los Angeles. More importantly, KJLH became part of the story as it attempted to serve as a community agency. When all was said and done, a grateful listener nominated the station for a George Foster Peabody Award, and KJLH was announced as the winner on April 1, 1993. KJLH's management and staff never anticipated any recognition for its efforts:

Yeah, [it was] kinda like baptism by drowning. You just get thrown in there and you swim and you look back and you go, "God, I can't believe I made it that far," but you don't quit; you just keep doing what you think is right and lo and behold you look back and you go, "Wow, it turned out." As a matter of fact, there was someone in the market at that time and they heard us, and they called in later and asked for a tape, so we put together a compilation and they submitted us for a Peabody Award, which we didn't initiate ... I didn't even know the significance of the Peabody until, of course, much later, and I was so honored, but once again, it wasn't even self-promotion. It was a listener that initiated that on our behalf because they thought what we did was so significant. So, you know, God bless them, you know, 'cause once again, being not necessarily naive, but staying so focused in the community, I didn't step back to see, what else — what other impact it could have had, because we had calls from other major cities. We had calls from as far away as London and Paris and Ghana because we've done a lot of outreach internationally. We've had interns from London come over here, and so they know us a little bit, and so we received calls from all over and we did a lot of broadcasting, a lot of updates [Slade, personal communication, 2002].

Nelson notes, "I don't think we did anything different than what every other radio station should have done during the civil disturbances. Most chose to play music rather than to be responsible to what was going on in the community" (Weinstein, 1993, p. 13). He underscored the importance of media, particularly Black media, to advance programming that deals with issues critical to the African American community: "But I think it is incumbent upon stations, especially those that appeal to ethnic minorities, to provide some kind of informational material" (p. 13)

Calls from listeners and reaction on the streets prompted other stations to respond to the verdict. In a number of cases, KJLH had set an example for them as its programming was simulcast or replayed across the nation and world. Unrest had occurred in a number of cities including San Francisco, Madison, Seattle and even the college town of Warrensburg, Missouri. When the verdict was announced Wednesday afternoon, an influx of listener calls came into Black and urban radio stations across the nation. KMJM program director Chuck Atkins recalls, "People were not calling for requests as they usually do at night.... It's the first time we've ever changed our format" (Hick, 1992, p. 25A).

Although KJLH's commitment to community is not unique, it is definitely part of the historical legacy of its owners — and Black radio in general. The station has been involved since its inception in the creation and execution of a number of community activities. Several events that occurred within the immediate years preceding and following the 1992 riots are worth mentioning for illustration. KJLH chartered a bus on December 28, 1989, for 35 homeless people and supporters of *Helpers for the Homeless and Hungry* to travel to Washington, D.C., to lobby and to attend a rally to draw attention to the needy (Mitchell, 1989). In 1991, KJLH, the California Afro American Museum, and the Institute for Black Parenting held a radio-thon to raise money and awareness targeted at the need for the adoption of Black children (KJLH, 1991). In another instance, KJLH joined with a Los Angeles baseball team in Simi Valley a few months after the Los Angeles uprising to bring the two communities together (Alvarez, 1992, p. 3). In December 1993, KJLH and RadioWest, a nonprofit organization of independent radio producers, worked together to prepare area students for careers in the media with the opportunity to produce and broadcast 30-second editorials on the air (Carr, 1993). In September 1995, the University of Southern California's Celebrity Softball Game was co-sponsored by KJLH to raise money for the Negro Baseball Leagues' pension fund (Dungee, 1995). KJLH has done a little of everything in terms of community service.

In January, the station typically organizes activities and promotions related to Martin Luther King, Jr. February is Black History Month, and KJLH typically broadcasts an inspirational role model campaign in which it features someone in education, entertainment, politics, or business, and asks, "Who is your hero? How did you get to that?" The station has asked five questions over five days for each person. Other station events have included gas discounts over three-day holiday weekends from Memorial Day, 4th of July, to Labor Day. In the past, KJLH sponsored candy giveaways at YMCAs and local schools, as well as turkey giveaways and canned food drives co-sponsored by L.A. Mission Downtown. Then around Christmas (since 1995), the station sponsors House Full of Toys, a fundraiser that provides toys and computers for 300 to 500 families every year. In addition, the station has sponsored a number of financial seminars on how to clean up your credit or how to buy a home — "whatever [the listeners] tell us is important" (Slade, personal communication, 2002). Other events coordinated specifically for *Front Page* listeners have included a trip "to the Motherland every year":

This year we went to Egypt. We've been to Ghana twice, Senegal, Ivory Coast — we've been to Gambia as well — and different places on the African coast. We've taken listeners back home 'cause anyone who's been to Africa — a Black person — knows that once you go to Africa, you're never the same person when you come back to the States. So we do that on an annual basis, and we let the listeners pick where they want to go as well, and we take them back and show them, instill some pride and try to take some young people too because they're our future. The show is really now focused on helping our young people.... So we've got to find a way how to reach our young people so they can understand, you know, what's going on and how they got to where we are in this situation. That's why we've sort of endorsed things that Dr. Claude Anderson is saying in his book, *Powernomics and Black Labor, White Wealth*, that explains clearly, very clearly, how we got to the situation we are in now and how we've become marginalized — what we can do to get out of it. You asked earlier if this could happen again in Los Angeles — could it happen again? It probably could, but it won't happen for quite a while, [Nelson, personal communication, 2001].

Stephens (2002) also relates, "News is defined as community service here, I feel. We also have a public affairs talk show, so, that kind of thing, when you don't have total latitude to do the full, full, full [program on-air], you can transfer it then to that one-hour talk show, sometimes run it two hours." KJLH has held town hall meetings on drive-by shootings as well as some topics on economics and more recently on terrorism:

They must start with the first one-to-two hours on air, and then they go off air. Traditionally, we've done them at different venues around the city, but primarily churches like the last one we did about terrorism, and the threats of terrorism in our city. We didn't have the turnout that we had hoped, but the officials came out. Well FBI, of course Chief Parks, and the Sheriff's Department, and so many people came, and then we had the religious aspect — Muslim, Christians, Catholicism. We had it at Crenshaw Christian Center.... But these are topics people ask for and we try to give them what they want [Slade, personal communication, 2002].

Another station-sponsored town hall meeting brought former CIA director John Deutsch to South Central. Nelson explains that KJLH broke a story on the government's alleged involvement in selling crack cocaine to the African American community:

So we really did a bang up story on that one. We had a town hall meeting at Marla Gibbs' place, Marla's Memory Lane, it was overflowing with people — a friend of mine, he was in Maui at the time, and he was watching it on CNN, and he was like, "Did you guys do that, did you guys break the story?" It came down — the community was really, really very upset with that. The jury's still out though whether the CIA actually was involved in bringing crack into the community. What it did, it did force the CIA Director John Deutsch, to come into South Central Los Angeles. Now Deutsch had to come in and try to explain away the fact that the government had nothing to do with bringing drugs into the community. But, at this point, I still think that the community believes that the CIA and some other folks are involved in bringing crack cocaine into our community [Nelson, personal communication, 2001].

The station's coverage of the "trafficking" issue drew national attention, and Slade recalled,

There was an article in a Bay Area newspaper that the CIA was involved with trafficking of cocaine, crack cocaine, and we got the author on air and that was a hot topic and so we did a town hall meeting on it and it was explosive. We had a 1,000 seat venue, and we had that filled to capacity, such that we had to put speakers outside because we had hoards of people that came and couldn't get in. We had everyone from Maxine Waters to ministers. When you pick a topic that's hot and that's of a concern to the community, you'll get a great turn out. The other side of it is, when I've tried to do town hall meetings on referendums or issues that I think are hot, they don't always, like the "Three Strikes Rule." They don't always get the response that you think — which doesn't mean that you're not right in doing it; it's just you may have done it a better way or used a better forum to get it done. Sometimes we do it on site either at a college campus or at a church, somewhere in the community. And if we don't think we're going to get the turn out that we need, then we'll do a two- or three-hour session on air; we'll just do a block of time with the artist, the guest [Slade, personal communication, 2002].

Their strategies, according to Slade and others, are similar to those of other Black and urban stations across the U.S. that have acknowledged relevant issues and cultural traditions unique to the African American, and in doing so stations like KJLH have celebrated the unifying concepts of family and community. In essence, KJLH's community outreach is not surprising when one considers the historical role of Black-targeted radio in unifying and serving its listeners. For example, WDAS-FM began Unity Weekend in 1978, and for more than two decades it has attracted up to one million people to its family-centered activities, health booths and cultural entertainment stages.

KJLH's commitment level to its community became particularly evident when the station raised approximately $55,000 during the course of the Los Angeles unrest, and in fact, the station never solicited any funds. People simply started coming down to the station and gave money, remembered Slade (personal communication, 2002): "We opened up a separate account at Broadway Federal, one of the Black banks, and we made micro-loan funding at the bank so small entrepreneurs could get some cash." Slade added, alluding to the station's bond with its audience, "You have a trust between you and your audience — just give it to KJLH — KJLH will know what to do with it. It was an amazing time how the city came together."

Determination Through Communication

Pierre M. Sutton, former president and chairman of the National Association of Black-Owned Broadcasters and president of Inner City

Broadcasting, states Black-owned stations have worked toward "developing a unity in the community so that actions can be taken to protect our community from itself in many cases. And in other cases from without" (*Pulse*, 1990, p. 19). Role models from inside or outside of the community who can spend time with youth appear to be the "only answer" to alleviating the drug abuse, violence, and other issues relevant to the inner city (Harvey, Bitting, and Robinson, 1989–1990, p. 127). KJLH has traditionally played a strong role in the community, and it has not ceased in its mission to reach out to listeners in tangible ways, ranging from sponsoring food drives to conducting economic seminars. KJLH is one of many social institutions in South Central — public schools, community agencies, and the churches. Its staff takes issues to the people over the radio and on the streets. It is more than just Black talk — it amplifies the community's voice by sponsoring community activism. KJLH is part of the community, along with other social and political infrastructures that shape the lives of those who live in South Central. As a guest on *Front Page*, a decade after the riots, CBS' KFWB reporter-anchor Larry Carroll observed that the first step in creating a relationship with the community is communication:

> I got to say that we have to lay a great deal of the blame for the lack of political and social focus on media, and in particular those media, which we can still call our own, if we're going to look at this from the perspective of an African American community, or even more globally as a minority community, or as community that is not in control. There is no way a community can create self-determination without communication [*Front Page*, 2002b].

We Are You

Since his purchase of KJLH, Wonder has remained engaged in its overall programming mission, which is to "entertain with the best music and to serve the African-American community in a socially responsible way" (Gronau, 2001, p. 2). One of its bannered themes, perhaps a moniker, epitomizes this heritage: "We Are You" (Barlow, 1999, p. 270). Former program director Cliff Winston reiterated the owner's commitment, pointing out that all the songs played on the station have "positive, uplifting lyrics," rather than those which promote violence and the "degradation" of women (Gronau, 2001, p. 2). KJLH has created its own music niche, targeting adult listeners with artists like Brandy and Usher as well as like-sounding contemporaries, and has fostered a strong community presence.

The station magnified its sense of community after the Los Angeles uprising by organizing two simulcasts with Korean KBLA (in conjunction with the Korean Grocers' Association) to discuss among invited panelists "the cultural divide that led to the Korean grocer shooting a Black young person to death, and subsequently the grocer's five-year probation sentence" (ibid.). In another instance, KJLH gave over the airwaves to three former gang members who hosted a call-in show during the aftermath of the 1992 riots (Gronau, 2001). Another program, *Black Viewpoints*, regularly aired controversial issues and opinions — and according to Winston:

> You might hear someone say, "The white man is the enemy." I don't think anyone listening to our radio station, blacks included, believes that, but that opinion may be expressed at one time or another.... That's one of the things that makes KJLH unique, and it's because we're owned by a gentleman like Stevie Wonder who's open to people dialoguing. He's up for people talking about things and finding a way for all of us to come together and live together in a peaceful manner while accepting one another's differences, because if we all admit it, we have more things in common than we do differences [Love, 1999c, p. 60].

Over the years, the station has demonstrated its strong news and public affairs commitment by adding reporters, discussion and call-in shows, encouraging community access to the airwaves, and providing "a number of services such as helping to pay electric and utility bills for destitute families" (Barlow, 1999, p. 270). In contrast, mainstreamed urban stations like KKBT-FM ("The Beat") targeted younger listeners interested in the latest hip-hop, rap, or other beats that blur racial and ethnic lines. Winton was hired by The Beat, leaving KJLH for its competitor. The station did not have the same local commitment as KJLH in the South Central community, and could not compete with KPWR-FM especially with its weaker signal. When Clear Channel sold KKBT to Radio One in 1999, it did so after flipping its frequency, keeping the better of two signals for another one of its stations.

KKBT's competitor, Los Angeles Hip-Hop Power 106 (KPWR-FM), won the Marconi Award for CHR Station of the Year in September 2002. It has raised more than $1.2 million for its Power of a Dollar community service campaign ("NAB Announces," 2002). Power 106 also donated $5,000 every month for a time to area schools (ibid.). Rated number one in Los Angeles in 2002, Emmis Communications' KPWR had attracted African American, Hispanic and other audiences away from Radio One's KKBT. Emmis is not a Black-owned company, and neither is Clear Channel, yet such stations compete for African American listeners similar to small independently owned operations like KJLH as well as the larger Black-owned radio corporations like Radio One. Urban radio in Los Angeles, in many respects, has lost its distinctive cultural edge over the past 20 years as it has embraced an increasingly mainstream audience. KKBT after 16 years changed its call letters and moved away from its then urban format. KJLH had one less competitor in the market; the larger African American community had one less voice.

One of the most influential stations among African American youth changed its format nearly 15 years ago, and as of 2004 it has resumed its presence in the market. KDAY-AM located in South Central Los Angeles achieved success as rap station with a strong commitment to street news. KDAY news director Lee Marshall wrote his news stories in street language, mainly directed at gang members involved in drugs and drive-by shootings, and encouraged youth to stay in school and off the streets (Love, 1990). KDAY emerged back on the air and the streets after nearly a decade's hiatus.

The following is an excerpt from one of Marshall's newscasts: "I come to you this morning with the truth! Alright, gather around all you young people who think that running around in a gang is just the right thing for you. It's time to run down what your role models did within the past 24 hours" (ibid., p. 50). Marshall told a story of how stray bullets from a gang fight killed a grandmother sitting on a porch. Marshall concluded, "So what is your new gang slogan — 'Join a gang and kill a grandma?!'" (ibid.).

African American voices have increasingly become a part of the White media infrastructure. In *Black Journalism Review Online*, Earl Ofari Hutchinson (1999) commented on the national decline of Black and urban radio, in terms of ownership and programming, citing the case of Atlanta-based Cox Communications that put "Los Angeles radio station KACE on the auction block." He noted, "Black leaders and activists in L.A. wailed that Blacks would lose a media outlet that had provided crucial information, news, and analysis on issues of grave concern to their community for nearly three decades" (p. 1). "There was some truth to this complaint," Hutchinson observed; "KACE, though not Black-owned at the time of the announced sale, is the latest in the lengthening line of Black-owned and 'urban format' radio stations that beam to a mostly Black audience to either change ownership and/or programming content in the past year" (ibid.).

One Voice, One Owner

Hutchinson, years later, would work alongside KJLH's new *Front Page* host, Dominque Deprima. He has become a regular contributor to the early morning talk program. It is also relevant — and significant — to note that KJLH ranks third overall in the Los Angeles market on Sundays and 6 A.M. to 10 A.M. That's when KJLH airs locally paid African American Sunday morning church services. The station has managed to survive through the rise and reign of corporate radio in Southern California. Its Sunday programming remains popular to date. It is the oldest black radio station in Los Angeles (Soul, 2001), and the only independently owned Black radio station left in the city. Formatted as adult rhythm and blues (or urban adult contemporary), KJLH's audience represents a minority mix: the listeners are primarily adult African Americans "skewing female, probably about 32 and up" (ibid.). About 70 percent of its audience is African American, and the other 30 percent is "probably a combination of Hispanic and then White and then maybe just a very small percentage of Asian" (Slade, personal communication, 2001). Ratings in the market confirm the station's demographic composition. KJLH's programming, particularly its coverage of issues, has reflected the diversity of its surrounding South Central neighborhoods.

KJLH is one of a dwindling number of independent Black-owned radio stations in small and large cities across the nation. KJLH, however, remains a competitive force within a highly consolidated major market. Los Angeles is ranked the second largest market in the U.S., yet this small neighborhood station has managed not only to compete against mainstream stations, but also to serve a localized and specialized community. The struggles and successes of this station seem relevant toward understanding the significance of community service on a local level within the radio industry and the necessity of providing a voice to those not represented by the corporate broadcast infrastructure.

Another station, WVON-AM, Chicago, projects a similarly credible voice to its audience with immediate "links to certain forms of political action and organization" (Squires, 2000, p. 84). WVON was one of two Black-owned stations in the Chicago market until 2006. Clear Channel bought the station with the former owner, Midway Broadcasting, continuing to operate the station under a licensed marketing agreement. WVON, promoted now as "Talk of the Town," remains relevant to its audience, still promoting discussion among listeners and community leaders; by doing so, according to Squires, it provides a "high degree of utility" (ibid., p. 79). One of its former slogans, "Bringing the community together," captured the essence of the station's historical mission; "[it] sponsors a number of community events, provides information about upcoming rallies, protests, seminars, and entertainment events in the Black community and Chicago at large" (ibid.). The Reverend Al Sharpton and Santita Jackson, the daughter of the Reverend Jesse Jackson, host daily talk shows on the station. Catherine Squires concluded, obviously not aware of the station's ownership transition in the years ahead:

> I argue that commercial media can play a positive role in forming and sustaining serious discourse within a subaltern[ative] public sphere, especially through a small-market or niche format like WVON's. By constructing and attracting a dedicated "family" of media consumers, WVON and its listeners created a media environment that's commercial and community goals overlap [Squires, 2000, p. 84].

The problem, alas, is what happens in the near future when and if the contract is terminated. In some cases, heritage stations cease to offer minority relevant programming immediately after ownership change. Other times, the transition from culturally relevant programming to mainstream is a gradual process, sometimes over a course of years. On the other hand, perhaps this time of financial agreement offers remedy for struggling independents.

KJLH created an environment that has continually prepared its staff to respond to community needs while surviving commercially as a business in the greater Los Angeles radio marketplace. Its independent status and ownership by an African American appear to be credible factors in its ability to relate to its listeners in times of crisis and when relaying critical information to its audience in a timely manner, which is daily through its news and information programming. KJLH management and staff are convinced that station ownership by an African American is integral to a keen perspective of issues significant to its listener base.

CHAPTER 5

False Prophets of Corporate Radio

The Business of Black Radio

In 2006, singer, songwriter, and record label owner Gary Taylor (EuroWeb, 2006) wrote an open letter to the Black radio industry, calling attention to the business forces driving its programming: "These people that are at radio right now — there's no way I can believe that Tom Joyner knows a store, let alone, any stores at all in Watts." Taylor explains, "There was a time when people hinged their whole musical process based off of what the radio personality had to tell them. They told them what [music] to buy and where to shop.... The perception is that it's better that you have one Tom Joyner than have 200 or 300 people who represent you and live in your community," Taylor observes, addressing the legacy role of Black radio in its heyday (2006).

KJLH is one of those stations that has tapped into the pulse of its neighborhood — the businesses, the people, and the problems. It's not about the music, solely; it's about the message behind the music. Location, location, location: the relevancy of KJLH's decision to broadcast within the African American community of South Central is integral to its non-music programming. One of the major changes for KJLH has been its move from its original location in Compton to Inglewood, with the studios in front of the local police station. Racial profiling has been directed at on-air personalities at times, as well as residents in the area, and a number of residents have moved away. Over several years, KJLH's community role has transitioned beyond its physical transmission limits to across the Internet. Its social and political mission for the radio station, meanwhile, is daily challenged by escalating deregulation and consolidation.

Stevie Wonder's invitation to appear at the 1999 FCC hearing on localism (amid rampant consolidation) is indicative of the station's symbolic role as one of the remnant Black heritage radio FM stations in the U.S. Throughout the hearings, Wonder reiterated his mission to serve the local needs of his listeners. It is evident in statements made by staff and management to the press and to the FCC (as well as in original data collection) that KJLH's mission has been, at the very least, consistent since 1979 — when Wonder purchased the radio station from Hill. Urging commissioners to reconsider trends toward consolidation, he warned that local radio, especially minority-owned local radio, could not sustain further economic challenges from corporate entities not in touch with the wants and needs of neighborhood listeners:

> Our concerns are not driven by remote stockholders who are looking at the bottom line for return on their investments. Our concerns are not dictated by the Dow Jones, but by the Mary Joneses who rely on our station as their source of information and entertainment. Public interest demands and public interest requires the protection of stations who stand alone like the dots in a Pac-Man game destined to be gobbled up by the voracious conglomerates. The big owners want more. Now they want TV and cross-ownership of TV and radio. Whose interest is served by allowing television stations to acquire radio stations? Can we honestly say that public interest is served when we stand mute? Can we stand mute and watch the single minority station owners be devoured by the relaxation of ownership rules? What is the standard? When do you say that a company has enough? Is four hundred not enough? Are nine hundred stations sufficient? Are you contemplating a future where one or two companies can own all the stations? Is that not the script of some scary science fiction book we read as children? Can we look in the future and see the voice of the people reflected in our precious airwaves? Or should we follow the stock market to understand what we hear and see? It is in the power of this Commission to protect the public interest. As a minority owner and a member of the National Association of Black-Owned Broadcasters, I strongly urge you to stop the grabbing of multiple blanket ravers, stop the consolidation and remember the community that has placed its trust in your hands. I thank you very much. God bless you ["FCC Proceeding," 1999, pp. 79–80].

Racism as Economic Loss

Forced to adhere to revised Equal Employment Opportunity policies in the 1970s, radio programmers then complained about the overall lack of minority talent available within the industry (Sweeney, 1975). By the early 1980s, urban radio, meanwhile, had become a major competitor in many metropolitan cities and was providing opportunities to African American radio personalities waiting on the sideline of mainstream radio. Within a few years, one woman would demonstrate the potential of Black and urban radio and its community service mission. Washington, D.C.'s, Robin Breedon, host of WPGC-FM, soared in ratings past her White male shock jock competitors, Howard Stern and "Greaseman" Doug Tract. With a decade of television broadcast experience and a degree from Howard University, she changed the way DC listeners listened to radio. Breedon offered her audience both compassion and commitment, and urged her listeners to follow her lead by getting involved in their community (Rosenfeld, 1991). *The Washington Post* crowned her the "Queen of Radio." During her 10-year radio stint, she won seven Emmy nominations and two American Women in Radio and Television National Awards; former mayor Sharon Pratt-Kelly even proclaimed a day named in her honor (Breedon, 1997). Breedon left radio in 1998.

Another Robin — Robin Quivers, Stern's articulate African American sidekick, became a dominant part of what was becoming known as "shock radio." *Private Parts* by Stern (1993) symbolized a turning point in modern radio history and inadvertently the book questioned conventional broadcasting practices. Stern and Quivers became household names. To some, they were American heroes, indeed defenders of free speech. By the late 1980s, Stern had waged war against the established East Coast shock jocks, such as New York's Don Imus and Washington, D.C.'s, Greaseman. His popularity set into motion a wave of racial epithets and lewd sexual comments targeted toward listeners, a style that became synonymous with the shock radio craze then sweeping the nation. The rantings of politically incorrect, White male radio personalities attracted large audience shares. Stern, most prominent among them, is one of the leaders of shock radio with more than 16 million people listening to his syndicated talk show every morning across America—first on terrestrial radio, and now beamed across satellite radio.

Shock radio flourished after Ronald Reagan's deregulation initiatives sparked new interest among investors. Stations were bought and sold to the highest bidder. In the midst of this buying frenzy, some stations would change formats several times within a matter of a few years. Also during this time, television talk shows began to attract female audiences away from radio. The Music Television Network changed the very nature of music listening and selection, yet it was criticized initially for its exclusion of many African American music artists. Mainstream music-oriented stations began to decrease news and public service in an effort to play more songs per hour. By the late 1980s, with the abolishment of the Fairness Doctrine, a wave of talk radio personalities surfaced in metropolitan markets (Zerbinos, 1995–1996), with some of the most popular shows eroding the ratings of music stations. By the mid–1990s, Rush Limbaugh, G. Gordon Liddy, and Bob Grant, and a host of right wing conservatives had been unleashed on talk radio. Grant was the host of the highest rated talk show on New York's WABC, and he earned more than $7 million in 1994. His program was controversial to say the least, and promoted racial strife, with his drive time show being described as "a Ku Klux Klan rally of the airwaves — cruel, racist, with hints of violence" (Cohen and Solomon, 1994, p. 1).

The problem was, and still is, federal law does not prohibit disparaging epithets, and the Bill of Rights guarantees freedom of speech. Local authorities may take action only if language clearly instigates violence. In most cases, the FCC has failed to find any "clear and present danger of imminent violence" despite reports of bomb threats made public through airwaves (*Anti-Defamation League of B'Nai B'Rith vs. FCC 403 F 2d 169*, 1969; *Brandenburg vs. Ohio*, 395, U.S. 444, 1969; Julian Bond, 69 FCC 2d 943, 1978; Letter to Lonnie King, 36 FCC 2d 636, 1972). In the 1990s, as a result of civil actions against broadcast companies that failed to control Stern's racial and ethnic epithets, African American groups were awarded money to set up minority training programs ("Traffic reporter," 1994; "WPGC/DC," 1994). That hardly solved the larger problem of inclusion of minority voices and representation to the point that they were not lost within the larger corporate infrastructure that serves the mainstream. That also does not take into account the difficulty of owning a station when the costs are prohibitive to many, particularly African Americans.

Symbolic Gestures

Historically, the FCC's role has been minimal in dealing with issues of discrimination and hate speech toward African Americans, and at the very most its efforts have been more symbolic than substantive (Fife, 1987, p. 488). The commission, for whatever reasons, has done little to address the lack of minority involvement, especially in key management positions within the radio industry. In 1998, the FCC struck down affirmative action policies, except as they relate to gender parity, in its Broadcast and Cable Equal Employment Opportunity Rules and Policies (FCC, 1998).

In a 2005 report released by the Radio-Television News Directors Association (RTNDA, 2005), African American journalists represented less than 1 percent of the U.S. broadcast news workforce (down from 5.7 percent in 1995). No African American radio news directors were reported in the 2005 report, compared to 5.4 percent from a decade prior (RTNDA, 2005). In 2008, less than 2 percent of African American radio news broadcasters were news directors, decreasing from more than 4 percent in 2007 (Papper, 2008).

Minority news broadcasters comprised nearly 8 percent of the 2005 workforce and represented mainly Hispanic Americans (RTNDA, 2005). Approximately 30 percent of minority employees are in large and major radio markets, with very few serving smaller communities (Papper, 2008). In 2008 the percentage of African Americans in broadcast radio news increased from less than 1 percent in 2005 to 7.8 percent in 2008; figures for African Americans working in TV news remained at about 10 percent (ibid.). What is missing among this data is the percentage of hiring of minorities by minority-owned or formatted companies.

In the late 1990s, research indicated not only had minority-owned firms consistently hired minorities more often than non-minority firms (and often in managerial and professional positions), but there appeared to be a direct relationship between minority broadcast ownership and minority-oriented programming, according to a report released by the California Institute of Technology based on responses from more than 7,000 commercial stations (BBA, 1997). Prior to that report, the FCC had issued a notice of inquiry in 1986 regarding race and gender ownership and employment policies in the awarding of station licenses. In a majority decision in the 1990 case of *Metro Broadcasting Inc. v. Federal Communications Commission*, U.S. Supreme Court justice William Brennan presented data that indicated that "minority ownership influenced the choice of topics for news coverage and a station's editorial viewpoint" (Kleiman 1991, p. 419). The court found:

> [T]he benefits of programming diversity are shared by ... minorities who gain access to the broadcasting industry through ownership [and] a causal link exists between minority ownership and broadcast diversity and therefore ... minority ownership policies were substantially related to the achievement of the desired end [Ivy, 2000, p. 144].

The National Telecommunications and Information Administration's (NTIA) Minority Telecommunications Development Program (MTDP) began to collect data on Black, Hispanic, Asian, and Native American ownership of commercial broadcast stations. When NTIA issued a public statement in 2006 that it would no longer track ownership trends for the broadcast industry, it caused concerns among the minority groups. The culmination of its MTDP's findings indicated that governmental deregulation led to a rise in station prices, less diversity of ownership, and limited access to advertising revenue (NTIA, 2001). Moreover, in cities across the U.S., ratings indicated that African Americans were more likely to listen to rhythm and blues and urban formats than other genres (*Black Radio Today*, 1996; BBA, 1997; *Radio & Records*, 2002). African American owners were found more likely than non-minority owners to possess a "less lucrative station" with inferior signal strength and reception, according to reports released through the Black Broadcasters Alliance (BBA, 1997, p. 5). That point is significant, yet ironic, when one considers that the strong community presence of Black and urban stations had translated into high Time Spent Listening (TSL), which is the amount of time that listeners have stayed tuned to a particular station (Love, 1999d).

Urban contemporary station WTLC-FM, owned by corporate Radio One, has historically found success in cosponsoring Black expositions that have attracted thousands of listeners and numerous business owners. Black radio, through event sponsorship with business, has advocated educational and financial empowerment. Radio One released its *Black American Study* (2008) results of 3,400 African Americans surveyed on a variety of themes, from media consumption to attitudes about life, education, and careers. The results indicated the rise of an optimistic generation of African Americans who sought self-empowerment over governmental assistance, and who embraced new technologies and media choices (*Jet*, 2008; White, 2008). African Americans engage on the Internet at levels comparable to other Americans, at approximately 68 percent compared to the national average of 71 percent (White, 2008, 6A). As of 1999, African Americans had buying power of more than $530 billion, ranking 11th among the top countries of the world (Love, 1999a). Today, that buying power is transitioning online, particularly among the hip hop generation, as the digital divide closes (White, 2008). The study also reaffirms that African Americans trust Black media over that of mainstream (*Jet*, 2008; White, 2008).

Dexter King, son of Martin Luther King, Jr., underscored radio's potential as one of educating the community on the need for economic empowerment: "I think black radio can play — or has played — a unique role in addressing issues and educating the community in ways that traditionally have not been addressed. That's something that needs to be continued in a big way particularly through economic change" (Love, 1999b, p. 48). Radio One, not surprisingly, initiated this survey coming from the perspective of an African American company that understands the legacy of Black radio. King continued, "That's the one thing that my father talked about in his later years of life — the fact that our community spends billions of dollars in terms of the gross national product, yet we still do not have an economic base, in terms of self-empowerment" (ibid.).

Preferential Policies Toward Consolidation

Several obstacles have impeded Black radio's success, especially for the independent African American radio owner. Columnist Walt Love (1999e, p. 56) points out, "A continuing problem for urban radio stations is that their often high ratings rarely translate into equally high revenues." Many discussions, few solutions, about minority bias exist among media buyers and advertising agencies (Ofori, 1999). An FCC study released in 1999 indicated top-rated urban and Hispanic formatted stations were forced to sell airtime for significantly less than mainstream entities with lower ratings and audience appeal ("Minority Stations," 1999; Mundy, 1999; Ofori, 1999). The increased buying power of African Americans did little to offset another problem that began to unfold for African American owners, namely consolidation. The media marketplace grew fiercely competitive as the U.S. government created conditions that would unleash corporate radio to swallow independents across local spectrums: "The first significant change occurred in 1990, when the Federal Communications Commission ("FCC") declined to extend enhancement credits for minority ownership" (BBA, 1997, pp. 1). "Enhancement credits," according to Black Broadcast Alliance (BBA) reports, "helped to make minority applicants more competitive in comparative hearings. Minority owners have argued that comparative hearings require that they expend an inordinate amount of time and money that may not result in securing ownership and that their chances of securing ownership have been lessened by the removal of this credit" (ibid., pp. 1–2)

According to the Black Broadcasters Alliance (1997), the "most significant change" (ibid., p. 2) occurred in September 1992 when the FCC relaxed national and local ownership caps to permit a sole licensee to own up to 18 AM stations and 18 FM stations, as outlined in the "Revision of Radio Rules and Policies" (FCC, 1992).

This new era of deregulated broadcasting ushered in the rapid growth of commercial radio empires. Ownership had been previously capped at 12 AM and 12 FM stations, with limits being raised to 14 stations for a single owner of two or more minority-controlled properties (BBA, 1997; NTIA, 1998). Only two years later, the commission extended the maximum to 20 AM-FM stations. Any financial benefits that might have accrued for minority owners in the past were virtually eliminated by the new ruling.

Concurrently, minority ownership preference policies became hotly debated among broadcasters in the early 1990s. The program was designed to provide tax benefits to owners who sold to qualified minority investors (BBA, 1997). Within a few years, the certificate program was repealed because of "allegations of abuse": some White owners reportedly made financial arrangements with minority individuals for the use of their name (Ivy, 2000, p. 141). The Supreme Court limited the federal government's ability to implement subsequent race-based programs via its decision to mandate with rigorous scrutiny any applicants for ownership (*Adarand Constructors, Inc. v. Pena*, 515 U.S. 200, 1995).

By this time, the FCC had already relaxed the duopoly rules and ownership caps within specific restrictions so that no licensee could own more than 25 percent of a market; by 1996, with the passage of the Telecommunications Act, licensees under specific conditions were permitted to own, operate or control up to 50 percent of the market. Ultimately the 1996 act "increased competition and drove station prices to their highest levels" (BBA, 1997, p. 3; Rathburn, 1996). In that a single company was allowed to control up to 40 percent of a market's advertising revenue, minority owners responded with concerns, suggesting that increased limits would "lead to media concentration, posing the single largest threat to minority broadcast ownership and the diversity of viewpoint that it brings to America's airwaves" (BBA, 1997, p. 3). "In 1992, when the FCC raised commercial radio ownership limits, it stated that an increase in the overall number of stations, or an increase in the national ownership caps, would not pose any threat to diversity of viewpoint," concluded the report (ibid., p. 3).

Why Is KJLH So Unique?

Regulatory attempts to ensure diverse viewpoints across the radio dial have been far from beneficial to minority owners. By the 1970s, Black music, as it was called, had become "integrated into the mainstream of American society," and unique concerns and issues relevant to African Americans began to blur into the larger fabric of mainstream radio (Cantor, 1992, p. 225). It was during this time that the FCC and the Office of Communications of the United Church of Christ called for an increase in African American ownership and management ("Coming Through," 1972). Stuart H. Surlin (1972, p. 297), in one of the few studies on Black-oriented radio, concluded that an increase in African American ownership, or, at the very least, in African American decision-makers, would be critical to establishing an "empathic relationship" with the African American audience. The following year, Surlin (1973) also acknowledged that Black-oriented radio devoted a significant percentage of airtime to call-in shows, personal on-air interviews, and community promotions not traditionally, nor previously, identified as public affairs or news in the radio industry, yet these activities fulfilled a service role among listeners.

In 1971, only 10 radio stations were African American owned (Meyer, 1971). In 1976, the National Association of Black-Owned Broadcasters (NABOB) was created with only 30 radio stations (Brown, Jr., 1990). African American broadcasters, the African American press, and Benjamin Hooks, the first African American Federal Communications Commissioner, called for increased Black ownership ("Coming Through," 1972). By 1981, there were 140 Black-owned radio stations, and that number increased to 182 within the decade (Schuyler, 1990, p. 15). Impacted by the deregulation of the late 1980s, approximately 120 stations were African American owned by 1992 (Johnson & Birk, 1993a, 1993b). From 1990 to 2000, minority owners represented approximately 3 percent (2.7 percent in 1991; 3.8 percent in 2000) of the U.S. broadcast stations (NTIA, 2001), although minorities account for 29 percent of the U.S. population. NABOB member radio stations are often "the sole broadcasters committed to programming music and public affairs geared specifically toward a Black audience, reflecting the cultural sensitivities and concerns of the community at large" (Brown, Jr., 1990, p. 22).

For instance, stations, like WOKS-AM/WFXE-FM in Columbus, Georgia, boasted "a community advisory board consisting of various civic and business leaders who lend their expertise to the stations so [they] can better serve the community" (ibid.). In a 1992 national survey of all African American owned radio stations, 98 percent of the respondents (station managers) indicated that their stations conducted community service promotions (e.g., education, substance abuse awareness, voter registration) on a regular basis (Johnson, 1992; Johnson & Birk, 1993a).

Access to the airwaves, however, is virtually denied to some individuals, particularly those with limited income and opportunity. In a rare move while responding to regulatory policy challenges, Clear Channel sold several spin-off stations to minorities, after it had merged with the company AM/FM in 2000. A number of stations went back into the hands of minority owners, mainly those who operate the minority corporate chains. The cost was still prohibitive to the independent African American owner. As beneficial as Clear Channel's decision was in somewhat boosting minority ownership, the likelihood of this type of deal happening again without federal incentive or intervention appears extremely unlikely according to some Black radio executives and analysts (Love, 2000).

Whose Spectrum Is It Anyway?

More than 25 years after NABOB was organized, the significance of Black radio in commercial broadcasting was a top issue of debate within the industry (NABOB, 2000a). The FCC (1998) stated in its Notice of Proposed Rule Making, dated November 20, 1998, that women and minorities are not likely to share one perspective; it is the multitude of viewpoints among them that will likely contribute toward overall diversity in broadcast programming and, as such, would increase the likelihood of targeting the needs and interests of any particular audience. Subsequently, this scenario would likely promote a diverse workforce within the radio industry.

In December 2000, the FCC contracted with the Ivy Planning Group to conduct a study to "identify and eliminate market barriers for small businesses" under Section 257 of the Telecommunications Act of 1996 (Ivy, 2000, p. 1). In *Whose Spectrum Is It Anyway?* (1950 to present) the following barriers to women and minorities mentioned included (1) discrimination in capital markets to obtain necessary funds to own and operate a business, (2) discrimination from the advertising industry by excluding women and minorities from information and deal-making, and (3) the subsequent market deregulation and consolidation from the 1996

Act. Other hindrances impacting women and minorities were lack of media experience due to industry barriers, inadequate or lack of lobbying before governmental bodies, and inadequate representation in the drafting of congressional laws, court rulings, and FCC rules, regulations, and policies "which have operated to the detriment of small, minority- and women-owned businesses" (Ivy, 2000, p. 3).

One of the key conclusions of the study was that "the relaxation of ownership caps has significantly decreased the number of small, women- and minority-owned businesses" in the industry; and further, this decline has "resulted in diminished community service and diversity of viewpoints" (ibid.). Finally, the report stated that the "FCC often failed in its role of public trustee of the broadcast and wireless spectrum by not properly taking into account the effect of its programs on small, minority- and women-owned businesses" (ibid.).

Waldfogel (2001) pointed toward a decline in minority-owned outlets, as ownership has become increasingly concentrated into the hands of a few players. This move toward expansive consolidation has not necessarily helped African Americans and other minority voices. According to Siegelman & Waldfogel (2001), a key factor in determining the likelihood of African American targeted programming is African American ownership — that is independent ownership, if one examines the fruit of Black radio at its genesis. Further, the power of Black and urban radio's influence has been demonstrated through its ongoing community service commitment to African American listeners, and by its ability to react instantly, as well as to provide guidance, during times of crisis as in the case of the Los Angeles riots. The 1997 BBA report also suggested that minority radio, in general, might be headed toward a state of crisis in and of itself:

> Given the continuing decline in the number of minority broadcast owners, it is time for renewed examination and public debate about the impact of media concentration, and the importance of minority ownership to localism, diversity and universal service [BBA, 1997, p. 4].

More than a decade since that report, a number of African American independently owned stations have fallen to the wayside. KJLH, alone in Los Angeles as one of those voices, is a member station of NABOB, and General Manager Karen Slade is the Far West regional representative on its board of directors. Other board members include President of Inner City Broadcasting Corporation and Chairman of the Board Pierre M. Sutton, Vice President Michael L. Carter, owner and operator of KPRT/KPRS in Kansas City, Missouri, and Alfred C. Liggins, president and CEO of

Radio One (and son of Radio One owner and Founder Catherine Liggins Hughes).

Approximately 240 stations are Black-owned in the U.S, according to NABOB data (Beresteanu and Ellickson, 2007). Inner City Broadcasting Corporation (in the radio business for 30 years) owns and operates 18 radio stations in 7 major markets, including New York's legendary WBLS-FM and WLIB-AM. Valued close to 1.8 billion dollars, Radio One is the largest African American owned company with 65 stations in 22 markets throughout the U.S.: arguably it is a corporate entity (Brosowsky, 2002, p. 1; NASDAQ, 2002). In late 2001, Radio One and ABC Radio Networks, the leader in urban programming, formed Urban Advantage Network to become the largest African American targeted radio network in the U.S ("Radio One," 2001). Hughes admits the 1996 Telecommunications Act "has changed everything so dramatically. If we'd have had the telecom bill 20 years ago, I never would have been able to finance a standalone 1,000-watter in Washington, D.C., called WOL. No bank would have financed me" (ibid., p. 1). Hughes began with the purchase of WOL-AM, Washington, D.C., in 1979, the same year that Stevie Wonder bought KJLH.

The problem, historically, has been that a significant portion of Black-oriented stations have not been owned by African Americans, dating back to when White announcers were taught to sound African American on the air during the early rhythm and blues days. Williams (1998) reported slightly more than 200 of approximately 600 Black-oriented stations were owned by African Americans in 1990. Black corporate radio chains, like Radio One, have contributed to the rise in the number of Black-owned stations; yet their number is comparatively small to that of White-owned corporate radio companies such as Clear Channel Radio, which owns nearly 1,200 stations across the U.S. The number of independently African American owned radio stations, meanwhile, has declined. In Los Angeles, KJLH remains amazingly independently owned — and continues to cater urban, gospel, news, and a strong sense of community to its largely African American audience.

Former FCC commissioner Nicholas Johnson, in a dissenting opinion on a case that involved the sale of stations to a corporate group when consolidation initially began to challenge the programming needs of minority audiences, made a statement not only reflective on the findings of the Kerner Commission report released one year earlier in 1968, but one that would be indicative to Black radio's fate:

I find this quasi-monopolistic concentration of control over a programming format to be particularly unfortunate in light of the lessons drawn by the Kerner Commission report on civil disorders. The report attributed the sense of alienation and helplessness felt by many black residents of this country's large cities in part to a failure by the mass media to offer them some access to the broadcast forums they control. I feel that one way to counteract this trend toward alienation and helplessness, at least with respect to the media, is to strive toward the goal of diverse and local ownership and control of community broadcast stations. In an area of discussion where little is demonstrably clear, I have operated on the assumption that a station which is locally owned and controlled will tend to be more responsive to the needs of its audience than one that is owned by an absentee, multiple-station corporation [FCC, 1969].

The 2007 FCC Studies

Among a series of 2007 reports commissioned by the FCC, one study focused on the relationship between station ownership and radio programming. Researcher Tasneem Chipty concluded in FCC Media Ownership Study #5 that consolidation of radio ownership did not contribute to less diversity in local programming offerings, and especially so when considering its impact on nonmusic programming. However, the report neglects to take a historical overview of marketplace offerings by Black legacy stations prior to rampant consolidation and deregulatory policies that shifted programming in local communities and metropolitan areas toward the mainstream. Further, if a local community never represented an audience segment in the first place, does that mean that a need does not exist for coverage of those issues? If corporate radio has subsumed local minority programming, upon purchase of an African American owned station for instance, will the programming remain consistent to the needs and interests of that original target audience and for how long? In some cases, transitions in programming are evolutionary, and not radical, depending on the station's success at attracting its core audience. This Chipty study dealt mainly with shifts in mainstream programming, and its definition of diversity was weak in relevancy to culturally specific programming, information, and issues geared to the African American community.

In the report *Minority and Female Ownership in Media Enterprises* commissioned by the FCC, Beresteanu and Ellickson (2007) provide a statistical interpretation of ownership trends. It becomes glaringly evident that African Americans are underrepresented, with African American ownership in 2002 of radio stations representing only 4.35 percent in the U.S.

Beresteanu and Ellickson (2007) use NABOB statistics to analyze ownership trends for a 15 year period. NABOB data indicates that 138 FM stations were owned by African Americans in 2006, compared to 111 in 2001, 91 in 1996, and 74 in 1991, compared to 105, 94, 129, 111, respectively for AM stations. AM stations usually represent weaker signals compared to FM stations; however, it is worthy to calculate the total number of African American stations: 2006 (243), 2001 (205), 1996 (230), 1991 (185). Of the 243 stations that are African American owned, 53 are owned by the African American owned corporate chain Radio One. Inner City Broadcasting owns 18 stations.

What is also not reflected in these numbers is the transition from independent African American ownership to corporate African American ownership, and what that has meant for programming diversity, if anything. Even major players like Radio One struggle to compete against mega conglomerates such as Clear Channel. Reporting a loss of 266 million dollars in November 2008, Radio One's CEO Alfred Liggins announced that his company would shift toward television and online revenue, while restructuring the company's radio workforce (*Radio One*, 2008). The Beresteanu and Ellickson (2007) report recommends that the FCC revisit its definition of minority and female ownership; the researchers admit that they did not have data to examine larger historical trends. The historical link between radio ownership and consumer preferences in programming, for instance, is not addressed in this report. Rather, they ask, "Would female or minority owners deviate from the profit maximizing choice and offer an alternative viewpoint? The Gentzkow and Shapiro results suggest not." The Gentzkow and Shapiro (2006) study they refer to indicates newspapers target the content toward their subscribers, not toward ownership preferences. However, parallels between newspaper subscribers and radio audiences should be made with caution. Radio's mandate is to serve the needs and interests of its community of license. Other studies (FCC, 1998; Ivy, 2000; Surlin, 1973) already discussed in this chapter point toward qualitative differences in programming commitments between mainstream and minority owned stations; these prior studies are not taken into consideration by Beresteanu and Ellickson (2007). The impact of local diversity in programming, as it relates to minority ownership, should be specifically addressed together in any future reports.

African American ownership, be it corporate or independent, seems to have a dismal future, unless acknowledgment of Black media's contributions to the social, political, and economic structure of American life, particularly in Black America, comes with legislative foresight to reverse its downward spiral (Curry, 2007). With the sale of Black Entertainment Television into the hands of mainstream media in 2000, a new flurry of discussion has increasingly centered on broadcast television ownership, and much of this dialogue is similar to Black radio's struggle to maintain an independent voice. FCC commissioner Michael J. Coops noted that African American broadcast ownership had decreased 30 percent since 1998. Coops called that decline a "national disgrace" and added, "The facts are downright chilling" (ibid.). He presented his case before the 10th annual Wall Street Project conference of Rainbow/Push, reacting to a report by the Free Press that indicated that African Americans own only 1.3 percent of all broadcast television stations, while representing more than 30 percent percent of the U.S. population.

Coops concluded, "This is grassroots, All-American, where people live. And it is, in an important way, the latest chapter in the long and often painful struggle to create equal opportunity. This issue is really a new civil rights battleground for America, and we all know that civil rights have to be fought for by every generation" (ibid.). Former FCC commissioner Gloria Tristani, speaking to Women in Ethnic Media, part of the First New America Media Awards, held 2006 in Washington, D.C., pointed out that ethnic minorities in general own less than 4 percent of the nation's television stations, and added that underrepresented communities tell her that "mainstream media is simply not covering the news of interest in [our] communities" (Vongs, 2006).

Rainbow/PUSH and NABOB challenged the commission's local hearings in recent years, pointing out that critical issues have not been addressed, notably an identification of market entry barriers, articulate definitions of qualified ownership with regards to socially and economically disadvantaged businesses, and ways in which to increase minority ownership. The idea is to stall any legislative action until a clear picture of the issues is identified. They also advocate that the commission's study of issues regarding ownership definition and market barriers, as well as policies favoring corporate media, are discussed thoroughly among minority communities (Lasar, 2007).

Black Radio Today: Ratings and Revisions

Black Radio Today: How America Listens to Radio (2003) provided a comprehensive study of African American targeted formats and its listeners in the top 100 African American Arbitron-rated markets. The study indicated that urban contemporary, urban adult contemporary, contemporary hit radio and gospel music ranked as top favorites among African Americans. Indeed, these formats have mass appeal often beyond African American listeners. *Disappearing Voices* is a documentary that was released in 2008 telling the story of Black-owned radio in the era of corporate radio, where the legacy of urban programming has evolved into mass commodity.

In August 2008, when the FCC approved the sale of XM Satellite Radio to Sirius Satellite Service for more than $3 million, concerns arose among minority owned stations that this deal would encourage a trend toward financial mergers and perks benefiting large corporate radio companies. Such initiatives as a reinstatement of the 1978 minority tax certificates repealed in 1995 have been advocated as an option to boost ownership among culturally-specific populations. Other issues that have confronted minority owners, particularly African American and Hispanic-American, have revolved around Arbitron's use of Portable People Meters (PPM) as its new audience measurement tool. NABOB has called for an investigation into Arbitron's methodology, given the substantial declines in ratings for minority audiences. The company responded that it plans to review its "recruitment and compliance methodology aimed at Black and Hispanic households" (Wade, 2008).

National radio host Michael Baisden, when asked about the impact of syndication (and also corporatization) on local radio, discussed the important relationship he has had with local personalities through his show, and elaborated on radio's role in the community: "What I think is cool about local radio is that they can talk about what's happening locally and things that matter in that town, be it [an event] at a high school or a crime in that area" (Alexander, 2008). He added, "You can even program the music according to the weather in your town, which I think is really cool. And you can be more involved on the ground with what's happening locally, like local benefits. That's something you can't do nationally."

CHAPTER 6

On-Air Vigil
KJLH's Transformation to Talk

God bless you, Dick Gregory talking to you about the Front Page. *Every morning radio station KJLH 102.3, you have to be part of it. Information is knowledge, hey for you.* —Front Page *program opener (Front Page, 2002b).*

Front Page began as an experiment during the fall of 1991 to create a dialogue within the African American community; initially it tended to address lighter topics of "romance and entertainment" for only 15 minutes weekday mornings (Slade, personal communication, 2002). The show was still under development about a month prior to the civil unrest, but it was then expanded and literally transformed on April 29, 1992, when the King trial verdict was announced across KJLH:

> Everyone was angry after the King verdicts last year, and some people thought we should have tried to just ignore problems in the city, or hush them up.... As soon as we went on the air with the verdict, the phones just lit up. Then people started coming down here. They wanted to voice their opinions so we put them on the air. We never got back to the music. We got so many calls from everywhere — London and Australia and Japan. I never knew so many people knew [about] KJLH [Slade, 1993, p. 22].

KJLH halted its music and commercials for four days of nearly non-stop coverage of the Los Angeles Riots. The station facilitated dialogue between staff and listeners, celebrities, and guest hosts. *Front Page* had already been extended into a 30-minute format a few weeks prior to the verdict. The show's structure provided the framework for the station's coverage of the civil unrest, as radio personality Eric "Rico" Reed explains: "[It] ran about 5, 5:30 in the morning, just before the morning show started, which I was hosting at the time. We started an extended version

106

of the *Front Page*, and little did we know that extension would continue over the next three or four days. It was just an unbelievable experience" (Reed, personal communication, 2001).

A former KJLH program director, Lee Michaels, brought the *Front Page* idea from Chicago to Southern California, and gave it a Hollywood spin. KJLH's audience, on the contrary, wanted to speak out on community issues.

> He wanted people to talk about what's going on in Hollywood, if we saw any celebrities in Hollywood the night before because you know, L.A. is trendy town, and he wanted people to talk about if they saw Eddie Murphy at the China Club.... When they went to the phones, people wanted to talk about Soon-Ja Doo. She was a Korean storekeeper who had shot Latasha Harlins (a 15-year-old girl) in the back of the head for allegedly stealing some orange juice and the people are pretty upset about that. So ... every time they opened the phones people could care less about Eddie or any other Hollywood celebrities, they wanted to talk about what the radio station was doing about what they saw as the real injustices in the community. It sort of fell on me and then we had a change in the program director and morning man, and Rico joined us, and I said, "Rico, we need to talk about this thing" because when we first started it was just like 15 minutes. Rico came on and was amenable for us doing more — so we ended up, you know, expanding the discussion to half-hour [Nelson, personal communication, 2001].

The guest list began to transform from Hollywood notables to political activists like Dick Gregory and the Reverend Jesse Jackson as well as lawyers Johnnie Cochran and Christopher Darden (Gronau, 2001). However, in a twist of fate, a number of celebrities came to KJLH during the civil unrest to speak out against the injustice of the King verdict and the violence on the streets. But, rather than the glitz and glamour of Hollywood, ashes and destruction consumed Crenshaw Boulevard and the South Central community. Some of the relief hosts included former MTV video jock J.J. Johnson, KJLH staff member Chris Lewis, and J. Anthony Brown from the *Arsenio Hall Show*, among others. Celebrities and political figures who spoke to the public through KJLH's airwaves included Barry White, Whoopi Goldberg, Bill Cosby, Oprah Winfrey, Rosanne Barr, Arsenio Hall, Denzel Washington, Stevie Wonder, Ice-T and the Reverend Jesse Jackson as the community sought "nonviolent solutions to the community's frustrations" (Weinstein, 1993, p. 13). Brandon Bowlin was also part of the KJLH *Front Page* team during the civil unrest, and since then has been on HBO and the *Tom Joyner Morning Show*.

Rapper and actor Tracy Marrow (personal communication, 2002a,

2002b), better known as Ice-T, came down to the studio to give money to the American Red Cross and other organizations. Marrow (personal communication, 2002b) explains, "It was a touchy situation — it wasn't like get on the radio and tell people that they're doing something stupid. It had to be done delicately, and they kind of brought it together." Previously, he had criticized KJLH for not airing his music, which spoke to some of the issues addressed on-air during the unrest. In the 1989 lyrics to his song "This One's for Me," Ice-T says, "I'm tryin to save my community but these bourgeoisie blacks keep on doggin me ... KJLH, you ain't about nuttin." In 1991, Ice-T performed "Cop Killer" on a summer tour with his heavy metal–rap band Body Count, and it was released in late March 1992, only about a month before the verdict was announced (Shank, 1996). By the summer of 1992, police organizations protested his violent lyrics. Tension remained high in South Central as residents faced a devastated community and only promises of community rebuilding by governmental agencies. Marrow (2002a) simply puts it this way: "We yelled, and finally people heard." In reality, KJLH had been listening and responding to its community's needs long before the Los Angeles riots.

In Pursuit of Context

What went down in 1992 has not been forgotten. "No one could be prepared for something like this — it just happened. Just rely on your instincts and what you feel and know is right in your heart and hope that what you're doing is the right thing," explained former radio host Eric Reed (personal communication, 2001). KJLH found its identity and purpose during that difficult time in history — and it has continually expressed itself through the dialogue exchanged within *Front Page*.

On March 3, 1991, police officers pursued a white Hyundai through the streets of Los Angeles. The license number, 2KFM102, ironically seemed to foreshadow KJLH-FM 102.3's coverage of the trial and the subsequent uprising that would occur over the next year. Fourteen months after the King beating, a not guilty verdict was announced around 2:45 P.M. on Wednesday, April 29, in the Simi Valley courthouse in Ventura County, California. Hundreds of protesters gathered outside the steps of the courthouse, and by 5 P.M. another crowd gathered near the intersection of Florence and Normandy in South Central Los Angeles. That evening, the streets became wild with violence, and bottles and objects were hurled at passing cars. Police officers withdrew from the area. Around 6:45 P.M., Reginald Denny was pulled from his car and severely beaten. The incident was caught on tape. About 15 to 20 minutes later, a state of emergency was declared when looting and violence broke out in Inglewood and the surrounding neighborhoods ("Legacy," 2002).

Hundreds of residents gathered on the steps of the First African Methodist Episcopal Church on South Harvard Boulevard, with as many as 2,000 people participating in the vigil by 8 P.M. ("Legacy," 2002). The First African Methodist Episcopal Church (A.M.E.) has a long history of community activism and celebrity activism. "FAME" is another acronym that has been used to identify the church, which according to Smith (1994) is "a center for political activity in Los Angeles. Many movie stars go there. On any Sunday you are sure to see Arsenio Hall and others" (p. 159). Smith described the A.M.E. church as "very colorful, with an enormous mural and a huge choir with very exciting music. People line up to go into the services the way they line up for the theater or a concert" (ibid.). As people gathered peaceably on the church steps, the mood on the streets began to turn for the worse. To the many stranded and displaced residents, the vigil was a safe haven from the dangerous storm that was intensifying around them — and the storm would gain momentum over the next few hours.

The Los Angeles Times reported that one of the first stores to be looted was a liquor store on Florence and Normandy, and the first fire call was received at approximately 8:30 P.M. By 9 P.M., Mayor Tom Bradley declared a state of emergency, and Governor Pete Wilson ordered the activation of 2,000 National Guard troops — a number that eventually increased to 6,000 by midnight. The South Central bus service was shut down, and the California Highway Patrol began to close freeway exit ramps to keep motorists from entering the mayhem ("Legacy," 2002).

After LAPD reports that a shot was fired at one of its helicopters, the Federal Aviation Administration redirected the landing pattern of incoming airplanes to the Los Angeles International Airport (LAX) near Inglewood. By midnight, 24 people had been admitted to area hospitals, and eight people had died (ibid.). A state of emergency was declared by the governor just a few minutes into Thursday, April 30, as well as plans to dispatch the National Guard and the California Highway Patrol. Minutes later, Bradley signed a curfew into effect that was eventually extended citywide (ibid.). Many South Central residents without electricity listened to the station on battery-operated radios.

At this point, South Central Los Angeles was in complete mayhem. Hundreds of people were displaced after stores were looted and burned down, and streets became dangerous. Reed, Carl Nelson, news director at the time, and others informed residents of places to go for help and places to avoid:

> *Co-Host*: The American Red Cross is attempting at this time to get into that area and provide the people with items so they can get through the night. They're going to set them up with cots and stuff like that. Some 5,000 South Central residents are now said to be without electrical power. We don't know if that was caused by the fire or if they've turned off the juice. Stores at La Brea and Rodeo, including Foot Locker shoe store and the Wherehouse Record Store have been set on fire, and so has the Thrifty Drug Store across the street from those stores; they're also on fire.
>
> *Rico Reed*: All right, we're expecting a call from Reverend Carl Washington — he just called through, I don't think he could make it; he'll call us right back in a minute. Let's take a call here from one of our listeners. Good evening, you're on the special edition of the *Front Page*. What is your name and where are you calling from? Hel-lo? Hi.
>
> *Caller*: Hi.
>
> *Host*: Yes, you are?
>
> *Caller*: Leann.
>
> *Rico Reed*: All right, Leann, go right ahead.
>
> *Caller*: Okay. I'm calling — I live, oh God, on Century. What I'm really appalled about is that they're burning down the AM-PM and they forget that we live, people live behind the AM-PM.
>
> *Host:* Thank you.
>
> *Caller:* They're trying to burn us down with it — okay? And also, we were standing outside and people are outside shooting, have they forgotten that we have babies here. We have children. Have they forgotten about the two little babies that got killed by cross-fire shooting?
>
> *Rico Reed:* I don't know; it seems like all that's gone out the window. We're looking at the police right now pulling up — there's about 50 people right across the street running inside looting a store. The police are pulling up with lights but that's all they're doing.
>
> *Co-Host*: Is the AM-PM still burning?
>
> *Caller:* No, they, I mean, I mean that was like the first building.... The AM-PM was the first one the fire department came to stop because of the explosion.
>
> *Rico Reed:* Okay, I've got you. Excuse me, we have to cut away; we've got another call.
>
> *Co-Host*: We've got to cut away now to Governor Pete Wilson. He's making a special announcement. Thank you for calling.

Governor Wilson: The question is South Central Los Angeles. There will be as many as 750 California Highway Patrolmen (CHP) made available. Their key purpose is to try to seal off the area and try to keep motorists from entering the area. They will also be able to, by their containment of it, assist the law enforcement personnel from LAPD and from the Sheriff's office in seeking to contain the area and ultimately to shrink it down. The problem with the fires, obviously, has been that in order to fight the fires, the fire-fighting crews have required protection themselves. We have had a couple of firemen shot this evening that we know about.... The bitter irony of course is that the injury that is being done to South Central Los Angeles will be hurtful to the residents of that area. It is our hope that people will not be injured by the actions of what are apparently comparatively few. The number on the streets is not great, not withstanding the number of fires, the deliberate arson activity, and the looting [*Front Page*, 1992b].

Residents peered from their windows in disbelief as their neighborhood stores went up in smoke, and many were overwhelmed with the images of children running alongside their parents to steal a television or food from a local store. Then, there were the outsiders, many from beyond the streets of South Central, who came into the area to loot and destroy for personal gain and satisfaction. As the violence intensified, so did the chemical fog (a mix of burning solvents and plastics) that filled the air. Within seconds, the needs of listeners changed rapidly as one phone call after another rang into the studio. It was around midnight when one listener called in and reported that a nursing home had been set on fire from an adjacent building. The neighbors were going into the building and pulling elderly people out of the building, according to Slade (personal communication, 1993), "as fast as they could, and laying them in the street. Trying to get them out of the building and medical attention. It was horrible." Slade (personal communication, 2002) recalls, "I was just going on the air with all the pertinent information that was happening. Where the fires were. Where to stay away from. Do not get in the streets."

By early Thursday morning, 5,000 homes were without electricity. By Friday, May 1, 25,000 people had no power ("Legacy," 2002), and much of South Central stayed home:

As of this morning, only the off ramps are closed between Martin Luther King, Jr. Boulevard and Imperial Highway. The on ramps are open but travel is not advised for the Harbor Freeway, absolutely, whatsoever. You can use the Long Beach Freeway, the 710 as an alternate. Freeways are very light though this morning, not a lot of people traveling and that's good. People are staying home. All policing agencies and the National Guard have asked citizens to restrict travel unless absolutely necessary. There's really no one to help you.... I'm Margaret LaPique with the traffic update for KJLH [*Front Page*, 1992c].

By the end of the civil uprising, 54 people had died, 2,383 people had been injured, and 13,212 people had been arrested. There were estimates of $700 million to $1 billion in property damage in Los Angeles County. Much of the damage occurred within 24 hours after the verdict ("Legacy," 2002).

Not Just About Rodney King

At 2:45 P.M. on May 1, 1992, Rodney G. King spoke out emotionally to the people of Los Angeles: "Can we all get along?" ("Legacy," 2002, p. 4). The agony of the South Central community was caught on tape with selected images broadcast across the world: "South Central residents have not forgotten the image that television portrayed. Cameras focused on looters and arson though the bulk of the population was not involved" (Rollins, 1993, p. A01). In the final analysis, "Other media found their disoriented, mostly white middle-class reporting staffs under attack by rioters. Police closed the freeway system, using it to ensnare the population. Electricity was out" (ibid.). KJLH provided the information and assistance needed when the services were down throughout the area. "People were confused and needed information. The mainstream media reported only on the carnage, and for the benefit of white suburbs" (ibid.).

It would have been impossible to prepare for the magnitude of the media barrage and mayhem that erupted on the streets and inside the station. The looting and burning of Korean stores was viewed by many African Americans as retaliation for Latasha Harlins' death (Jackson, 1992; Lacey & Hubler, 1992). The pain inflicted by the loss of the young girl's life was evident in comments made by *Front Page* listeners calling into KJLH during the Los Angles civil unrest. One caller, for example, who commented on the King verdict, also expressed her outrage at the Harlins case:

Okay, I just wanted to say that the verdict today shows that the life of a Black man in America is worthless. It shows that they can just take advantage of us and do us any type of way and they expect us to be passive and just accept what they do to us. The Latasha Harlins case, they had — I mean there's no justice anywhere. I mean, Latasha Harlins, there was evidence, I mean, a videotape — that was rare. They had evidence that it was murder, but they gave her probation, no just sentence. You kill a dog, you go to jail. You kill a Black teenager — nothing [*Front Page*, 1992a].

Slade, Nelson, and others on the KJLH staff and the streets agreed that the King beating was the "last straw." Slade (personal communication, 1993) states, "All indications in hindsight were that there was going to be a riot ... not so much as saying, 'I'm going to go out and burn down a building' [but saying] 'I'm tired of this. I can't believe this.'" The department heads had discussed the possibility of unrest in the streets early on in the process, and reporter Jacquie Stephens was assigned to cover the trial. Nelson (*Front Page*, 2002b) explains that the jury's release of the "four officers was not the real reason why folks were mad." His impression that something was going to happen came during the trial, when people called into *Front Page* to express their views:

> When we were doing the show, people were saying that things were going to happen. They didn't say exactly Florence and Normandy, but they said that people were going to "act up" to put it mildly. But they were more concerned with what had happened with Latasha Harlins.... People were very upset with what happened with the judge's ruling on that one [*Front Page*, 2002b].

Nelson (personal communication, 2001) also pointed out, "People started going after Korean stores during the uprising, and that was probably an offshoot of what happened to Latasha Harlins."

Verdict in Rodney King Case

KJLH-FM was prepared to respond to the verdict to the extent that the station "had stayed pretty close to the trial," says Slade (personal communication, 2001): "We were doing daily updates from the trial, and we really integrated it into our public affairs and our news program offerings." Moreover, Slade said, the feedback from the trial, "the daily accounts of what happened," indicated that the station had to be prepared to discuss the issues once the verdict was announced. Denny was pulled from his truck and beaten at the intersection of Florence and Normandy Avenues soon after the acquittals were announced:

> Reginald Denny was the guy who was driving his truck through the intersection and a young man hit him with a brick and knocked him unconscious and beat him horribly, and that was what they showed over and over, and ultimately these four young men who did the beating, cause it was all caught on tape, they were convicted and they did time for it [ibid.].

"When the decision came down," explains Slade, "we were going to do some editorials, and that kind of thing and take some listener feedback. We had no idea that.... Mr. Denny was going to be hurt." She adds, "We had no idea of the magnitude, that it was just combustible. But, having the editorials ready, having the additional news updates, we really were prepared to cover it" (ibid.).

The Fuse Ignites

Greg Johnson, KJLH marketing director, had not joined the staff in 1992, but he lived in Los Angeles at the time:

> I was with a record rep that is now the president of his own marketing firm out in New York — Sincere Thompson.... Anyway, we were going to Roscoe's, and Sincere was driving a rental car, he honked and somebody cut him off. He honked the horn, cussed the guy out, next thing we knew we're getting hauled out of the car by LAPD. You know cops.... Philosophically, I think that we all witnessed what happened in the rebellion in '92 and there was a lot of social issues in Los Angeles that really needed to be addressed that just weren't being, and that's the cause of that, I think Rodney King was just the fuse — there was already a lot of stuff happening in the community and some of the stuff is still happening, you know, today [Johnson, personal communication, 2002].

Nelson explained that there were rumbles on the street about what would happen if the verdict came back "not guilty":

> We knew that something was going to happen if the jury came back and found those police officers not guilty, or innocent, if you will, of beating Rodney King. We just did not know where it would come from. We had people who'd call the station, on the air and off the air as well, and they would say, "You know, if they find those cops innocent and da, da, da." Some you'd take with a grain of salt, but there were too many and they were from different people.... After awhile of being in the business, you could tell when you're getting a set-up call or organized call. These were just different people from different persuasions and age groups, you could tell, and backgrounds, articulating the same frustrations about the situation in Los Angeles as far as they felt [about] the treatment of African Americans [Nelson, personal communication, 2001].

Stephens started observing the first signs of unrest after the verdict came down, as she headed toward First A.M.E. Church to interview city council members for their reaction:

> I had kept hearing rumbles and rumbles and rumbles, after the verdict, and I kind of felt after the verdict, that verdict was going to be a problem. I knew at that time that some city council members were meeting at First A.M.E. Church

for something else, so I decided that should be a key point. Go down there and get some sound from them on what they expect and how they're going to handle the city if there is an eruption. And as I'm driving there, I'm starting to see little fires here, people gathered on corners over there, and it was really kind of scary. And I get to the church and they're just getting ready to start [and they did not know that] the verdict had been rendered, nor the little incendiary happenings around the city that I encountered. Anyway, yeah, so that was mine [Stephens, personal communication, 2002].

Slade noted that KJLH's former address was 3847 Crenshaw, which is basically on the main strip — "actually further north" — than her Inglewood location. It was mid-afternoon on Wednesday, April 29 when Slade prepared to respond to the verdict:

We had just done the interview with one of the police officers. We got a lot of feedback from that. And the jury verdict was coming down ... I aired my editorial, and Steve [Wonder] prepared his editorial. While we were preparing our editorials, the city [finger snap] just ignited. We were prepared for it, but not for what happened. We were prepared to respond to the decision [Slade, personal communication, 2002].

The intent of KJLH to establish a significant dialogue with its community of listeners was evident within minutes after the verdict was announced over the station's airwaves. Nelson details the initial setting:

I was actually at home when the verdicts came down, and I heard it on TV and I switched to the All News station and I listened to a friend of mine and he was getting pummeled out at Florence/Normandy — and so I decided to go to the station because it seemed like ... it was so spontaneous — folks were just doing things all over the place. So I drove to the station. When I got to the station, passing so many demonstrations — by that time the looting and the fires and all that — had not started, but people were just running up and down the streets. As soon as I got off the freeway on Crenshaw, there's crowds of young people, male and female, Latino, African American, Whites, you know, just shouting and screaming. We got a report in the station that there were shots being fired at Florence and Normandy. I managed to get our security chief, Sonny Williams, to take me down to Florence and Normandy. At first Sonny didn't want to go, and I said, "Sonny, you live in that neighborhood, the guys know you and we're going to take the station van anyway." So we took the van, rolled down there to the corners of Crenshaw, down to Florence and Normandy and it was a whole bunch of young folks out there in the street, fighting, throwing things and even guns were firing. Now when the guns started to fire, that's when we decided to get out of there — but they embraced us. You know ... people saw that we were from KJLH. They said, "Aw c'mon, you know, why don't you guys tell the real deal, what's goin' on." On the way there, there was a camera crew from one of the local stations and they took over the TV van, turned it over, set it on fire, and they hit the camera guy and he was "getting out of Dodge," so we decided to go back to the station and report on what was going on. By the time we got to the station, it seems like there were these mini-riots or scrimmages, if you will, just going on all over the city, not just in South Central and at Florence and Normandy where they claim everything started, but they were all over the city, East L.A, West L.A., in the Valley — it was just all over [Nelson, personal communication, 2001].

It was about three o'clock when KJLH began putting listeners on the air. Nelson called Reed and asked him to come to the station immediately. Reed (personal communication, 2001) explains that he was on his way home when he heard the verdict:

I was coming from the mall with my wife — and we were at a gas station getting some gas and I overheard a couple of people talking about the verdict — and as I was listening to a news station, I heard the verdict when it came down and they read the "not guilty" verdicts on the police officers that were involved in the Rodney King beating — and I guess you could say my heart just sank and my stomach sank and it's like, unbelievable.... People who were around me of various races were making different comments — I really couldn't tell you exactly what they said, but you know, it was mostly disbelief from what I remember — and as I got home, I turned on the television set and I could see things that were going on, and it seemed like as soon as I walked in the door, the phone rang, and it was Carl Nelson on the line. He was at the station and he asked me if I was watching what was goin' on, and I said, "Yeah, this is crazy." I couldn't believe it. And he said, "Well hey, you know I'm reporting now, and you know, [you] should come on down and do something. We need to talk about what's going on." I said, "Why don't we just go on the air and break into the music programming and do something." So as I got down there, they had already begun to put things together for that — our program director at the time, Lee Michaels, was on hand, and I walked in and we started talking about it. We just decided to call it an extended version of the "Front Page" [Reed, personal communication, 2001].

Callers were angry and frustrated with the system, according to Nelson (personal communication, 2001), and the events began to spiral out of control. KJLH staff was on full alert, and even sales people turned into reporters. "We even had our General Manager Karen Slade in the newsroom, pulling stuff off the wires for us, and, you know, handing it to us in the studio. We just used everybody, everything at the station," said Nelson:

The coverage was spontaneous as was reaction to what was going on in the streets. We had our reporters, Jacquie Stephens, myself, Rico. We deputized people in the sales department to go out and just interview people. Mayor Bradley had a meeting at First A.M.E. Church, trying to calm the community down, but the folks who were tearing up Los Angeles, they were not at First A.M.E., and we knew that [Nelson, personal communication, 2001].

Slade pointed out that the station's "call-in" strategy proved to be an effective and a powerful outlet for the community, at least in terms of addressing the concerns and outrage among KJLH's regular listeners:

> When you're frustrated and angry, and you can't release it or vent, then you tend to do something destructive depending on how angry you are. It's almost like a valve, you know, on a teapot. It whistles before it blows, so if you can get them to release or relieve just by venting, you know, and then you hear other people vent, and they may go too far, and you go well "No, no, I wouldn't say that." You know, it helps bring you back down. Because there is a time to say well let's pray for enemies, but initially you don't feel that, that's not your initial reaction. Even, I won't say it's the most Godly, even those that believe in God and have a great deal of faith, your initial reaction, out of frustration and anger, is not always forgive them, it's, "how can they do that?" "I don't believe this." And then it goes from there; you're either egged on to violence or you can be calmed down, if that makes any sense. And I think that's the role that we try to play, to give them a resource to vent and to hear themselves vent, and sometimes just hearing how crazy other people sound, it makes you step back and go, wait a minute, "No way." And it evolved to that, it really did, but for the first couple of hours, it was explosive [Slade, personal communication, 2001].

Beyond that, Slade and her staff, however, did not have the luxury of time or context to analyze the situation comprehensively as the mayhem unfolded before their eyes. Her first impulse was to send home most of her employees:

> I sent a couple of my guys out to get some actualities, and they came back.... They weren't gone 30 minutes and they came back very fearful saying "You don't pay me enough. I think I saw a dead person out there. I'm not going out there." I didn't realize how the city was at that moment going up in smoke and that was before I realized that there were fires and, you know, I was just trying to get feedback ... I sent my non–Black folks home first and then I sent my Black folks home, my staff home second, because first I thought, "Well, oh God, if they're going after Denny, they may go after you. You need to go home, get out of this neighborhood." Then I said everybody go home and check on your families and secure your property and we'll be okay, so I kept a skeleton staff for awhile. If I had it to do over I would hire more folks and be a little better prepared, maybe even have some security there. But, it did work out; they didn't touch us. They amazingly kind of considered us their resource — even people who called in. They respected our facility and what we mean to the community, which is a blessing, because that is the time when you find out what you're made of and what people think of you, and they really protected us [ibid.].

Because of KJLH's location and the immediacy of what was taking place on the streets (the Reginald Denny beating was only one of many scrimmages going on in the community at the time), it became difficult for some staff members to stay on the sidelines and watch from inside the KJLH studio. Nelson (personal communication, 2001) remembers vividly another incident: "One of the things that I'll never forget was the young Asian man who could have suffered a similar fate [as Denny]. His life was spared by somebody from our radio station, Gregory Allen Williams." (Williams, then KJLH production director, would later leave radio for acting, becoming a cast regular on *Baywatch* and *The Sopranos*.) He was "one of the guys" who "saved" a young Asian man who was driving through the neighborhood when the violence erupted in the city: Williams "pulled him away from this group of young men who were about to attack him and beat him up" (ibid.).

KJLH listeners heard the riots unfold as they tuned into the station — Carl Nelson, Eric Reed, Karen Slade, and number of the staff had a front row seat. They described on the air what they saw, as news media around the world reported from the KJLH studios. The intensity of the coverage increased moment by moment, as the world listened to the historic events. KJLH was one of the few stations that provided context to the riots — as they talked one to one with listeners and residents, allowing airtime to vent the anger and pain heard in the voices of the callers, making on-air pleas to stop the looting and chaos on the streets, arranging for emergency assistance at various hotspots, and announcing prayer assemblies at churches and throughout the city.

CHAPTER 7

Tuned In and Out Front

Communicating Social Responsibility on Black Radio

So basically, what you end up getting is a mist of hate that is welling up from all these fires and all of these buildings burning. For instance, we saw the one particular part of this mall across the street from us — the tailor shop was the one that burnt the longest. I mean those clothes, the chemicals in those clothes were just really smoldering. — Brandon Bowlin [*Front Page*, 1992b]

Mainstream media had no idea how to grapple with the unfolding events that filled TV screens and radio airwaves. Black radio had been here before — the night that King died, the Watts riots, and a variety of events only superficially contextualized by White media. From coast to coast and throughout the heartland, African Americans assembled — literally and figuratively — around the radio dial. Urban Radio KMJM-FM in St. Louis suspended its format to take phones calls from listeners. One female listener commented, "We're so passive, that's the thing that kills me. I would be willing to protest ... in front of the Federal Government building or wherever. We can't let this lie. It's not something new." Across the U.S., the music stopped, and the dialogue began. The following excerpt is from the morning program on KMJM, Wednesday April 30, 1992, beginning at 8:44 A.M.:

> *Tony Scott:* People are venting their frustrations on the air, and what's going to happen. Are we going to get anything out of this, or are we just going to be pissed off?
>
> *Kevin Woosten:* I'm taking a lot of calls. A lot of people are giving me experiences that they've gone through as far as racism, but I haven't heard a lot of anger.

Tony Scott: Only a few people. This is one of many theories that could be used to explain it. I think the majority of Black people really know what time it is; it is hard for a lot of people to come to grips and be honest with themselves, and admit, yes, this does happen.

Kevin Woosten: You're talking apathy. What you're saying is if people know what time it is and they're willing to accept this, then tomorrow, it's going to be Friday, it's the day before the weekend — let's kick it. This is forgotten. If that is the case, then what happened to Rodney King, the decision that came down yesterday, it shouldn't even have happened because it didn't affect anybody except the man who got the hell beat out of him, and the guys who got off. So that's five folks, and the attorneys are getting mucho dollars.

Tony Scott: But you know it's funny how things come together. It's National Honesty Day, and how honest can it be than the slap in the face that has happened in this country.

Kevin Woosten: It's an affront to all Americans.

A few minutes later:

Tony Scott: We're encouraging you to drive with your headlights on today in support of the protest.

Kevin Woosten: Non-violent.

Tony Scott: Non-violent for Rodney King, the acquittal there which makes absolutely no sense at all. We're getting your phone calls this morning, and we're telling you sound off this morning on how you feel about it [KMJM Transcript, 1992].

The *St. Louis Post-Dispatch* reported that KMJM inserted listener comments between songs beginning mid-afternoon (Hick, 1992). WGNU-AM, Granite City, Illinois, was overwhelmed with phone calls on Onion Horton's call-in show on Thursday morning, April 30, 1992. The afternoon personality, Charles Geer, reported that 90 percent of the calls that he received "expressed outrage and shock ... and resignation" (Hick, 1992, p. 25A).

From Los Angeles, KJLH would simulcast its frontline coverage to news and urban stations — WGN-AM, Chicago, WLIB-AM, New York, and WDAS-AM/FM, Philadelphia — as well as to Black-targeted stations in Houston, Seattle and across the nation. As the world listened to KJLH, it had a rare opportunity to get to know South Central listeners, many of whom were still without electricity. The listeners discussed how they were not only horrified by the events taking place in their own backyard, but also by mainstream's assumptions of what was going on in their community. One listener said:

The media and the reporters, I don't think they really understand the frustration that these people are going through and the violent reaction, I think, is a reflection on those people in the South Central area, the LA area, that were going to get into trouble tonight. They were going to do violence anyway tonight. I think they're using the Rodney King situation as just a vehicle. And I don't think that the media really understands it. I think that they're trying to find direct relationships between the violence and the case. And that's not it. I think people were going to get into trouble tonight anyway. It's just heightened because of what's going on with the case [*Front Page*, 1992b].

By May 1, many people heard KJLH's perspective about the uprising on radio stations across the world. In particular, Black radio stations came together to help KJLH broadcast the story of South Central across the nation. At one point, Arsensio Hall began to broadcast a message of peace across Los Angeles' KPWR, in an effort to solidify the African American community:

Arsenio Hall: ...This is Arsenio Hall tryin' to increase the peace. This radio thing is new to me and it's scary. All these people around me throwing signals to me and I'm just trying to hang. I want to mention that I'm at Power 106, but everybody's come together tonight. Let me tell you who we've got: Kiss-FM, KBTT–The Beat, KJLH, KGFJ. Pirate Radio is in the house. KLOS, K-Rock, KFI, KABC, KMPC, K-LITE, KCRW, KWNK, and by the way, that's in Simi Valley. KGIL, is that Johnny Gill's radio station? I don't know. KKXX, Bakersfield and we're around the country, too. Q-106 and Z-90 in San Diego. 106-KMEL, WILD 107 and KGO Newstalk Radio in San Francisco. WGCI Chicago, I've listened to that when I've been visiting Chicago. WRC-AM in Washington, D.C., Chocolate City, love it, love it. KUBE 93 FM in Seattle. WMXD "The Mix" in Detroit. 102 Jams in Orlando; we're down there jammin' with them tonight, trying to increase the peace. FM 102 Sacramento, 97.9 "The Box" in Houston — ooh I won't even question that. 100.3 Jams in Dallas, XHEP Mexico City, and the ABC Radio Network, which of course, is nationwide. I'm Arsenio Hall, trying to increase the peace. I'd like to give my listeners out there the phone number that we're working with. Area code 213–520–1059. Area code 213–520–1059 or 1–8 or 818. I'm dyslexic. I'm so nervous. I'm dyslexic. Okay, take a chill pill and just relax. It's just like television, just they can't see how nervous I am. 520–1059, that's the 818 area code and 714–977–1059. Do I have any callers ... that I can put on the air? Tryin' to increase the peace, we're going to turn a negative situation around into a positive situation. Martin Luther King used to say, "We'll take a dungeon of shame and turn it into a chamber of human dignity." That's what we're going to do. And this young lady's from Glendale. What's your name? Angela?

Caller: It's An-ge-la.

Arsenio Hall: Angela, Hi Angela. This is Arkenio — No, I'm just kidding.

Caller: The one and only. How you doing?

Arsenio Hall: Oh, I'm hanging in here. Let me have some comments on what's going on around the country.

Caller: Okay, great. Martin Luther King is fine. Like other Americans in earlier times, he had a dream of a better America. We must not fight or use violence nor other ways to protest. We cannot solve this problem through violence. We, as a community, must stop and let peace take its part. And I'd like to ask the City of Los Angeles, if Martin Luther King, Jr., was still to be alive, what would he have done?

Arsenio Hall: He'd be very angry and he'd probably, gosh, feel that all of his work was in vain. I really thank you for calling. And like I said, we're all one gang tonight. Black, White, male, female. We've got to team up on the issue and increase the peace.

The black media worked together in Los Angeles and across the nation. Celebrities calling for peace helped to get the attention of listeners, but it was the reporters and station employees who worked hard at sorting through the details from listeners and officials calling into the studios that were critical to providing an accurate and timely information flow across the airwaves. Without the people behind the scenes, at the desk and on the phone, it would have been impossible for the on-air hosts to keep up with the events unfolding quickly. KJLH employees worked day and night during the on-air vigil, sometimes only taking a short one or two hour break in the middle of the night, and then starting all over again:

> The talk consisted of, you know, quite a bit of things, from listeners calling in to making sure that the Fire Department was where it needed to be, and where aid and blankets and food and shelter, whatever people needed, we made sure that they got that information. We had ministers on, we had attorneys on.... We had someone call in from across the street from a nursing home where the fire looked like it was going to join the nursing home and people were nervous and they couldn't get the patients out of the building. We really had like a call, a community wake-up call [Slade, personal communication, 2001].

The station's Hispanic audience turned to the Spanish-speaking stations, while both White and Black listeners stayed tuned to KJLH. Listeners of Korean-owned KCB-FM similarly called into their station, which alerted merchants and residents of the events transpiring on the streets. KJLH listeners called into the station to respond to the verdict — in an attempt to provide context to the mayhem that was occurring in their neighborhoods:

> *Caller:* I was at work when the verdict came through, and my work place is full, like with White people, and you know, different races, Filipinos, and

when we heard the verdict, they don't understand that this is something that's been put on us time after time after time, and it's just accumulated. They feel it's an isolated incident, because one guy was like, "well that's good, he got what he deserved, he deserved to be beat," you know.

Rico Reed: Oh boy.

Caller: It's like we couldn't respond, the Black people there, we couldn't respond in a way that we wanted, which was to lash out in anger....

J. Anthony Brown: It's so weird that every Black man is subject to what happened to Rodney King, it's —

Tyrone: Absolutely, it's just the norm.

Rico Reed: And it's not just African Americans now, it's all minorities.

J. Anthony Brown: All minorities.

Brandon Bowlin: It could have been anybody. The beautiful thing was that the whole movement, right after it had taken place, was that everybody was involved. And, actually, I saw in the eyes of some people, like non African Americans, who knew exactly what it feels like to have to put your hands behind your head, kneel down in your suit on the freeway at two in the afternoon.

Rico Reed: Yeah, it certainly is. 520-KJLH, 977-KJLH, we have a special bulletin here from Carl Nelson.

Carl Nelson: Yeah Rico. L.A. police advise us some 200 people have gathered near Sunset Boulevard and Gardner Street in Hollywood, where members of Queer Nation and Act Up L.A. are staging a protest, and uh, those two groups have been violently opposed to Chief Gates and the LAPD. Also, an angry mob converged on the Hall of Justice in the Criminal Courts Building downtown tonight, hurling rocks and bottles, setting small fires and taunting deputies before moving on. Mobs set fires in the Criminal Courts Building lobby and in the exterior courtyard [*Front Page*, 1992a].

By 10 P.M., April 29, 1992, as the situation intensified on the streets, the range of topics initiated by listeners jumped from discussions and criticism of the verdict and police to misrepresentation of the events on mainstream media, to personal shock and disgust about what was happening on the streets of Los Angeles. The listeners were struggling to cope with events that had already transpired within hours of the verdict — as well as with the events that continued to take place within feet or blocks of their homes or workplaces, while the station provided continal updates:

Carl Nelson: Okay, Rico. Several L.A. Unified School District campuses will be closed tomorrow due to the rioting by the verdict in the Rodney King beating trial. Superintendent William Hampton has called for the closure of all schools and offices tomorrow within the area of Adams Boulevard to the north, Imperial Highway to the south, La Cienaga Boulevard to the west and Alameda to the east. So we'll give you those directions again a little later on.

Rico Reed: That's all the high schools, elementary schools, everything.

Carl Nelson: All high schools, everything — even district buildings, school district buildings....

Brandon Bowlin: ...Remember when the Watts riots took place, a lot of the Jewish businesses were burned — and here, a lot of the Korean businesses are burned, and then there, the lines were drawn over what the Black community actually was, and now you've just seen, when you discussed the schools, it almost draws the exact block of the Black community that's in the riotous state [*Front Page*, 1992a].

Behind the scenes, the general manager with a skeleton crew of sales, office, and air personalities coordinated the hundreds of incoming phone calls, the news reports, and influx of celebrities, politicians, and news crews from other media. Nelson and Jacquie Stephens, then a reporter and anchor, struggled to keep on top of the situation as it changed from moment to moment, as evident from this conversation around midnight, April 30, 1992:

Jacquie Stephens: I'm just trying to put the information kind of sort of together so we can see based on where we've been, where we might be going. The troops are now coming in, Rico, from the L.A. County Sheriff's Department. Two platoons of National Guard troops have been dispatched and they're in route to Crenshaw Boulevard and Slawson Avenue and they're also going into the city of Carson. They were dispatched about, right now, about 40 minutes ago to assist with the LAPD in handling the looters. I had to find out a platoon means one lieutenant, 5 sergeants and 50 deputies. Now this proves that the mayor has made good his threat to halt some of the violent activity.

Mayor (actuality): Anybody out there who believes that they can take advantage of this situation and create havoc for the law abiding people of this community, we're going to put you on notice. We're going to be out to arrest you.

Jacquie Stephens: Also, 13 deaths have [been] tallied from all the community disruption from overnight into this afternoon. That number, of course, could increase as shifting is done through destroyed structures and authorities are admitting that at this stage, with so many officers deployed and so busy, it's difficult to actually secure an accurate count. Now police do say that most of the injured died of gunshot wounds. We have a list of some of those and when their deaths occurred; an 18-year-old died after 8:00 last evening. fatally wounded at Vernon and Vermont avenues. Around that same time, a 42-year-old man fatally injured at Martin Luther King Boulevard 400 block at 8:30 at night as well; a 15-year-old boy injured at

Vernon and Vermont showing that a lot of activity going on in that area overnight and right after midnight. This morning, a 45-year-old man was fatally injured at 102nd street and Avalon Boulevard. We had around 10:30 last evening a 21-year-old man fatally injured — that happened at 78th and San Pedro Street. Now from the White House and from his presidential campaign, President Bush has sent a word — violence won't be tolerated [*Front Page*, 1992b].

Listener after listener called into the KJLH studio to express frustration with the King verdict and Police Chief Darryl Gates' handling of the violent outbreaks in South Central Los Angeles. Later that morning around 6 A.M. on April 30, the dialogue continued:

Caller: My name is Bella and I'm calling from Los Angeles. I was real upset about the verdict, but what upset me the most was the senseless violence. And I was speaking with my son last night and he's 13, and I said Gates is clever. I mean Gates is very clever. He sets the stage; he was telling everyone how he was going to prepare the police force for violence. And it just seems like we just played right into his hands.

J. Anthony Brown: But the ironic thing about it was that they were not prepared for it. We were down here all night. Something was happening and you could see that the police never even showed up. There was no readiness. They weren't ready for this. They were talking about being ready but they definitely weren't ready for this.

Carl Nelson: Gates admitted last night that he was too slow in sending in his officers and that's just kind of strange, to me, to make that admission. Since he made these preparations beforehand, and now he's ... "well I was kind of slow, I think I was kind of slow, I could have sent my boys in quicker."

Caller: I don't think he had any intentions on it.

J. Anthony Brown: Now that I believe. He had no intention of sending people into this neighborhood. What they did was cut it off. We've been cut off since about 2:30 or something like that. They started cutting the area off, not coming in and dealing with some of the problems that we had [*Front Page*, 1992b].

Keep the Kids Off the Streets

Slade recalled that many teenagers "just sort of cut loose, but the younger kids, I imagine, would have been scared to death. I was afraid. But I had a duty to do, so I just forged through — you don't realize until you sit down and see everything visually that you were really in some dangerous time" (personal communication, 2002). On the first night of the unrest, listeners, shaken audibly, called KJLH for answers or just to seek solace in another voice. One caller, expressing her mixed emotions of fear and outrage, said:

> I've gotta tell ya, I went to the church at A.M.E. today because I'm really angry and I'm really very scared. You know, I just spent the last ten years of my life in college. I went to one of the best law schools in the country, Hastings, up in San Francisco (very angrily). But it doesn't really matter, because even with a briefcase in my hand and a suit on my back, I'm still just another nigger to the cops out there and to the redneck White people, and not all White people, but there's people out there who don't really care who you are and what you're about. And I know that I'm not the only one who feels helpless. But I can say that. You know, we do have something that we can do. We can look inside of ourselves, not at just our neighborhoods. When I drive down the street at 9 o'clock at night and I see a 12-year-old child out there riding around on a bicycle, there is something very seriously wrong. That child should be at home. Not sitting in front of a television, but sitting in front of the parents with conversation happening or sitting at the kitchen table doing their homework.... And to this "gentleman," I'll call him, who says there's a revolution happening ... a revolution happens if we're fighting the enemy. We're out there tonight fighting each other; White people coming into our neighborhoods, burning up our stores. You know, we just got that Crenshaw Mall put in there and they're burning Sears?... It's ridiculous. Stop it people. STOP IT. We've got to be together [*Front Page*, 1992a].

There were nearly 50 mentions of concern by hosts, listeners, and others for the welfare of children and teens in the *Front Page* transcripts. In every case there was a sense of urgency to keep them off the streets and to provide them with positive role models within the community:

> *Arsenio Hall:* ...We don't want to become like our enemies. And this is not a White or Black thing. It saddens me to see people pull White people out of the cars based on the color of their skin.
>
> *Whoopi Goldberg:* When in fact, that's what we're saying is so wrong about what happened. You see, so we then become the abuser. And another thing that I think people really need to take into consideration are two things: if we burn and loot and destroy, how do we feed our children? How do you cash your check? Where do you find your way to work? How do you find the way to look for work? The other thing is machismo does not begin at the end of a gun. You see, guns don't make you a man. Intelligent thought makes you a man. A gun makes you a thug and an animal and sadly tonight we're faced all around the nation [with] the idea that if we don't pull this thing together and pull it together real quick, we're going to be gunned down in the streets like animals. So this is all about our families. And the families of the people who aren't going to come home, as Rodney King said earlier today. It's about all those kids, kids looting along

with their parents. You know, how many TV sets can you have if you don't have a house? Somebody said to me, "you need to appeal on television." I said, "Honey, those people are not watching television, they on television."

Arsenio Hall: Check that out. I hope we can get them, and they're in their cars right now and I plead to the parents. Whoopi, you're a mom, I plead to the parents all around the city — know where your boys are tonight. Keep them at home. Watch *Wheel of Fortune*, do anything, but don't go out tonight. I'm a graduate of Kent State and I know what the National Guard are all about, and I don't want you to lose track of your sons tonight and have to go identify them in the morgue tomorrow.

Whoopi Goldberg: Not only that Arsenio, but you need to remind people too that these are our children, these are our children, and the example that we set regardless of what the government does, it's what you do as an individual that teaches your children how to act. You want them in on time? Then you need to set that example. This is not the way to do it because these minds are young and fresh.

Arsenio Hall: I saw parents taking their children looting today, it was sad [*Front Page*, 1992c].

Callers reiterated concerns for children in the community, and especially for their future, as illustrated in these comments from listeners:

I'm calling from Los Angeles. I just want to appeal to the parents. The parents are out of hand. They have to get in control and control the children. This is one of the problems; there were so many children out yesterday, looting and everything. When your child gets hurt, don't blame it on anyone but yourself because that is wrong. You are supposed to be the leader to guide your children. They are wrong. The parents are wrong. My son is here and he's going to be here by me until this thing is over [*Front Page*, 1992c].

I have a 1 year-old son and being that he's going to be a Black male in America, what chances does he have for the future. What about our kids? This is not helping our kids. We got a whole bunch of little confused kids out there, 8, 9, 10-year-olds who don't completely understand. It's hard for me to be an adult and understand fully [*Front Page*, 1992d].

Nelson reported that a number of teens participated in the youth assembly outside the First A.M.E. Church on April 30, 1992:

You know, L.A. City Councilman Mark Whitley Thomas made a profound statement during the assembly at First A.M.E. Church this evening, and that was looking at the large number of people there and I'd say over half were young adults, under the age of 21. And his statement was, "Take a look around you. Not all young African-Americans are out there being destructive in this city" [*Front Page*, 1992b].

Now nearly 14 hours after the King verdict was announced, hosts and the callers were becoming more articulate in their pleas for voter participation, and it became obvious that the community was beginning to reorganize and respond to the needs of their neighbors (*Front Page*, 1992b). KJLH callers were angered and disheartened by the one-dimensional depiction of the African American community in the mainstream media, as indicated in the following excerpt:

> *Caller:* [There are] certain people who are reaching out for the moon, certain people who are satisfied with their morals, living right, raising their family right. Then we have the people who are just out there and they are trying to survive. Now, you look at the ones who are making it, and they're upset. You look at the ones who are trying to raise their children right. You know, I have a 6-year-old son; I have a 4-year-old daughter. I'm trying to tell them what is right. Not only by man's law, but by God's law.
>
> *Rico Reed:* Good for you. And in that sense right there, when you're trying to teach these kids right and they see wrong just blatantly put out in front of their face, then that's another level of ethics and morals that we have to deal with our children, and to try to put everything in perspective in our society — and then society is trying to half-way work for us.
>
> *Carl Nelson:* Yeah, we have to try to put some faith in something, man [*Front Page*, 1992b].

Media Reaction Across the United States and the World

> It was a third world rebellion for the first time in recent history where people of Color united against common symbols of oppression. But more importantly, and you yourself Carroll, Jamaal, and Carl said the same thing. You keep calling it a L.A. Rebellion. I remember vividly, and I have it on videotape that within the first 24 hours of the Rodney King decision, I think it was ABC television [that] had a map of the United States as a still print on television. On that map, they had fire icons on 23 cities in the United States that were up in urban rebellion within 24 hours. After 24 hours, the media was censored by the Federal Emergency Management Act, and they said, "No call this the L.A. Rebellion, and do not give broadcast coverage of the rebellion of any other city [Caller cited in *Front Page*, 2002b].

News reporters who had never stepped foot into the neighborhoods of South Central were overwhelmed by the rapid and rampant violence sweeping through the streets. The neighborhood was particularly dangerous for these journalists unfamiliar with the area or issues, as demonstrated in the following excerpt:

Rico Reed: I just talked to J. Anthony Brown. He called me from Arsenio. They're over there talking about the issues, what's going on right now. I don't know if you saw the issue; there was a big double 16 wheeler or a big 40-foot truck with the trailer behind it and the guy — blond hair, shaggy — was beaten.

Jacquie Stephens: Hmmm hmm. His eye is out.

Rico Reed: His eye is out and it's a very good possibility he's going to die.... He lost so much blood right there while people just walked by and watched him.

Jacquie Stephens: That's so sad.

Rico Reed: I think one lady did die, was beaten.

Jacquie Stephens: One of the UPI reporters, also a victim of that type of harsh treatment, stomped in the face while attempting to file in a report.

Rico Reed: Oh boy, what does it all mean? What does it all mean? It's 12:45, 15 minutes away from one. We've received a letter from a German magazine. It's a press agency out here covering for a German magazine and they faxed us to applaud what we're doing, they really appreciate what we're doing. They'd like to commit their support. They said that when the news of the riots were heard in Europe a few hours ago, Germany and France, England, everybody was concerned. At the same time they support the cause of Black people here in the U.S. in Los Angeles. It's going beyond the borders of the U.S.; it is traveling across the country right now and it's all over the world [*Front Page*, 1992a].

Reporters camped out at KJLH especially the print media, *USA Today*, *Chicago Sun Times*, and The *New York Daily News* to name a few. They papered "over the logos painted on the sides of news vehicles" and hid their identification "under blouses and shirts" (O'Neill, 1992, pp. 23–25). A Crenshaw shopping plaza across the street from KJLH burned the first night of the unrest, and it was one of more than 150 fires that night ("City under Siege," 1992; Lacey & Hubler, 1992). Camera crews arrived from all over the world to the Southland, and, at one point, the beginning of *The NBC Nightly News* with Tom Brokaw was broadcast live from the KJLH studios.

KJLH was the only station licensed to Compton, and at the time it was one of at least 60 radio stations in metropolitan Los Angeles, including at least five Spanish stations and three Black and urban stations (*Broadcasting Yearbook*, 1993). Its unique vantage point in South Central quickly made it a focal point of the media, and Reed recalls what flashed across his mind:

A lot of things were going through my head, as in the other hosts and co-hosts that were in the studio and other guests. You're looking out of the window and first, of course, is disbelief. You're like, well, you kinda feel like you're watching a movie. We're so desensitized by watching movies and television with all the special effects and things that are out now. It's just like you know, nothing really shocks you, but then you kinda look at it and it's like, nobody said "cut." No commercial came on. This is real, and as you're looking at it, once again, it's disbelief, that people [were] doing things they would normally not do: going through windows, breaking windows out, running trucks into windows, trying to break bars out to steal, you know, insignificant items out of the liquor stores — like toilet paper and baby diapers ... I think [our coverage] was extremely effective. I think it opened the eyes of the world per se because we pretty much became Ground Central for the world as far as accurate news reporting. What you were getting on the news stations, just from the helicopters flying over and the police reports, in my opinion, wasn't necessarily accurate. It was just you know, "well they're looting, they're rioting, they're doing this, they're doing that," and it wasn't really a one-on-one birds-eye report or view of what was actually happening [Reed personal communication, 2001].

On the morning of May 1, 1992, a Dallas radio personality called into KJLH, live from his show, to share his views with Reed and Nelson and reiterate the importance of responsible journalism:

> *Russ Parr:* And I think part of the problem is, I know, [they] have got TV cameras sitting in your face right now, and I'm sure ABC and NBC, everybody's there, but I think right now we don't need that kind of exposure. I know it's sweeps week and everybody wants the ratings and everything, but where is the responsibility? Where are journalists? When are the journalists there going to take responsibility for what they're doing? They're whoring the public. And, to me, I think that's a travesty. You're only inciting, and it's wrong. Forget your ratings, you know, because these people are not representative. I've been trying to tell people here, these people who you see running like animals in the streets are not representative or indicative of the kind of people who are in Los Angeles.

> *Rico Reed:* Well Russ, just to reiterate on what you're saying and to add something. No, the people who are running the streets are not the total view of what Los Angeles is all about. There are good people out there. We have hundreds of phone calls. I guess by now, thousands of phone calls that we've fielded over the air and we've talked to people off the air that are concerned. They don't like the violence in the streets; yes they're upset about the King verdict [*Front Page*, 1992c].

During the heat of the unrest, a number of celebrities — Carl Weathers, Ice Cube, Jody Watley, Denzel Washington, and South Central's own Barry White, as well as some of the players from the L.A. Clippers ("Celebs Pitch," 1992) dropped into the KJLH studio, often unannounced, in an attempt to calm the city without any regards to their personal safety. In one instance, Slade (personal communication, 1993) explained, "Barry White came down here ... and he was pleading for them to stop [the violence]. Well, Barry White's from the neighborhood. And I'm like, "Mr. White please — I appreciate you coming down but please go home. I cannot guarantee your safety." He's like, "I'm not afraid." Other celebrities, like former football star Jim Brown, called into the station to express concern for the safety of listeners and their families:

> *Carl Nelson:* We've got Jim Brown on the phone. Good evening Jim.
>
> *Jim Brown:* How are you, Carl?
>
> *Carl Nelson:* Oh, I'm pretty good. Jim, what is your assessment of what's going on in the streets tonight?
>
> *Jim Brown:* Well, naturally, I'm very sad about what's going on because it's self destructive, and I know that the police have a master plan. If things continue, there's going to be a lot of unnecessary bloodshed. On the other hand, I just came out of Imperial Courts [interruption] Gardens and the guys out there have kept to their truce.... So it is ironic that when Crips and Bloods make history, coming together, the news media and all of the other leaders in the community are trying to overlook that and go to that general kind of conversation about stopping something. These brothers are stopping something themselves. I'm proud of them because as I said, I just came out of the projects and the brothers are working together, both Crips and Bloods, not to do anything crazy [*Front Page*, 1992b].

Another one of the celebrity guest hosts, J. Anthony Brown, commented that the outside media seemed to focus only on the destruction:

> I feel bad about the fact that the news stations, the television stations were showing a lot of the violence, but there were a lot of churches and there were a lot of civic organizations that were doing things to calm the people, along with the radio station — and none of that was broadcast. They really focused on the violence and there was a lot going on, but there were some things that were going on across this city to try to calm people and get their heads calm [*Front Page*, 1992b].

By Friday, the events happening at the KJLH studio had been aired globally. KJLH's coverage was transmitted via satellite across National Public Radio, CBS Radio Network, British Broadcasting Corporation (London), as well as to outlets in Japan, Italy, Germany, all over the world. Stephens and others assisted the influx of reporters from all over Los Angeles and the world:

> We allowed them to come on in and, yeah, everybody was basically professional, so it was okay. We just had to take turns, and we were the point. We were the information point, and I guess because we worked with that commu-

nity, it was our community. We were the information providers for a lot of the media because they didn't know. You know [they'd] pull out the, I can't think of the book, *Thomas Guide*. [It] tells you what streets intersect and where they are, that's how they found out; whereas for us, we could go straight there, know the short-cuts, so we were their source [Stephens, personal communication, 2002].

The station's events were simulcast to Chicago, Philadelphia, Houston and Seattle, and several other markets. In a 1993 interview, Nelson explained, "There were so many stations that we had to just assign one person to deal with the media.... We didn't really care about the media.... They'll be gone tomorrow and we still have to work here. You see, we have a vested interest in this community. If this community burns, they can't advertise on this radio station" (Nelson, personal communication, 1993).

In all this confusion, said Nelson (personal communication, 2001), and with all the national media coming down to South Central, "I remember getting different calls from all over the city from people cause you got to remember now, there were lights out. There was no power." Nelson continues, "One guy called and he was scared; he was listening to us on his transistor radio in his closet and he said, 'that's the only thing that's keeping my sanity.'" And many stayed inside their homes, and just listened to the radio because they were scared of the looters, the police, and, to some extent, even their own neighbors:

> *Caller*:...I mean I'm scared to be out in the street myself. A female out on the street? I mean, I'm afraid of the police.
> *Rico Reed*: Well don't be out on the street tonight.
> *Brandon Bowlin*: Well just remember "April 29th" — do not forget why it happened.
> *Caller*: Oh, we won't. Believe me [*Front Page*, 1992a].

Incoming phone calls streamed into KJLH's studio as listeners vented their frustrations or reached out for a soothing voice in the midst of the mayhem, and they exclaimed, "I can't leave the radio."

Organized Chaos Caught on Tape

On Wednesday, April 29, 1992, Reed and Nelson called the Reverend Jackson to ask for his help in calming down the people of South Central, and neighboring communities. It was as if all the problems of urban America cried out when the King verdict was announced to South Central residents. For some, the season for listening had passed by, and now there was hell to pay for the longtime, often ignored, social ills that had taken their toll on a community. On the other hand, a number of people came from other parts of Los Angeles into South Central to gawk, to loot, to instigate violence and to ignite neighborhoods, with little regard to the emotional and physical safety of families and residents already distressed by the destruction of their homes, businesses, and lives. Goree began to observe "some things [that] would make [him] wonder if there was not some other element, maybe a clandestine, very organized, element that was going around burning some of these buildings." He remembers:

> I had been in a building, I remember on 43rd and Degnan during the day, maybe the second day of the rebellion. It was a grocery store. It was still conducting business. I remember the next day, maybe, that building was being blocked off by the police, and that evening it burned down. Now I say, OK, wait a minute, now the police at some point had made a decision that this building may be targeted. They were protecting it and it still burned down. OK, so it made me wonder. I saw an interview — folks at a senior citizen's home, and I believe that was at 83rd and Vermont, and they told them that they saw law enforcement, or what appeared to be law enforcement, going to a small mini-mall, run some of the young people out who were looting, and the next thing they know, the whole mini-mall went up in flames.... You know, there's a phrase, and I'm not sure who I can accredit the source to this, but it says "It's order out of chaos," that once you create a chaotic environment, that you can start now to repeal certain laws or implement certain legislation that may infringe upon certain rights and people will go for it because they're afraid. I mean [that's] what's happening right now after September the 11th — with the anti-terrorism legislation [Goree, personal communication, 2002].

Goree also observed that some people "seemed to be ready-made for the chaos that took place out there; they thrived in it. And obviously some people were horrified." He explained that there were other inconsistencies:

> I was also shocked at the response by some law enforcement that either took it upon themselves or [were] instructed [to] "simply do nothing," and watch certain business establishments burn down. Now I don't know what their reason was. I also know that there were cases where shop owners used the '92 Rebellion as an opportunity to burn their own establishments down to collect insurance money. That was documented [ibid.].

With so many fires seemingly starting at random in the area, many of the radio hosts and celebrities began to question how the fires had begun. On Friday, May 1, 1992, Bill Cosby and Arsenio Hall spoke to the newly emerging theories that many building had been intentionally set on fire, and attempted to provide some sense of reason behind some of the looting that continued throughout Los Angeles:

> *Bill Cosby*: I'm calling from a pay phone booth out here. I'm in New York City. And you know what? It was very, very respectful back here. But the thing about being in New York City, I don't know, there were rumors going around and these rumors had to be squelched. There were things coming into the newsroom, out of the newsroom, that there was a bus turned upside down and burning on 5th Avenue; then there was another that Macy's was on fire and that Bloomingdale's had been bombed. So, a lot of stupid people were just having a ball. And along with all of what we see on TV, I must also add that some of these fires, I would be willing to bet cannot be blamed on just folk out there angry about what happened. You know, there are some sick people out there and they call them arsonists, and once they see those things up in the sky on the news, you know, these people start to come out.
>
> *Arsenio Hall*: A lot of the fires, I talked to a couple of police officers yesterday, a lot of the fires have been professionally set. These aren't fires set by gang members. We have a tendency in this town to blame everything on gang members. I'm not trying to defend gang members, but the bottom line is they were talking about gang members looting and I turned on the television and saw a lady stealing diapers. We can't blame everything on gang members [*Front Page*, 1992c].

After the National Media Went Home

For many reporters and residents, their world had changed in a matter of days and, in some instances, minutes. The King verdict was announced on April 29, at which point KJLH hosts urged listeners to stay calm and talked many callers through the confusion. The next day, the National Guard and federal troops were called to active duty. On Friday, May 1, the hosts were trying to help the city cope with the power outages and find shelter and food for the homeless:

> A lot of folks in the inner-city area for a few days really couldn't get food, and that is actually why some people started to loot; it's because they couldn't go shopping; they couldn't get food, so they said, "Well, if everyone's taking the food, then I've got to get some food." The buses didn't run; there were no taxi services, and if you didn't have a car ... [Goree, personal communication, 2002].

KJLH had returned to regular programming on Saturday, May 2, 1992, except for periodic updates on road and work conditions. When all was said and done, KJLH maintained its credibility among listeners and residents, and provided an opportunity for reporters outside the community to observe this type of relationship:

> While other stations were playing music, I may add, this is where the difference was actually, other stations went back to regular programming. We did not go back to regular programming. We were discussing issues. We weren't even playing commercials, you know. For that matter, you know, if you look at it from a financial standpoint we were losing money. We said, "No, our community is much more important than playing a few commercials," cause we say in our slogan that, "We are you," so whatever the pain that's going through our community, goes through us too. And if we don't have a community, we don't have a radio station, and we made that perfectly clear, and I think that the people understand this [Slade, personal communication, 2002].

Indeed, on Saturday, 20,000 people came out to participate in a voter registration rally that had been promoted by KJLH since the unrest began only days earlier. For the most part, the weekend remained calm as the city began to rebuild, and by Monday, many schools and businesses had reopened. However, a number of businesses also had burned to the ground and the smell of war still lingered in the air:

> When you're in the middle of it, it felt like a war zone to me. I don't know if anyone's ever shared that with you, but when the whole city was burning, there was a smell that permeated the building. It's something that you don't forget. And when I worked 26 hours straight and when I went home to shower and change, it had even permeated my house. The smell is the thing that made me think of war and the troops. It's hard to describe when we were under martial law — it's like God, South Central's become a war zone [ibid.].

KJLH was left to pick up the pieces with the community. The station began immediately to seek ways to bring the African American and Korean-American communities together in the rebuilding of South Central. The station also encouraged activities and forums that would attempt to alleviate the tension between the police department and the residents. *Front Page* found its identity as a strong issues forum during the crisis.

A few weeks after the unrest, the second trial in the Rodney King case was announced. Its coverage of the first trial and verdict and unrest that followed, as well as KJLH's timely interview with King, was pivotal toward demonstrating its credibility as a necessary and significant voice within the community of listeners and the larger political and judicial systems:

> We had Rodney King in studio. We had had, who else did we have? We had one of the police officers that was involved in studio on one of our public affairs shows. We were afraid for him, but he was determined to come and he came

and I thought he really showed great courage and we couldn't get the others to come, but he came. And, you know, and it helps, the unknown, you're afraid of the unknown or you can build up animosity or anger towards the unknown because it's ignorance; you don't know any better, but once you put a voice with the name and you hear this person speak and their views, then you kind of ... you may not agree, but you have a better understanding. So that's, I think, a benefit of broadcasting, it allows a two-way communication. It's not just one-on-one, it's one-on-one heard by the world or, you know, as far as your listening audience extends. And people get to understand the other person's point of view in the safe environment of their home, listening to it on the radio or in their car. It's a great way to explore differences and to try to get a better understanding of someone or something you know nothing about without subjecting yourself to any ridicule [ibid.].

The Justice Department "guaranteed two minorities a seat inside the federal trial." One was from KJLH and the other was from the Latino newspaper *La Opinión*. *Newsweek*, the *Washington Post*, the *Los Angeles Times*, and *USA Today* had to share a seat on alternate days, and numerous other media outlets were not allowed inside the courtroom. Their reporters were stationed in the media room (Stein, 1993). Slade pointed out that long before the Los Angeles Riots, KJLH had proved that a small neighborhood station could effectively serve its audience and bring the world to its listeners:

When Nelson Mandela was released in 1990, I sent my news director, Carl Nelson, over there to South Africa. And everyone was saying: "Wait a minute. You're just a little Class A station, with a single station outlet. Why are you doing that?" Because I felt it was important. He went with Jesse Jackson's contingent and filed two to four reports a day. And it worked out very well. It was very pertinent information. Now we're covering the new trial of the four Los Angeles police officers charged with violating Rodney King's civil rights. We're respected enough, or lucky enough, to get a seat in the courtroom [Slade, 1993, p. 22].

KJLH became an important source for its listeners during the second trial. As she awaited the outcome of the civil trial, Slade stated in April 1993, "Even if this is partial victory, it is a victory because we have stopped erosion of our civil rights" (Du Brow, 1993, p. 6). In April 1993, KJLH also had reporters covering the Denny trial: "In the African-American community, there is much more apprehension about the Reginald Denny trial.... The defendants remain in jail while the King beaters have been free on bail the entire time," explained Nelson (Rollins, 1993, p. A01).

KJLH has received local and national media attention for its coverage of a variety of issues since 1992, especially given that the efforts of most local radio stations rarely reach beyond their neighborhoods. However, the station received very little commendation among its media brethren for its heroic efforts during the Los Angeles civil unrest and its service to other broadcast outlets across the U.S. and the world:

> We really didn't. *L.A. Times* did an article, but they didn't do it in their core magazine; at that time they had a community offshoot. I'm trying to think of what it was called. It may have been called *City Times,* which was the offshoot of the *L.A. Times,* that did an article. One of the Black newspapers did a pretty in-depth article — *L.A. Sentinel.* But other than that, no, we didn't get a lot of press. I think one of the trade publications did a nice write-up too. They came out and took a picture of one of the rallies that we had, and got all the folks around the station, which turned out nice. But no, we didn't get a lot of publicity and I wasn't really thinking about how I could probably use it to my advantage, which I probably should have. As a business person, I should have stepped back and said, "Ok, how can I work this to my advantage?"— but I was so caught up in, you know, caught up in the activities of broadcasting and operation of the station, I didn't have the foresight to try to market it. Even as far as the Peabody, I didn't even seek that. Someone else submitted us for an Image Award as well and we got a NAACP Image Award after that, which thank God, people did, but we just weren't savvy enough to use it to our advantage [Slade, personal communication, 2001].

KJLH hosts, listeners, and others reiterated the need to come together as a community. The station not only reported on the uprising, it also provided context to the events as they occurred on the streets. The violence and looting in the neighborhoods (as well as the motives of those involved) and the need for restoring safety and peace in the community were unavoidable topics of discussion. KJLH also provided listeners and staff with opportunities to vent frustrations concerning the King verdict and question the role of media and authority in handling the civil unrest. Even more importantly, Black-owned KJLH, as an independent voice in Los Angeles, was a companion to many listeners during one of the bleakest moments of Los Angeles' history.

KJLH-FM was the pulse of a peaceful revolution that elevated community needs over ratings, and as such extended its bond with the African American community across the world. "Most people in our community do not trust the mainstream media," said Nelson (Rollins, 1993, A01). KJLH provided a means to vent for listeners who needed to verbalize their fears and concerns over what was going on in their neighborhood. As Nelson, Reed, and a slew of celebrity hosts looked out the KJLH studio window, they watched a living drama play out before their eyes. Yes, a few people called the station, perhaps, to rationalize or justify their participation in the looting and vandalism on the streets. Yet, the hosts and the majority of the callers made a plea to them (and others on the streets) to stop and think through their actions, in an effort to keep the community together — in essence, unified.

CHAPTER 8

Change the System
Politics of Empowerment

"We're out to do what's right for all people. We want to show those people we're all about a human movement." — WPEG-AM program director Michael Saunders (cited in Love, 1991, p. 36).

On April 29, 1992, only several hours before the riots, the Los Angeles Country Task Force on Health Care Access gathered to discuss the crisis facing urban communities. During the Los Angeles uprising, many physicians' offices, pharmacies, drug rehabilitation clinics, and federal program sites were destroyed. When the County Task Force met again a week later, some health care leaders blamed the riots on health care injustice, "the chronic diseases of racism and poverty," and the exclusion of African American leadership from the development of heath care policy (Cotton, 1992, p. 2719). The solution, according to some, can often be found in partnerships between local health agencies, law enforcement, schools, churches and other community groups as well as culturally-specific media ("Homicide," 1991; also see Best, 1989).

KJLH's role created partnerships with city agencies, churches, and social organizations. Within the midst of the mayhem, KJLH contacted the phone company and requested a toll-free number for people to dial to get information and help. Indeed after the looting and the fires stopped, much of South Central Los Angeles was without electricity, water, and medical attention, in some cases for several days. Many people without electricity listened to the station on battery-operated radios. KJLH responded quickly to the changing events. People had no way to cash their monthly assistance checks. Gas stations were burned down. Banks and post offices were closed. Without money, many people, now homeless, had

139

no way of getting food, finding shelter, or replacing clothing. KJLH responded to the community needs by working together with area churches to create a resource center. Indeed, KJLH was awarded a Peabody for its "timely, exhaustive and important coverage" of the 1992 Los Angeles Riots, and was heralded by the *Los Angeles Times* and Associated Press (Weinstein, 1993, p. 13).

"We tried to have the neighborhood churches be the focal point because we couldn't have everybody coming down here. Plus it was not safe to move about in the street, armed guards were coming in," said Slade (personal communication, 2002). Her then news director Carl Nelson explains:

> For a major market station in a big city, we went into a small town radio. "Can somebody out there volunteer to go down to 121st street and Normandy, and take so and so to the doctor? She's an old lady. And there's no buses running. There's no transportation." People calling up, "where can I get gas?" "Okay, where do you live? You'd be surprised. We had so many files that the phone company gave us an 800 number" [Nelson, personal communication, 1993].

Over the days that followed, KJLH interviewed attorneys, who told listeners on-air that they could not get fired if they did not go to work during the unrest. Another attorney called up, and explained martial law to listeners. One of the police officers involved in the trial was invited on the air. Psychiatrists talked to parents on KJLH, and advised them on how to explain these images to their children: "One guy called up, and his son was missing. We tracked his son; he was picked up in a gang round-up 'cause they were just rounding up young African-American men at the time, and he called back to thank us" (ibid.).

Politically Connected

On October 27, 2000, during a special one-hour telephone conference call to 40 NABOB stations, the Reverend Jesse Jackson, Jr., and Bill Clinton, with the endorsement of NABOB, urged African American voters to go to the polls and to spread the word to other Black radio and television stations. Jackson ended the conference by encouraging people to go to church on November 5, and get others to vote on Election Day or what he called Dignity Day (NABOB, 2000b). Clinton agreed to produce a public service announcement urging African Americans to vote in the upcoming election. Barabak (2000) reports that African Americans comprised approximately 12 percent of the eligible voters in 2000, and Black radio played a large role in encouraging voters to participate in registration drives and the election turnout: "The Republican Party launched its biggest minority ad campaign ever, budgeting more than $1 million for commercials on black radio stations across the country" (p. 1). On the other hand, Democrats positioned "designated field workers in more than a dozen states, part of an unprecedented effort targeting black voters with phone calls, mailings, door-to-door visits and advertisements taped by a range of celebrities, including actor Will Smith, singer Stevie Wonder and author Maya Angelou" (pp. 1–2).

Discussions of community empowerment through political and civic activity among its personalities and listeners filled much of the airwaves during the riots and aftermath. Of course, immediate attention was directed to the safety and physical needs of listeners. Yet, KJLH has a unique prominent position in its community in its ability to draw celebrities and politicians into major events and discussions. Perhaps this prominence is somewhat the result of its owner's celebrity fame or its larger role as a Black heritage radio station in America. KJLH was instrumental in its call to unify as a community and specifically served as a vehicle to empower listeners through voter registration and participation. Even before the verdict in the King trial was announced, Slade (1993a) was preparing an editorial on the importance of getting involved in the community, getting registered to vote, and participating in the political system.

Continuous references, nearly every hour, were made regarding the need to register to vote in the upcoming June election and in all elections — local, state, and national. Again and again, the hosts reiterated the need to participate in the system — "if you want to change the system, get involved in the process" (Slade, personal communication, 2002). KJLH listeners caught on early to the message, a message that was also echoed by celebrities, community leaders, and public officials over the next week. Listeners were encouraged to register to vote on May 2, 1992. KJLH's proactive approach inspired listeners toward voter registration and information about the political process. Newspaper articles dating back to 1987 indicated that KJLH had a strong track record when it came to informing its audience on issues through forums and community events. KJLH management knew early on that its strength as a community voice was dependent on its ability to become a political player not only in the media marketplace, but more importantly to its listeners within its city of license.

Black Radio Politically Defined

Coretta Scott King praised Black and urban radio for its leadership on issues and events that affect the African American community, but, at the same time, she expressed concern that Fortune 500 companies have not encouraged a "wider observance" of Martin Luther King, Jr., Day: "One thing I would like to see is the American Flag being flown from every home and every workplace, just like on the 4th of July. We need to be clear that this is a patriotic holiday in the truest sense of the word" (Love, 1992c, p. 46). In essence, Black-owned radio has embraced Scott's plea for political and economic acknowledgment of the King holiday. It has often provided voice to its listeners' concerns, and has encouraged participation in the political process. KJLH listeners' interest and willingness to participate in rallies and voter registration drives have become unifying forces within the African American community in keeping with the station's mission. The electoral system is a politically-motivated, economically-fueled mechanism that drives the American agenda in the media and society, and provides unique challenges to minority groups seeking voice on often ignored specific concerns and needs.

Shoemaker (1994) and Wittebols (1993) point out that mass media tend to reinforce majoritarian political viewpoints, while de-emphasizing grassroots alternatives. Mainstream media, according to some interviewees, remained narrowly sighted on the social and political reality of what was happening in South Central, for they lacked a certain historical frame of reference upon which to evaluate events. Larry Carroll, Los Angeles news anchor for KFWB-AM at the time of KJLH's 10th year commemoration of the 1992 uprising, elaborated during the show about media's responsibility in addressing social issues through political communication:

> We need to communicate intramurally within this community in order to create the kind of critical mass of thought that creates movement that creates political agenda. As long as we are not talking issues, issues are not going to be addressed. As long as we are not framing the problems, the problems will not be addressed. And as long as we are not visionary, then we will not have a picture of the future toward which we are working. That only happens when media become responsible to carry on that dialogue, that community dialogue which becomes a municipal dialogue, which becomes a state-wide dialogue, which ultimately becomes that national or the international debate; we're not in that because our media are not committed to carry those messages [*Front Page*, 2002b].

Carroll left KFWB in October 2008, as part of the CBS/Infinity Radio lay-offs. He had joined the station in 2001, bringing with him more than 30 years of news experience, including 17 years as a prominent African American TV news anchor on KABC-TV in Los Angeles. He served as the West Coast correspondent for *NBC Nightly News* at one point in his career. Carroll views *Front Page* as one of a few programs in the U.S. "that exist certainly in the [African-American] community at large, that is brave enough, that is committed enough to doing that, in order to make that happen, but this has got to happen on a broad scope" (*Front Page*, 2002b).

Call to Participate in the System

On April 29, 1992, the first day of the Los Angeles civil unrest, Slade (1993a) wrote and aired an editorial that told listeners the only way to change the system was to be part of the system. That became one of the main topics of the night, among other things. Rico Reed, along with several station personalities, kept the dialogue going through the night, while fumes and frustrations filled the air — outside and inside the studio:

Brandon Bowlin: You know, the person who was talking about political puppets — Malcom X. In his book, *By Any Means Necessary* — it's a companion to the *Malcom X Speaks*, he calls them "chicken wing" politicians because they go wherever the food is. That means wherever the money is, they're right behind them, and if you want to make a difference, hey — vote, learn, educate yourself on the issues and go out and take care of that business.

Rico Reed: Alright, let's go to another phone call. Ten-o-three on 102–3, KJLH — that's a coincidence. Good evening, what is your name, and where are you calling from?

Caller: My name is Samuel and I'm calling from Inglerock and I just want to say, "thank you KJLH," and I want to say how devastated I was when the decision was handed down, but by the same token, had we united in peace, the way that we united to violate our selves in our community, a whole lot, that would have made a tremendous statement to the world.

Rico Reed: It certainly would have —

Caller: It just sickens me beyond belief, the devastation that is happening in our own community. But thank you to KJLH that we can voice these opinions and you guys are doing an awesome job.

Rico Reed: Thank you so much for calling. Here's a number to call if you're looking for some place to register to vote or you need more information, write this number down — 7–2–1–1–1–0–0. That is 721–1100. You must be registered by May the 4th, that's coming up — what is that, Monday?

J. Anthony Brown: Monday.

Rico Reed: Monday, you must be registered by Monday to vote in the June election. If *anything* can move you to vote, this should do it right here.

J. Anthony Brown: If we could get as many people out who are riding right now to go out and register to vote....

Rico Reed: It would make a big difference.

Brandon Bowlin: A lot of people don't realize you don't have to go Democrat or Republican.—

Rico Reed: You can go Independent.

Brandon Bowlin: Independent.

Tyrone: Just go vote.

Brandon Bowlin: Right — and take care of your stuff, but know what you're voting for [*Front Page*, 1992a].

Even so, Slade (personal communication, 2002) noted, listeners "were emotional; they were upset; they were not going to be appeased by a voter registration drive." Some listeners vented, still confused about what was happening around them, while the reaction from others was one of peaceful organization:

Caller: I just want to say that as long as Black people have been in America, we have not been able and it's not going to work for us to try to work this situation out in a European form. It doesn't work for us to vote — we can vote, but it's not going to work for us, 'cause as long as particular Europeans are in power —

Rico Reed: Well that's what voting is. I hate to interrupt you, but that's how you get 'em out of power, by voting. It will help.

Caller: Another fact I want to articulate is this. That I'm for all the people uniting and all that, but this time around, we tried the passsive way with Martin Luther King and it seems like every time, sometimes, somebody goes about it in the form of the regulations and the judicial system and the legislation and all that, somebody gets knocked off and the whole situation dies off. This way we should go about it as Malcom X would have went about it, and that is, by all means necessary.

Rico Reed: But he would not destroy his own communities.

Tyrone: Naw, brother, you got that backwards.

Brandon Bowlin: The rebuttals from Malcom X probably would have come right after the Rodney King situation and not at this late date where you're destroying your own property, your own community. One of his tactics actually was to make sure that they understood the threat that we posed. The same stuff that they do to us, things can come right back to them. Not necessarily the situation that we see right today.

Rico Reed: Certainly. KJLH. Good evening, thank you for calling, you're on the special edition of *Front Page*. What is your name and where are you calling from?

Caller: Hi. My name is Lydia and I'm calling from Lakewood.

Rico Reed: Yes, Lydia.

Caller: I'm sitting here watching TV and I'm so shocked at what's going on. Right now we should be focusing our energy as, you know, marching, doing something positive. You know the NAACP is supposed to be having a, a, some kind of organization going on at Parker Center Saturday and I think everybody should go down and really just get involved. Focus your anger on something positive [*Front Page*, 1992a].

Now nearly 14 hours after the King verdict was announced, the hosts and callers were becoming more articulate in their pleas for voter participation, and it became obvious that the community was beginning to reorganize and respond to the needs of their neighbors:

J. Anthony Brown: I feel bad about the fact that the news stations, the television stations were showing a lot of the violence, but there were a lot of churches and that were a lot of civic organizations that were doing things to calm the people, along with the radio station — and none of that was broadcast. They really focused on the violence and there was a lot going on, but there were some things that were going on across this city to try to calm people and get their heads calm.

Rico Reed: And we're going to continue in that vein right now. We were on the air non-stop with nothing but phone calls and information from about 4 or 5 o'clock yesterday afternoon up until 2 or 3 o'clock this morning and we're right back on. It's 5:16, 16 minutes after five. This is KJLH. 102–3 and we're going to extend *Front Page* throughout the rest of the morning time. Give you an opportunity to, number one, get information; number two, vent your frustrations and number three, maybe, just maybe out of all of this we can come up with a solution or some direction. One suggestion that has come out in the last 15 minutes — write your councilman, write your senator, register to vote — it's very important. You have until May the 4th to register to be a part of the next election in June. If you want the number to call, it's 721–1100. That's 721–1100 to get more information on where you can register to vote and if you need information on how to fill it out, what to say, what to do, call that number. Flood them with phone calls. That's what we need to do. That's something we can do as a community.

Carl Nelson: Because one of the ways where you can make a change is Proposition F on the ballot which calls for a change in how the L.A.P.D. is run.

J. Anthony Brown: I mean even the fact that it's taken so long to get Darryl Gates out of office and the mayor is powerless — I mean stuff like that. The change is only going to be made by us going to the polls and voting. That's the only way.

Carl Nelson: A great deal of that stems from the early 50's when there was a big corruption situation in the L.A.P.D. It was nationwide and people were quite embarrassed about it, so they wrote in a situation where the police chief was pretty much impervious to being controlled by anybody at city hall. Unfortunately, that gives the chief a chance to wield a great deal of power.

J. Anthony Brown: Totally, totally — much more power than the mayor and this should not be, this should not be at all.

Rico Reed: All right, let's go back to the phone lines. Good morning, you're on KJLH....

Caller: My name is Joey and I'm calling from Los Angeles. I'd just like to say that, you know, of course I'm hurt by what went on and very frustrated and disgusted. I'm not a registered voter. I do intend to register. One of the things that I tried to do, my son is 21 years old and I *dared him* to go out into that community. I *dared him*— he needs to stay here. I was here in the Watts riots. This is the ugliest, most disgusting thing I've ever seen. And this is not the way for us to vent our frustration. This is what they expect us to do. And the other thing is, I don't know why people are so surprised. The police have been whupping us down for years [*Front Page*, 1992b].

Politics and Pews

Church leaders worked with KJLH management and staff, in both the location of resources for the homeless and displaced and the search for peaceful solutions during the unrest. KJLH Reporter Jacquie Stephens stated that she was heading toward the A.M.E. for reaction to the verdict from community leaders, and along the way she heard rumblings on the street that there might be a violent response to the unrest. The church immediately organized a peaceful rally that became a haven for those residents unable to safely return home after work.

That evening, Angela King, Rodney King's mother, thanked a crowd of 2,000 people for their support at the Reverend Cecil L. Murray's South Central church in Los Angeles (Wallace and Ferrell, 1992). After the vigil, many residents who attended the peace rally at First A.M.E. Church decided to camp out at the church. Here's an excerpt from the KJLH transcript:

Co-Host: Hundreds of people went over there and then they found they couldn't go home because of what's happening in the streets

Rico: Of course not, can't get back in their own communities.

Co-Host: So, they are camping out at A.M.E., First A.M.E. Church.

Rico: Is it safe over there?

Co-Host: At First A.M.E. Church? Yeah, it's fairly safe, fairly safe, I should say.

Rico: What's the location. I thought it was over near the....

Co-Host: It's on Harvard [*Front Page*, 1992a].

KJLH, like other Black heritage radio stations, carries forth the church's mission. With very early roots in Colonial America, the Black church rose out of the post-plantation era, when freedom was overshadowed by fragmented families, poverty, racism, and a need for civic and political empowerment (Erskine, 1991–1992). The Black church has historically promoted the family through song and prayer, and provided members with social support and economic security (Scott and Black, 1989). It follows that KJLH should have been influenced by these values, evoking a strong commitment to the African American community.

KJLH's "core block of churches" has aired since the mid–1960s, "which was about 16 or 17 churches at the time" and that continued through 1992 (Slade, personal communication, 2001). KJLH now airs about 10 church services and related programming every week:

> We've had church programming on pretty much since the inception of the radio station, but what we were trying to do from a programming standpoint was make a smoother transition from church programming — or gospel or not gospel, but ministers speaking, preaching — to our regular format which is R&B. We wanted to be respectful of the churches and that audience, and yet bring our current audience back because it is a switch. So as a segue we put in a gospel block, an inspirational block of music programming, to go from the churches back into the regular programming; and that's basically how it started, trying to make a smoother transition. So the hour extended to two hours and now we're now up to six hours on Sunday. From noon till six, we play gospel — and then we do a church call-out so some of the other churches can get on that can't do block time; and it's an underserved audience because there's not a gospel-formatted station in the market so it's worked really well for us actually [ibid.].

Spread the Word is one of the most popular programs, and it airs on Sunday afternoons. It began in the mid–1990s when a local gospel station went off the air. It was an "outgrowth" of KJLH's church programming (ibid.).

The foundation of the Black church, historically a strong political and social institution in the African American community, has encouraged liberation from racism, illiteracy and poverty. Richard L. Allen and his collaborators (Allen, Dawson, and Brown, 1989) assert that the African American community is strengthened through positive experiences with the Black church and Black media:

Indeed, the message of spiritual, social, and political liberation from bondage may be strongest in blacks who have been socialized in religious denominations that encourage a sense of racial solidarity. In essence, we think that the communal aspect of black religiosity will manifest itself mostly in black churches that preach as part of their gospel message, social liberation based on racial group membership [p. 436].

As heard through KJLH's on-air coverage, religious leaders were among the first in the nation to organize non-violent rallies protesting the 1992 acquittal of the four officers involved in the beating of King:

> *Rico Reed:* All right. Hel-lo, is this Reverend Carl Washington?
>
> *Reverend Washington*: Speaking.
>
> *Rico Reed*: Okay, Reverend Washington, thank you for calling us back. Go right ahead. Are you over at the First A.M.E. Church?
>
> *Reverend Washington*: No, I'm at....
>
> *Co-Host*: Reverend Washington, I should point out, is with *Peace in the Streets*.
>
> *Rico Reed*: Okay, I'm sorry. Alright.
>
> *Co-Host*: He's the minister with *Peace in the Streets*.
>
> *Rico Reed*: Exactly.
>
> *Co-Host*: So Reverend Washington, what do you think about what's going on here tonight?
>
> *Reverend Washington*: Oh we absolutely ... it's outrageous. I am totally — words cannot even express the dismay that I have.
>
> *Co-Host*: You went, you went out on the street and you met with people and tried to tell them there were going to be no riots. You said yourself there wouldn't be any riots or any disturbance. How does this make you feel?
>
> *Reverend Washington*: Again, we are dismayed, but we believe this is from the so-called "trouble makers" of the community. Those who we have come in contact with have maintained peace. We allowed them, and we left the doors of the church open. What we tried to do is send a message that if you want to express anger, don't tear up your own community doing it. You have the church where you can come and in open forum, discuss your anger [*Front Page*, 1992a].

Meanwhile in Atlanta, Bernice King, Martin Luther King's daughter, an attorney and minister, spoke to 400 people gathered at her father's tomb: "If Dr. King were here today, I'm almost certain that he would have been on the first thing smoking out of Atlanta on his way to L.A." (Treadwell, 1992, p. A–9). "God has created us, and if nothing else we owe it to God Almighty to do something about this tragic situation" in Los Angeles, continued King.

Jackson's Tour of South Central

The demarcation between church and politics is not clearly delineated in South Central. Black radio, in general, has aired the messages of unity and empowerment at times voiced by the Reverend Jesse L. Jackson, Sr., founder of the Rainbow/Push Coalition (RPC). His offices are located in some of the largest radio markets — Chicago, New York, Los Angeles, and Washington, D.C., Jackson's mission calls for a revival of the American Dream, a message voiced by King, Jr., in the 1960s, and now echoed through the coalition:

> The American Dream is one big tent of many cultures, races and religions. Under that tent, everybody is assured equal protection under the law, equal opportunity, equal access and a fair share. Our, struggle demands that we open closed doors, extend the tent and even the playing field [Jackson, 2002b].

The RPC has been specifically involved in the civil education as well as the registration of hundreds of thousands of voters, and has assisted in the election of hundreds of local, state and federal public officials. Jackson states: "I started Push in Chicago to help build from the bottom up in Chicago, sustaining a weekly meeting and hundreds of local projects for over thirty years now." He continues, "To draw a line between local commitment and political involvement, to urge one and condemn the other, is wrong headed. Ask anyone who runs a food bank, anyone who builds low-income housing, any minister who creates a day care center — all will say the same thing. Private charity cannot do it alone."

Through his One Thousand Churches Connected Program, one of his goals "has been to ensure equal employment and ownership opportunities in the media, as well as equal opportunity through 'shared economic security and empowerment'" (Jackson, 2002a). The Reverend Jackson has been a major proponent of Black radio and its ability to impact an audience socially and economically. In 1988, he spoke to a crowd outside the Crenshaw-Imperial Shopping Center, saying, "You can vote for houses, decent health care, day care; you can vote to raise the minimum wage.... Your vote counts, and you count," in an effort to encourage African American voters to register for the general election in November (Boyer, 1988, p. 15). His message was aired over KJLH, as well as three other Black and urban radio stations, KACE-FM, KGFJ-AM, and KDAY-AM. Nearly four years later — on Wednesday, April 29, 1992, Reed and Nelson called Jackson to ask for his help in calming down the people of South Central and neighboring communities:

I said, "You know, you need to get here 'cause this thing is totally out of control. I see no ending, 'cause they're not listening to the Mayor — obviously, they're not listening to the Mayor and they're not gonna to listen to Pete Wilson." And actually he was lying down in bed when I called him. I think it was East Coast time, at 8 or 9 o'clock [Nelson, personal communication, 2001].

At 10:44 P.M., the Reverend Jackson spoke to KJLH listeners:

> *Rico Reed*: ...Good evening, Reverend Jackson, are you with us?
>
> *Reverend Jackson*: Yeah, I am with you, I'm with you with my prayers, with my thoughts. I've been on the phone with the ministers, nearly all of the night long, and I just hope that something will happen that will allow us to break this violence, this cycle of killing and hurt and self destruction.
>
> *J. Anthony Brown*: (In the background) They're right across the street.
>
> *Rico Reed*: Yeah — I'm sorry Reverend Jackson, something's happening directly across the street — had our attention for a moment. This is, this is absolutely ridiculous.
>
> *Carl Nelson*: Might as well tell you, there's a liquor store over there and a lot of people are just crowding around it, Reverend.
>
> *Rico Reed*: They just broke in. I can see people inside looting the store. They're looting the store right in front of us.
>
> *Carl Nelson*: If there's something that you could tell the people here in L.A., Reverend Jackson, what would you like to say to them.
>
> *Reverend Jackson*: The verdict on Rodney King was unjust. It was wrong. We must not compound that pain now by killing each other and by destroying where we live — we simply must know that to violate each other is no solution to what happened in that situation today. I am going, for example, with Congressman Wallace tomorrow morning to meet with the Justice Department at 8:30 because justice must be done. Those police must face the judgment bar, but I would hope, for those who are listening, who can hear my voice, do not risk your life. Do not take someone else's life or their property in the name of, "We're upset because of Rodney King." We've got great reason to be angry, but we must also seek our way out, and not just burn our way out. I make the spiritual appeal to you tonight.
>
> *Rico Reed*: Thank you Reverend Jackson for your thoughts and your prayers, and we'll certainly join you tomorrow.
>
> *Reverend Jackson*: I'll probably see you tomorrow.
>
> *Rico Reed*: Okay, I think....
>
> *Lee Michaels*: Reverend, this is Lee Michaels, how you doin'?
>
> *Reverend Jackson*: Aw man, I don't know.
>
> *Lee Michaels*: It's wild, Reverend, I mean we're right here in the heart of the community, and right across the street from our studios, right now, as we speak, there's looting going on. There's a....

Rico Reed: (In background) Tag's Liquor

Lee Michaels: A liquor store....

Rico Reed: Tag's Liquor

Lee Michaels: ...that's being looted right now as we speak. As you know, we lived through the '60s, and I don't believe that I'm seeing this again in my lifetime.

Reverend Jackson: Well, here it is.

Lee Michaels: It's unbelievable.

Reverend Jackson: Well, keep me in your prayers and you're certainly in mine.

Lee Michaels: Alright.

Reverend Jackson: Okay. Bye.

Lee Michaels: Thank you.

Rico Reed: Thank you Reverend Jackson.

Lee Michaels: God bless.

Rico Reed: 10:44, 1–0–2–3, KJLH, Compton/Los Angeles, discussing the aftermath of the King trial, we'll take a short break, coming back with your phone calls next, 5–2–0–KJLH, 9–7–7–KJLH [*Front Page*, 1992a].

Jackson left on a plane that night, and arrived early Thursday morning, April 30, 1992:

> It was sort of funny 'cause next morning I was still at the station. The craziness was still going on in the streets and he walked into the studio and there he stayed with us for the three-day duration. I remember him vividly having a conversation with Pete Wilson, the governor at the time, 'cause they had burned down a post office in one of the communities and there was a local election coming up. Reverend Jackson turned to him and said, "You know what, let's call a halt to the registration 'cause these guys can't get their votes registered because they've burnt down the post office so they can't register to vote. So let's have a two week delay in the process while we sort this out so they can be registered to vote." Pete Wilson just verbally snapped his fingers to his aide and it was done. And I'm like, "Wow, that's what you call power" [Nelson, personal communication, 2001].

Reporters and politicians were geared up for the June elections. Reporters were all over the place. A media crew filmed a medical building burning in front of the Reverend Jackson and the fire was within view of the KJLH studios on the second day of the uprising. Nelson and Reed were overwhelmed with the media response to his arrival. It would be another 5 minutes before they would have an opportunity to speak with him over KJLH. Meanwhile, Nelson and Reed were taking phone calls from listeners:

Carl Nelson: ...I see three members of our esteemed California Highway Patrol with their shotguns and riot gear out here now. The looters are gone.

Rico Reed: That was two days ago.

Carl Nelson: They've raped this community already. Now they're here protecting the fire fighters.

Rico Reed: Well actually, I think that and if you've noticed, they're escorting a little bit of traffic through every 5 minutes — they let about 10 or 20 cars through, then they stop — then they let 10 or 20 more cars.... I guess that's the way to stop the looting. Just a few cars at a time. KJLH. Good morning, you're on *Front Page*....

Caller: ...The Black leaders in the city and the country, we need to get together because Black people are tired of being suppressed and being abused.

Rico Reed: Well the main thing is we have to get together as a people first, sir. We really do. We have to get together as a unit and not for any up-rival or upheaval or anything like that, but just to learn respect — to respect ourselves. We don't respect ourselves. We don't love ourselves.

J. Anthony Brown: Yeah, we really have to get past the part of, "it's the Spanish people," "it's the White people," it's the Black people." The main thing is, we need to stop. It doesn't matter who it is now. The thing is, it's got to stop. It's ridiculous out there. It's gotta stop.

Carl Nelson: You know, I'm just watching the crowd here. They stopped the traffic to allow Reverend Jackson to cross the street — and so it's just a crowd of people with him. You know, we're speaking about our leaders, here's a chance for you people on the phone to call and ask a man who's — the media has anointed him — a leader, I guess. You can ask him what's going on....

Rico Reed: You want a leader? We've got a leader for you.

Carl Nelson: He's coming in right now as soon as he gets through these camera crews that are right in front of the station. They're holding him up. But he'll be here in a few minutes so we'll take a few more calls until he gets here.... Good morning. You're listening to 102.3 KJLH.

Rico Reed: The fire department is coming in — a fire that we've been looking at for the last hour. Jesse Jackson's on TV, then the fire department comes. I mean, I'm glad they're here, but....

Carl Nelson: All too often in the community that's how problems get solved you know. These things happen. Until a so-called "celebrity" comes along, it goes unnoticed.

Rico Reed: I mean we're looking at this fire; we're talking about this fire....

Carl Nelson: For the last what? Two or three days.

Rico Reed: Yeah, I mean, this is the same fire, ladies and gentlemen, that started late yesterday. It makes you want to laugh. I hate to laugh, but it makes you want to laugh, it really does. Let's continue on with the phone calls. 6:45, 16 minutes away from seven o'clock with Rico, Carl Nelson,

Brandon's in here. I believe J. Anthony Brown is coming in from the Arsenio Hall Show shortly. "J" graciously got Arsenio to call us yesterday right out of a meeting. We really appreciate that for happening. Thank you for that. KJLH. Good morning, you're on *Front Page*. What is your name and where are you calling from?

Caller: My name is Lita and I'm calling from Compton. I'd like to commend the firemen and the police department of the City of Compton. Our family has been on a watch for our neighborhood on the east side of Compton for at least 48 hours. I haven't had any sleep all night and just the corners that are at the intersection of Compton and Sante Fe, we've been watching the Milk Palace that has been looted, ignited and the same crazy people who have been out there have come back to re-ignite the same buildings over and over again. We've had to water down our roofs to keep them from catching on fire. And I just want to say for the people who are out there, who are sincere about their community, that you have to work with the police and the fire department to ensure that you protect your community. All of them are not our enemies and it's unfortunate with what has happened, but we must work together. The people who are destroying the communities do not care. They have never cared and they will never care. In the end, it will be people like me, my family, and others who will have to put the city back together without the help of those who destroyed it. I suggest they pray to a heavenly father and keep the strength and just keep on trying to keep it together and work together. That's all I have to say.

Rico Reed: Alright, thank you for your comments. It's 6:45. 14 minutes away from 7 o'clock. A lot of folks are out of power. Unfortunately, we have no good news for you. They are trying to restore power as expediently as they can, but it's taking time. They're still trying to put out fires. It's a major fire right across — I just went outside — I ran back in, excuse me for being out of breath — cause we're smelling smoke inside here. We want to make sure that everything's okay. They're trying to put the fire out now in front of Reverend Jackson. If you watch Channel 7, you can see exactly what we're looking at. That's what's going on right outside the window. That's what we've been seeing for the last day and a half — just one fire just burning, burning, burning, and burning. So hot we had to move the cars off of the street because we were afraid something would happen to our own cars, not just damage, but maybe the gas tanks exploding or something. It was that hot. You could feel the intensity of the heat and it's still burning. They don't seem to be able to put it out [*Front Page*, 1992b].

The Reverend Jesse Jackson, Jr., made his way through the cameras and the questions of the reporters to the KJLH studios, and there he gave an interview with Rico Reed and Carl Nelson. They provided him an open forum to talk to the listeners directly. Reed introduces him momentarily once Jackson enters the on-air studio:

Rico Reed: We have Reverend Jesse Jackson in [the] studio, Senator Diane Watson in studio, quite a few people. This is 102.3 KJLH, Compton/Los Angeles. It's Rico, Carl Nelson, J. Anthony Brown, Brandon, we're all in here. We've got the phone lines hot. 520-KJLH, 977-KJLH, for the 714. We're calling it, *Front Page—A Continuous Thing*, and Reverend Jackson, welcome.

Carl Nelson: Reverend Jackson, I'm going to put the question to you that I put to Senator Watson yesterday. A lot of people are calling and they want to know what can they do. What are our leaders doing?

Rico Reed: What's the next step?

Carl Nelson: What's the next step. It's on you.

Reverend Jackson: Well, first of all, I have with me, Monique Matthews and Darlene Webb, here in the station. Two young women who care, and I'm concerned that as we look at a situation this complicated, it's like you would look at a body that's bleeding on the outside and cancer on the inside. You don't just say, "What you going to do?" and take an aspirin real fast. It defies that kind of simple response. We're looking at the Crenshaw Medical Center right now go up in flames. Last night we systematically, when Congresswoman Waters and I got to town, watched how Thriftys had been very systematically burned and 7-Eleven's. Some of these fires are too systematic to be the work of "teenagers or gang bangers." Some of these fires are profiting somebody. They had some fire insurance connected to some of these fires. When I look at the way this medical center is burning down right now, you could not just throw a brick through the window, a Molotov cocktail and it burn down this systematically. You could throw a brick through a window or a fire bomb through a window — it would hit a certain spot and that would be limited. And so I say that we must not in this, allow the media to keep any longer calling our youth "thugs." Some people are looting and the looting is wrong, but you know, desperate people do desperate things. And what we're looking at now are the fruits, the bitter fruits of alienation — what was once grapes of hope have become raisins of despair and hurt. And while we must appeal to them to help us break the cycle of pain — when I walked these streets today, if you will, déjà vu, I walked them in 1965 and Watts was on fire at that time. And I'm now looking at the grandchildren of some of those who burned in '65, walking those same vacant lots that have been vacant since 1965. So there must be a renewed commitment to justice. The Rodney King verdict was a grave miscarriage of justice and it was the spark that offset a kind of spontaneous combustion. What is spontaneous combustion? A lot of discarded stuff. Discarded stuff. Over a length of time, it just kind of, with a spark, explodes. We're looking at a generation of youth whose education has been discarded. Fifty percent youth unemployment, 20 percent adult unemployment, health care facilities closing, school options cut back. They spend $5,800 to send you to Cal State L.A. Forty-thousand to send you to Soledad — better treatment in jails than there are in schools. I was here with Arsenio Hall just two weeks ago. We went to the Center for Correction for Youth downtown.

Rico Reed: The Excel Program

Reverend Jackson: Down there, just two weeks ago. And if you go to Dorsey High, for example, they spend on you, 5,000 a year. You go to the Center for Corrections, 30,000. For a generation of our children, people must hear this. For them, going to jail is a step up. Step up? Once they're in jail, they will no longer be hit by drive-by shootings. Once they're in jail, they're no longer homeless. It's warm in winter-time; it's cool in the summer-time. Adult supervision, organized recreation, balanced meals, access to medical care. There's every provision for them in jail that should be for them in their communities, and so we must seek to offset the alienation with a national plan for development. This is not just L.A. We met with the Attorney General yesterday — Congresswoman Waters and I did in Washington. He has prosecuted 128 cases of police brutality since 1988. It's Rodney King in L.A., but what about Phillip Parnell, a young Black teenager in Teaneck, New Jersey, shot in the back. There were no video cameras there but there were bullet holes in his back. Yet the two police who killed him, they walk free. So that's where there's a sense of national outrage about the situation. We urge the justice department to now pursue civil rights statutes, 241 and 242 and prosecute these four officers on that basis. They should never walk these streets again with a badge on their chest, a nightstick in their hand and a gun on their sides. But beyond that, Mr. Bush's commitment in investing and rebuilding Eastern Europe and the Russian Republics, that same amount of money must be spent investing and rebuilding urban America. There should not be another dime in S&L bailouts — now they're asking for 25 billion, that does not have with it a rider to invest in educating our children and rebuilding and building urban America.

Rico Reed: I'm with you Reverend Jackson. Carl, go ahead.

Carl Nelson: Would you like to take some calls? Let's take some calls and see if they want to ask Reverend Jackson or Senator Watson a question.

Rico Reed: It's 7:06, 6 minutes after 7 with Rico, Carl Nelson, Reverend Jackson, Senator Watson in the studio. We call it the *Front Page* and good morning, I must say you're on it. What's your name and what city are you calling from.

Caller: Hi, my name is Cathy and I'm in Hollywood. I would like to say that this has got to stop. Last night was so bad. I think the message has been made and now it should stop and everyone should come together. I don't think a march — the only way that I think a march would help is if everyone comes together and march and shut the city down. To me, that would be the only other message.

Reverend Jackson: You know, Cathy, riots in many ways cannot be controlled that way. It's like a cycle of pain. It's like poison going out of your body.

Riots are not plans, they're not strategies; they are reactions and we hope that there would be sufficient deterrent by our moral appeals, by our reaching out to defer expansion of the riots. What I see already in the burning of these Thrifty stores so systematically burned down with a kind of organized arson or 7-Eleven's or the Crenshaw Medical Center are, some of these, are inside jobs.

Caller: Yes.

Reverend Jackson: And while the media can rather immediately take a broad swipe of our youth, our youth are not so irrational as to burn down the medical center in their own neighborhood that pregnant women go to and their grandparents go to. They're not so irrational as to make it more difficult for us to get access to medicine and to food. And I hope that those who come here, if you will, the National Guard — while they keep looking at our Black youth — move real fast on looking at the systematic arson of certain businesses.

Caller: Well this has moved further from just Blacks, and at the beginning, the media just said South Central, saying we're going to curfew South Central when they should have been curfewing all of L.A.

Rico Reed: I agree, it's not just South Central.

Reverend Jackson: And, I must tell you, it's not just L.A. and it's not just Black. That's why when the police threw a back hand statement that said, "it's a kind of rainbow coalition," he was trying to take a swipe at us but it was his way of saying that they're White, and they're Brown, they're Black. I was in Washington when this verdict came down and I tell you that we marched in front of the White House yesterday trying to get President Bush's attention. There's an unusual level of rage by Whites across the country who simply themselves have lost more confidence in the judicial system as a result of this decision. That's why moving to prosecute these four officers must be a real priority. But then, even to put them off, the police department and they must be put off, does not address the need for a plan for rebuilding and hope for the entire community.

Rico Reed: Reverend Jackson, question. I heard Mayor Bradley allude to something last night. I believe you were part of the meeting with the governor and Sheriff Block, and everyone.

Reverend Jackson: No, I was not.

Rico Reed: Okay, I thought I'd heard you mention that. They were discussing something about coming up with a plan or some type of agreement. That's all I heard. He was on Arsenio last night and he had mentioned something about an agreement. I was wondering what that agreement is, we haven't heard anything else.

Reverend Jackson: I know nothing about it, except the agreement must be to implement the Kerner Report. That's why I say we don't need to do any more studying; we need corrective action. We need a commitment. "A," we're spending 150 billion a year defending Europe and Japan when they are no longer under the threat. "B," they can afford to defend themselves. "C," nobody is after them and "D," we need the money to reinvest in our own country. And I tell you, people who have a stake in things, people who have a good job, whose children are going to school, and whose children are in school, and who have a piece of property, and who see a future for themselves — they have hope. People full of hope act one way. People full of fear and rejection act another. The cost of alienation is expensive.

Rico Reed: When we were looking out here, it's amazing we were discussing amongst ourselves on the radio when things were happening across the street with the fire and when you pulled up, all of a sudden fire department battalions came and television cameras.

Reverend Jackson: Man, don't make that connection. We were on the way to the station and we saw the burning take place and Channel 7 was there and we stopped, and then in a few minutes because we were talking on air live on Channel 7, then other channels saw that, of course, and the helicopters started swarming around and the fire department came, so ... I do not see myself in this situation as a fire stopper....

Rico Reed: It just happened that way; it's nice to be protected.

Reverend Jackson: ...but rather, the youth of whom I have worked in Nickerson Gardens, in Imperial Courts, in the schools, at Dorsey and around. We're reaching out to our youth, "A," because I want to protect them. They cannot be just left out here and be run over. You know, after the '88 campaign and people have seen my family on television and there was all this excitement about Jackson and all of that, that year Jesse Jr. graduated from college and we bought him a car as a gift. He was on his way from the house to the pancake house to get some breakfast, he and another friend of his —

Carl Nelson: Was this in Chicago?

Reverend Jackson: In Chicago. In a new car, and he was immediately pulled over. He had not put his sticker on the car but he had it in the glove compartment. These two cops pulled him over and said, "Out, and no damn talking," "Out, and no damn talking." He got out, "Now spread eagle." He spread eagle. "Hands up" — "No talk back" — and then hands behind your back, handcuffs, threw him in the back of the car. And then on the way to the police station they started taking their names and he gave his name. He did not scream, "I'm Jesse Jackson, Jr.;" he just "Joe Citizen" — and finally, the guy said, "Jesse Jackson, Jr." you mean your daddy — he said, "yeah" — they said, "Oh shit." But then he stayed in his place with his partner and then called us from the police department. Now, these two police officers were Black. This disease of using that badge and using that gun to violate people is not limited just to White. It's White, it's Black, it's Brown, it's wrong everywhere all the time. Those police, whether White, Black or Brown, who do care must separate themselves from those who don't. If not, they'll be lumped in together. I mean rotten apples, whatever color those apples are, red or green, must get out the barrel so we can have a civilized relationship between police and people since we pay the police to protect and serve, not to abuse and violate.

Rico Reed: You brought a couple of young ladies with you.

Reverend Jackson: And I want them to talk, because really what touched my heart about Monique and Darlene was that they were saying to the camera, "You know, we are intelligent people, don't treat us like animals, don't stereotype us, we're not burning." They have not slept for two days, walking Crenshaw, protecting properties. And yet, somehow, out of nowhere, with no youth running up and down the street, at 6 A.M., the Crenshaw Medical Center is burning from all four corners.

Rico Reed: Out of nowhere.

Reverend Jackson: That's an inside job, and that's their real point, and I think Darlene needs to be heard.

Darlene: My concern is the way the media is portraying us as these pillagers and looters and, you know, if we use 1492 as a working date, then pillaging and looting is nothing new. That's what this country was created on. So, the whole thing of violence begets violence; people don't know any better. Ideally, you want people to read the paper to become aware of what's going on, but that's not how it works because these things aren't accessible to everyone and when you're compact, you're in a ghetto, these are the things that you create. People would like us to believe that people from other parts of town — I grew up here in Leimert Park — that people from other parts of town are coming here and doing this. There is such a thing as small business rebates. There's such a thing as people wanting to buy out; there's such a thing as this particular neighborhood, and I'm including Inglewood and Baldwin Hills, Ladera Heights — these homes are worth a lot of money. These kids know that, so why are they going to destroy their own, and not in all instances it is Blacks. It's not Latinos. There are other people who have interests in this community, in the residential, in the property. They have an interest to burn their own property [*Front Page*, 1992b].

At 9 A.M., Jackson was in the KJLH studio, listening to President George Bush who urged for peace in a speech carried by radio and television stations nationally. Bush also condemned "the murder and destruction" by looters and rioters in South Central Los Angeles. This was the first time that KJLH carried a presidential speech. Jackson, who was in the studio, reacted immediately to Bush's announcement, refuting his condemnation and arguing that the president had not addressed the problems and plight of those living in poverty and inequality. Jackson's message resonated throughout the nation. On Saturday, May 2, 1992, thousands came out to register to vote amid the confusion and destruction on the streets.

Grassroots Empowerment

The general consensus among KJLH staff and community leaders is that the mission of Black radio is not to teach or preach, but rather to inform its listeners. The station has empowered its listeners to participate in the political process by informing them of the power of their vote and its ability to change the system. Overall, the importance of the station's community mission became clear throughout all the interviews, especially with regards to the role of independent Black radio to work on a grassroots level to serve its audience through information. Civil rights activist Dick Gregory illustrates the KJLH mission by pointing out the station's coverage and investigation of controversial allegations against the Central Intelligence Agency for its involvement in illegal drug activities:

> When they were talking about the Freeway Rick (about the drugs that the CIA, the government, had brought into this country), if you weren't listening to KJLH you wouldn't have known it was happening. I mean the *L.A. Times* didn't touch it. Maxine Waters was bringing 5 to 6 to 7000 people out for rallies, and they were getting the information from the radio station; and so I feel sorry for almost the rest of America who don't have a voice like that [Gregory, personal communication, 2002].

In another instance, third-term Congresswoman Maxine Waters and other politicians drew 2,000 people to one Crenshaw rally sponsored by KJLH and the Congressional Black Caucus in October 1996. Her theme that day was investigating the CIA's alleged involvement in the selling of crack cocaine in her district: "If I never do anything else in Congress, I am going to make somebody pay for the destruction to my people.... This is my number-one priority ... I've made a commitment to myself and to God."

It is through the church that KJLH was able to mediate differences among political and community leaders and unify the African American community to work together to change the system. Black churches, like the A.M.E. in South Central, have served as the meeting place for town hall discussions and voter registration rallies. The church is also a vehicle of economic empowerment for many residents. The church serves to inspire social, political, and economic freedom among its residents, and its message is voiced through stations like KJLH.

The structure within the African American church has provided a foundation for "effective political action in the secular realm" (Hill, 1990, p. 132). Johnson and Birk (1992) reported that voter registration was mentioned as one of the top three themes of promotional events conducted by gospel stations owned by African Americans. Jackson served as not only a political voice across the airwaves, but also as a symbolic figure for the Black church and present-day civil rights movement. According to Lorn S. Foster (1988), Jackson's political campaigns were "an extension of the civil rights movement [and] the black church" rather than an attempt to engage in "electoral politics" (p. 204). In 1988, his candidacy drew 7 million votes — with 2 million new voters registered through his campaign efforts (Catania, 1996). Jackson was one of the first political leaders to arrive on the scene of the Los Angeles civil uprising. He camped out at the KJLH offices over the next few days.

Black-targeted local media actually increases the likelihood of a greater voter turnout among African Americans, according to Oberholzer-Gee and Waldfogel (2001). In particular, Black radio has historically contributed toward increasing voter participation among its listeners. In 1983, four Black-targeted stations — WBMX-FM, WGCI-FM, WVON-AM and WJPC-AM -along with civil rights activists sponsored a massive voter registration campaign that led to the Democratic Party nomination and eventually the election of the first African American Chicago mayor, Harold Washington (Zorn, 1983; Sheppard, Jr., 1983). Eric Zorn, a radio columnist for *Chicago Tribune*, credited Black and urban radio "with galvanizing the mayoral campaign of Harold Washington and supplying him with the winning edge." Black talk shows on WVON (James Rowe's *Hotline*), WJPC (*The Vernon Jarrett Report*) and WXOL (*On Target*) promoted "the black voter registration drive and generat[ed] pre-election hoopla" (Zorn, 1983, p. 8). Years later, WGCI-FM, along with other area African American–owned and –formatted stations, was instrumental in disseminating voter information and coordinating registration drives during the 1992 presidential primaries and election campaign. The stations worked together to organize a massive voter registration drive and an information campaign as well as to encourage voters to go to the polls on Election Day.

Likewise Black-targeted stations in Memphis played a key role in the dissemination of voter information and in the promotion of voter registration during the 1991 Memphis mayoral race between incumbent Dick Hackett and Willie W. Herenton (Caffey, personal communication, 1992; St. James, personal communication, 1992). Herenton became the first African American mayor of Memphis (Arndt, 1991; "Herenton Elected," 1991). Rick Caffey (personal communication, 1992), former vice president and general manager of WDIA/WHRK, recalled that listeners called his stations when they had questions about the voting process or when they were not treated properly. The station's airwaves were dedicated to voter information, such as what you need to know when you go to the polls, and subsequently its switchboard was flooded with phone calls.

The political activism in the City of Brotherly Love can be traced back four to five decades when the African American community had one elected city councilman yet represented 35 percent to 40 percent of the total metropolitan area. According to WDAS' talk show host E. Steven Collins (personal communication, 1993), "tremendous decisions were made without the input of the Black community." In 1981, Frank Rizzo was defeated by William Green with nearly 85 percent of all African American people voting on Election Day (ibid.). In 1984, W. Wilson Goode, Green's managing director, became mayor after winning the vote of African Americans and White liberals (Beauregard, 1990). The African American community responded with a voter registration record of 99 percent (Beauregard, 1990; Collins, personal communication, 1993).

Collins underscored Jackson's significance as a political voice to Philadelphia's African American listeners in the 1980s, and recalled when

> Jesse Jackson was running one year, and we put together a hastily coordinated, at least from a technical point of view, live remote from a Center City park where he was addressing union workers. And we just stopped music which is just unheard of in a very competitive urban radio environment. We just, on the FM and AM stations, stopped music to put Jesse Jackson on the air live [Collins, personal communication, 1993].

Subsequent to the Jackson campaigns of 1984 and 1988, other community events and activities unified and defined Philadelphia's political activism and empowered its local civil rights movement. In September 1991, WDAS, along with Project VOTE, held a "parliament folkadelic voter registration rally" in a city park with music and a picnic (ibid.). WDAS conducted a vote-a-thon that encouraged listeners to beat the registration deadline for the presidential primaries on October 6, 1991, by filling out their voter cards at various locations in the Philadelphia area, but principally at the WDAS lobby. Boxes and boxes of completed forms were taken to the voter registration office before the midnight deadline.

In June 1992, a WDAS morning personality announced that he was the self-proclaimed mayor of Philadelphia radio, and he would go at least twice a week to various locations with the WDAS van to register people. His monthly goal was to register 3,100 people. WDAS also presented voter information via public affairs shows and featured interviews with Project Vote representatives, city election commissioners and the secretary of state in an effort to increase voter registration activity, as well as to explain the infrastructure of the political system, everything from the election of ward leaders to mayoral candidates to presidential candidates. Collins recalled another incident when he questioned the political process within metro Philadelphia in an effort to address community concerns of his African American listeners:

> And I'm coming way off the wall with questions like "Why are drugs such a major uncontrollable problem at 32nd and Dolphin?" It changes the course of a news conference or a newsmaker that is used to the pat questions and the pat responses. And for a mayor of a big city, it's like "well there's so many streets in our town, why are you focusing there?" "Because Black people live there. They've been complaining for a long, long time, and nothing's been done." Or this housing project, or this school has been dilapidated, or whatever it is, Black policeman aren't being treated fairly in promotions, "what are you doing about it?" [ibid.].

He continues, "And all of a sudden it sounds like I'm being the Black representative, but I believe really I'm articulating the view of 43.7 percent of metro Philadelphia." Collins (personal communication, 1993) concluded by saying, "Black radio therefore has a responsibility to really help examine who these people really are and what they bring to elected office, and how they propose they can deal with the myriad of problems that are facing people that live in our neighborhoods." Collins helped to orchestrate the KJLH broadcast of the 1992 riots across Philadelphia's airwaves, and somehow the historical role of Black radio made complete sense:

> I remember the Rodney King event, I had all this sound from Los Angeles, and we had the news director from KJLH, Carl Nelson — KJLH is like a sister station in L.A.— on the air, and we had Jesse [Jackson] on, and we had Willie Williams, the outgoing Philly police commissioner who was going to take over the LAPD, on. All of this stuff going on, and then we opened the phones. Four to five other radio stations in the market put our program on their air — live — which was unheard of. And so, we were literally speaking to the largest audience we could ever hope for about the L.A. "eruption." And the other stations in the market immediately recognized that they couldn't do that. Half the people called in angry, really intensely angry, about the way this jury had gone about its responsibility of finding these officers not guilty. It was an all–White jury, an all-White city. All of that created a tremendous anger on the part of Black America. And a lot of Whites just did not understand the level of intensity of that anger. And so we dealt with it thoroughly and straightforwardly. To me, that's what Black radio is [ibid.].

Years later, Barack Obama's victory in the 2008 presidential election was celebrated across Black-owned stations, and those formatted to serve the African American community. Web sites like those of KJLH had served as informational portals on how to register and the voting process and provided a place to find out more about candidates' positions and elaborate on pertinent issues discussed previously on the air. Flashing across the KJLH Web site, the station headlined words of encouragement to listeners, reminding them to step out to vote and make a difference and then to plug into the station for results:

> Keep it locked to 102.3 Radio Free KJLH on Election Day as we move out and about in the community to observe history in the making!! Cast your vote and then join us as we watch and pray for change!!!
> HISTORY is at our fingertips ... as we go to the polls [KJLH, 2008].

KJLH programming had been geared up toward educating the listener. After the announcement of the presidential election results, sweepers between songs over KJLH congratulated Obama's success. Music and message — KJLH once again served as the tribal drum for its community.

CHAPTER 9

Owning a Legacy — And Hanging Onto It

KJLH aired its 10th year anniversary edition of *Front Page* on April 29, 2002 — a decade after the Los Angeles riots. Nelson provided a rundown of the major players from back then:

> Some of the players in the riots are no longer with us. Ten years have passed, and Mayor Bradley has passed on, died of a heart attack in 1998. Reginald Denny has moved now to ... Arizona actually. Daryl Gates has retired. He had a short life as a radio talk show host. He's retired down in Orange County. Rodney King, now according to *[The] Washington Post*, ... won 3.8 million dollars from the city in a settlement from the beating. They said, Now he's what we call "cracked out," folks — you know he's on PCP, he's broke and living in a rehab center [*Front Page*, 2002b].

Slade (personal communication, 2002) said that the station intended to bring together some of the community leaders that helped unify South Central Los Angeles in 1992. KJLH opted for a more subdued approach than was originally planned when the 10th anniversary finally arrived. The program invited listeners to call into *Front Page* to speak with Nelson, Goree, and special guest KFWB news anchor and reporter Larry Carroll. Initially, the hosts and callers addressed the difference between a riot and rebellion and concurrently reviewed the events leading up to the verdict as well as present conditions favorable toward another outbreak (i.e., poverty, unemployment, race relations, inadequate housing). *Front Page* producer Jamaal Goree also related some statistics provided by Loyola Marymount University in Los Angeles, namely that 50 percent of all looters had been Hispanic or Latino compared to approximately one-third African Americans during the 1992 civil unrest (*Front Page*, 2002b; also see Briggs, 2002). Subsequent discussions centered on the rise of Hispanic political power and the acknowledgment of and need for more African American political leaders. A significant portion of the program criticized failed economic initiatives over the past 10 years, and a need to replace area liquor stores with more laundromats and banks in the community than presently exist in South Central. The African American churches' efforts to empower people financially and politically was integral to the discussion. Much of the devastation to South Central and neighboring communities impacted minority-owned businesses, both African American and Korean-American. Reports on the burning of businesses filled the airwaves, night and day from April 29 to May 1, 1992. One caller related:

> You know, that really hurts. It's like, all those people now are going to be displaced, they don't have [homes, jobs] ... as if we all weren't suffering before this burning. You tear up the economic foundation, I'm really upset and I can't believe that people would resort to violence to help solve the problem. This isn't doing anything but creating more of a problem for us. Now, we've got to fight two things [*Front Page*, 1992b].

Specific discussions underscored the economic and regulatory impediments facing KJLH and similar stations toward achieving equity in advertising dollars, preserving Black ownership, and responding to the needs of a diverse audience — in 1992 and in 2002. When people on the streets began to get out of control, Slade made the decision to pull the commercials for beer and malt liquors, and at one point virtually all KJLH's commercials were removed from the air: "I just made some executive calls; some worked out to my favor, and some didn't. But I didn't think it was appropriate to have rappers on [the air] talking about drinking malt liquor ... when all hell was breaking loose" (Slade, personal communication, 1993).

That particular decision, when its service mission conflicted with its business goals, was a costly decision for management. Beyond that, a number of national advertisers were no longer willing to invest money into South Central: "It was a difficult period for us. A lot of the advertisers called to cancel their advertising. After that, they did not want to be associated with the unrest. They felt we were too closely tied to it, and they just stopped advertising; they stopped booking advertising on us" (Slade, personal communication, 2001).

Just like any family-owned store or neighborhood gas station, KJLH is a community business. There is no dividing line that separates listen-

ers and staff. Its business is not music or talk, but rather its ability to provide a service to its listeners. As the riots subsided, people began to send
KJLH money:

> We didn't ask for money. We did not do a cash call. We didn't do anything like
> that. Denzel [Washington] came down and wrote a check. Quite a few people
> came down and wrote a check. The community churches started sending us
> checks. Because we knew where the need was and they were saying, "Well, get
> this to where you think it would do the most good — so that was kind of amaz-
> ing, where the entertainment community kind of rallied around us and the
> business community kind of stepped away from us because they didn't under-
> stand. And I think that the lack of sensitivity is really a fundamental problem
> with business, and that's why diversity and diversity training is key to all busi-
> nesses to thrive" [ibid.].

Slade said that she has advised business owners on several occasions that
it would be financially wise for them to support the communities in which
they are located: "Many sell products and make profits from minorities
who purchase their goods; however they fail to circulate money back into
the same communities they take money out of" (1993a, p. 22).

Rebuilding South Central

On May 2, 1992, city councilwoman Ruth Galantes, state legislator
Marguerite Archie-Hudson, and former governor Jerry Brown discussed
their push for economic development in South Central. The need to
rebuild businesses, homes, and lives became increasingly apparent as residents began again to move about on the streets (*Front Page*, 1992d). One
year after the Los Angeles civil unrest, many businesses remained covered
in ashes and rubble, and there seemed little likelihood of another uprising, as KJLH and other media awaited the verdict of the Denny trial and
second King trial. Rollins conjectures, "Part of the reason for a more subdued reaction may simply be that little reconstruction has taken place in
South Central. There isn't a whole lot to burn down." He goes on to
describe the area: "Blocks around many major intersections still are only
foundations and concrete floors, with a hint of rubble, wrapped in chain-
link fences. Fiery neighborhood meetings focus on demands for the eas-
ing of planning and zoning restrictions so grocery stores can be rebuilt"
(1993, p. A01).

As an African American owned business, KJLH was financially injured
by the 1992 uprising, especially in terms of its ability to generate adver-

tising revenue after local businesses were torched and looted: "Rebuilding our city from the inside out is going to take financial support of the businesses that operate within those communities. If our businesses fail, our communities fail. We must rebuild by rejuvenating our community businesses." Slade continued, "I can't emphasize this enough: It is essential to buy products from black owned and operated businesses. Thus our businesses will have the necessary funds to hire from the community and continue to offer quality products and services." Concluding Slade said, underscoring KJLH's role as core within the business community, "We are committed to quality broadcasting and service. In turn, we need our listeners and clients to work with us. After all, we're all in it together" (Slade, 1993, p. 22).

One of the major themes that emerged in this study was KJLH's community service mission of economic empowerment. This theme was present in interview and program transcripts and documentation within the KJLH file. A number of community service activities and discussions have dealt with issues of personal finance and the importance of recycling Black dollars within area neighborhoods. The station, in and of itself, has ascertained economic empowerment as a major theme during its self-studies throughout the years. After the uprising, KJLH also produced a 20-page brochure *Building with KJLH* regarding the potential of the 11.6 billion dollar Black consumer market. The brochure emphasized its coverage of the riots and the role of *Front Page* as a community forum, as well as the need to reinvest Black dollars back into South Central ("KJLH Communicates," 1993).

The significance of African American ownership, in terms of media and other businesses, was considered essential to any plan to rebuild South Central. A decade after the 1992 Los Angeles uprising, it would be easy to mistake the hustle and bustle on the streets and in the stores of Crenshaw and Inglewood as indicators of a viable economy within the South Central area. Carroll points out:

> I think without question there are too many liquor stores and too few banks. And I was at a hearing the weekend before last with Congresswoman Diane Watson with members of the Federal Home Loan Bank Board and community financial institutions — a grassroots capital formation of organizations looking [toward] the development and redevelopment of the South Los Angeles community, in particular. You know, we look at issues such as the proliferation of liquor stores and we can focus on that. But the larger issue is the economic development of this county, the economic viability of a community where the unemployment rate is still 25 percent. That's outrageous that there should be that

level of underdevelopment in a community with so many tremendous resources [*Front Page*, 2002b].

When Greg Johnson, marketing director, joined the station around 1998, he was "very familiar" with KJLH's award-winning community coverage of the civil unrest, as well as "with knowing where they were physically located ... right on Crenshaw Boulevard." They had "an eyewitness view of the rebellion," explains Johnson:

> Whether they're aware of it or not, [the station] has participated in the aftermath of rebuilding the community, in more ways than one —financial [and] just being there as a, you know, a beacon of communication. So it's a legacy that we have to uphold here, we have to continue to build, we have to continue to work with ... I just keep going back to it, the churches, to me, have the most money to do things.... If you just join shoulder-to-shoulder with them, you know, you're going to effect change. It's just that easy [personal communication, 2002].

The ability of KJLH to serve its community and to survive in an increasingly corporate environment definitely makes for an interesting analysis of local radio's viability to compete amid the radio giants. The music format is urban adult contemporary, with a targeted audience of 35–54 years old (Slade, personal communication, 2001). The station also plays gospel music on Sundays. But, what differentiates KJLH from the 60 plus signals in Los Angeles is its commitment toward news, information and service. KJLH ranked 24th in its metro market with an overall share fluctuating between 1.5 and 2.0 since the 1980s (Duncan, 1983; Duncan, 1992; Sanders, 2002). For KJLH, a strong commitment to the legacy of Black and urban radio might very well be that magic ingredient that historically led to its high Time Spent Listening (TSL) rating compared to other formats, and comparable to corporate-owned stations targeting similar audiences. In 2007, for example, KJLH's ratings positioned it as one of the leading urban stations in Los Angeles. As discussed in a previous chapter, Arbitron's new ratings tool, PPM, unfortunately has not been as urban-format friendly in terms of audience measurement as the diary method that preceded it.

Community Service Role in the Future

KJLH's ability to participate financially in the near and distant future within the larger corporate radio arena is definitely a concern of its owner.

Stevie Wonder's invitation to appear at the 1999 FCC hearing on localism (amid rampant consolidation) is indicative of the station's symbolic role as one of the remnant Black heritage FM radio stations in the U.S. In this way, the station's mission appears inadvertently to transcend its community borders; yet even saying that, its strategies to survive deregulation and consolidation when against the radio goliaths of America need further elaboration and investigation at this point. The station's success has not been merely measured economically by its owner, but rather through its impact on the community of people that listen and live in South Central. KJLH is Stevie Wonder, explains Johnson, and his compassion for his listeners helps to define station goals:

> God lives inside of KJLH. I think the spirit of the Lord flows into this radio station through Stevie Wonder, and being a very, very spiritual man ... I think it's a divine intention that we tithe maybe 10 percent of our playlist to gospel music. I think that's ... it's all there. Why is the Gospel Sunday the most listened to time on this radio station ... God is moving through Black people in America. You can tell it by, he's making churches that are going on, and, you know, there's an argument that every pastor's not honest, whatever, whatever—that's God's judgment to make, however, if the word of God is going forth. Now Black churches have 65 million dollar facilities. The Faith Dome right over here in the 'hood, and you can go all across the country and see these mega-churches, 20,000 members, four or five services on Sunday. Plus they're on television, international television, Internet, the whole thing—it's big business. But, the business of it, yes, they're asking you for money, okay because it takes money to buy the food that they need to feed the homeless, to run those programs to teach people how to be entrepreneurs, or how to buy a home, how to get an education. It takes money to operate that stuff, and so, yeah they're asking for money, duh! You know, they just kind of need it, but I think God is just working right now through Black people [personal communication, 2002].

However one articulates and identifies the sources of inspiration and motivation driving and connecting KJLH employees to their community, the station has tapped into the hearts of its listeners. KJLH strives to achieve its famous owner's goals: to entertain with the best music and to serve the African American community in a socially responsive way. "It is a family operation, with a personal touch," former program director Cliff Winston once explained: "It's like a neighborhood grocery, as compared to Ralphs" (Gronau, 2001, p. 1). Johnson (personal communication, 2002) also points out that radio is still a business, but it is in the business of serving the community:

A lot of times because we are a community station, that fax is going off all the time with people wanting us to do something for free, or whatever, you know, you adopt and pick and choose — you adopt them, but then you know, this is a business, so you have to go find out how you can get some money attached to it, some sponsorships, and it always works. It always works, you know, but you got to change the thinking of a lot of people [personal communication, 2002].

Nevertheless, when massive deregulation had financially challenged the very existence of independently and locally owned media, KJLH managed to secure corporate sponsorship of station events and to participate in innovative cultural grant programs. Similarly, Johnson adds:

You have to look at it a lot differently. There's a lot of budgets out there now that you can go after that are expressly set aside for community relations — you know, sponsorship of events that's going to benefit young people, you know, whatever. So, yeah, it's an interesting balance. It can be done though; it can be done [ibid.].

KJLH had always sought creative solutions to remain competitive in the Los Angeles marketplace, yet it became even more imperative to think strategically after the events of 1992. Obviously, corporate sponsorship of community programs is not a unique concept in business, but it has been a strategy used particularly well at Black heritage stations. Slade passionately speaks from her experience of what Black radio, and media in general, can mean to its audience and the African American community, and how its ability to make a difference, as cliché as that may sound, is often underestimated by those in powerful positions. At one point, Slade had an opportunity to reexamine her perspective as someone who had been on the front line of the riots, broadcasting live, managing an enterprise in the heat of a crisis. She did so when attending a meeting with a number of radio managers who had been called together into this forum along with her by the mayor.

Her perspective would be framed by her gender, race, and experience — all intersecting to provide her with a unique hearing of the problems and issues in the area: "I'm somewhat of a rarity as a Black female general manager. Mayor Tom Bradley had a meeting of radio general managers after the riots. So I went. And I looked around, and I was the only Black woman in that position in that room." As she sat listening to the male managers, "hair started rising on the back of [her] neck because [she] thought they were missing the point." She explained, "Buildings were burning across the street from my station during the riots. So I couldn't talk as lightly as they did, with a sense of humor and letting things roll off me. So I spoke my mind." At first she had some misgivings about speaking up, but it was her understanding of the community that had provided her station the means to persevere through hard times. She continued, "And afterward, I thought, 'Oh no. I hope they don't think I'm just another emotional female.' But yes, I'm passionate. And I don't feel so bad about it, because I care. So what if I'm not cool and I'm not a member of the old boys' club? I will never be" (Slade, 1993, p. 22).

Stevie Wonder answered the call toward Black ownership when he bought KJLH and has remained committed toward serving its audience. His hiring of Slade would become instrumental to the success of the station. Intelligent, motivated, and passionate about the station's core beliefs, she has been primarily responsible for execution of that mission. Yet, the KJLH struggle to remain an economically viable entity in the late 1990s, while serving its audience's needs, prompted Wonder to take a more active and vocal role in speaking against conglomerate ownership at the exclusion of minority voices than he had in the past. In a 1999 FCC congressional hearing, both Wonder and Slade pointed out the difficulties of competing since the Telecommunications Act of 1996 opened the way for massive consolidation:

> *Wonder*: Consolidation of radio ownership has made it difficult, if not impossible for the single owner. Competition with conglomerates who own several stations in a single market does not allow for fair access to advertising dollars. This is particularly true when conglomerates pursue a format that has been traditional domain of the minority owner. Survival becomes a game of deep pockets. Often many single owners cannot afford to survive. In a scheme of free enterprise, I suppose this is fair game [*FCC Proceeding*, 1999, pp. 77–78].

> *Slade:* Because as a small operator, I'm the one competing out there. And it's very difficult to compete with conglomerates. Just a case in point, I have a finite amount of inventory. I pitch, do my best. My numbers are what they are. I get the buy or I don't. If I'm competing with someone who owns five, six, seven, eight radio stations and a television station and a billboard company, they're packaging it all together. They've got one-stop advertising. It's very difficult to compete. Now, we do okay. But as you raise the bar and raise the bar, at some point you'll go under. When I came into this business ten years ago, there were five black-owned and operated facilities in Los Angeles. We are the only one now. And that's because the owner made a commitment to stay in the business. We are committed to this industry. But the bar keeps raising and my competitors are not playing with the same rule book. I have a finite amount of inventory. They buy another station. It's very difficult [FCC Proceeding, 1999, p. 105].

Wonder, nevertheless, urged the commissioners to reconsider the trend toward consolidation, and he stated during the hearing:

> History has taught us the danger of monopolistic control of the means of communication. Legislators consider these dangers. And even in this era of deregulation and laissez faire, the public interest is still protected in the Communications Act. The public interest cannot be protected when waivers are granted to allow multiple-station owners to own more stations. How are the single owners to compete with this — the owners who stand to own more than nine hundred stations? Consider the value of the single radio station owner, particularly the ethnic minority owner. Ownership diversity makes a difference in the mission of the station [FCC Proceeding, 1999, pp. 79–80].

Slade concurs that KJLH has been "sensitive and conscientious about more than just the bottom line and that comes through in different ways." For example, KJLH has been proactive in its hiring decisions, and that element distinguishes it from many corporate and non-minority-owned outlets:

> I mean we do play the same music pretty much, but our hiring policies, we hire a great deal of minorities regardless of what the EEO says. We hire from within the community, and I just think we're a little more sensitive to what we need to do for our community, rather than the shareholders and the "corporate suits," if you will, primarily because we're a single station facility. We're not one of the major groups and we're not required to deliver a certain return on investment or return on equity to the owner [Slade, personal communication, 2001].

Opportunities and Impediments

As opportunities for minority ownership continued to decline (and no signs of change when Michael Powell was at the helm of the Federal Communications Commission), KJLH sought ways to financially empower its audience, such as through its affiliate agreement with the Bloomberg Urban Business Report, which was the first syndicated financial report targeted toward African American audiences. Moreover, KJLH began defining itself beyond its 5,600 watts, even as a Class A licensed station, by streaming across the Internet as a way to remain competitive and, more importantly, bring the issues of its South Central audience to other African American communities across the U.S. Many of the issues in South Central would relate to other African Americans outside the city; however, each group would contribute its own local perspective through discussion and information sharing. *Front Page* has been the main source for information transmission beyond the local community, beginning in 1992.

According to MeasureCast Top 50 (2001), for the month of June 2001, KJLH ranked 42nd of the 50 top streamed radio stations in terms of hours streamed and number of unique listeners (3,207) who stay tuned for at least one to five minutes or longer at any one time period. New York's legendary urban giant WBLS-FM came in at 39th with a June audience of 4,546, and the only other urban presence was for Internet Radio Inc. (ranked 13th, with 34,638 listeners). KJLH is a small station, if defined by its physical limitations. But, in terms of personality and purpose, KJLH continues to move ahead against the market barriers defined by the 2000 Ivy Report. Slade also testified to the FCC that radio, for all its community good, is still a business, and must meet certain revenue and profit requirements to survive in the market: "Few of us encounter all aspects of Los Angeles — Hispanic, Asian, whatever. We just go about our lives. We don't intentionally not integrate but we just do our thing. So we need to know how we all, as responsible adults, feel about things." Slade continued, "As a broadcaster, if I can balance out that information, and encourage listeners to tune in, and understand, and then maybe read more, maybe I can open that window and we can get back to a more open society." Yet, saying all that, KJLH is still a business, and that is a significant factor in its survival and its ability to serve in the public interest: "So many times we get caught up with the entertainment or informational aspects of the business, many forget it is still just that — a business, with revenues and profit requirements (Slade, 1993, p. 22).

KJLH's commitment level to its community became particularly evident when the station raised approximately $55,000 during the course of the Los Angeles unrest, and in fact, the station never solicited any funds. People started coming down to the station and giving money: "We opened up a separate account at Broadway Federal, one of the Black banks, and we made micro-loan funding at the bank so small entrepreners could get some cash (Slade, personal communication, 2002). She adds, "A trust existed between the station and audience, and basically listeners and community members were saying 'just give it to KJLH.'"

Black ownership appears to be the driving force behind KJLH's community service activities and discussion. In particular, its role as an independent station has provided incredible latitude in freely discussing issues often ignored in mainstream media that have had significant relevance to the African American community, and actually to every citizen within the melting pot of the U.S. It is no secret that it takes millions of dollars in today's corporate environment to buy and launch a radio station. So far,

KJLH has managed to survive in this new era of mega-consolidation, and perhaps lessons learned along the way have shaped its message of economic empowerment within its community.

The station's desire to empower listeners is actualized through workshops and relationships with lending institutions, as well as strong African American owned churches that provide loans and financial services to jump-start new businesses in the community. This scenario was especially the case during the rebuilding phase after the Los Angeles riots. The government never followed through on many of its monetary promises to rebuild the area and, as a result, few external resources were directed at African Americans that comprised 35 percent of the residents in the South Central area (with a number of them moving westward toward the original KJLH location in the Crenshaw District) (Foote and Murr, 2002, p. 44). Other African Americans have relocated to suburbs, miles away from the vacant lots of former businesses. Aside from those circumstances, KJLH has managed to expand its reach to beyond Southern Los Angeles to across the world through the Internet. Its community is both South Central and the larger African American audience within the United States. Furthermore, Johnson articulates his views on the mission and outreach of KJLH, as one of social and political equity that can be achieved only through economic empowerment. His point is illustrated in this passage:

> Our men — drug addicts, prison, there's a million brothers behind bars, a million — just think of all those minds that could be out here effecting change, you know. So then, you know, what do you say to the men that are out here, how do we galvanize? I don't know, but we need brothers to come step forward and be real men, and if I can help speak that through these airwaves, through the stuff that I'm doing as a marketing director here. And, you know, if I'm at the Rec Center in Nickerson Gardens and the guy tells me, you know, Greg, I need volunteers, I'm on the radio saying, "I need some men down here to help coach these kids," you know, or be positive role models, something. We need that. So, the revolution's not over, but it's not guns and burning down the stores, *the revolution is economic* (emphasis added) [personal communication, 2002].

Slade adds that the economic struggle has remained a relevant issue in South Central, as it was in 1992:

> At that time, Tom Bradley was still in office and he came up with "Rebuild L.A." and a lot of efforts were made, but I think it's back to business as usual. It does sound unfortunate, but this is the business that we're in and we must show that we are different. We are not just an R&B station, I mean, that is a wonderful thing to be, an R&B station, because that's the format that we've selected, but we're so much more. I think part of it is because of the collective

consciousness of the staff, but it's primarily because of Stevie Wonder, the owner. I mean he has set the stage and the tone of what he wants and what he expects, so it's easy to do the right thing when you're not being stressed out about profits and profit margins and financial ratios. It is good business to do right by the community in which you do business [personal communication, 2001].

Admittedly, Slade, as manager, still worries about everything from advertising revenue to meeting the needs of her staff and listeners. It is no longer possible to ignore the economies of scale enjoyed by the radio giants, with their corporate programming attempting to absorb her comparatively small community of listeners in South Central. These are the same giants that are eager to redefine listening habits in large and small communities across the U.S. The price of admission into this arena is to be the highest bidder in the market, due to the deregulatory actions of governmental agencies that once advocated preferential ownership polices for women and minorities so that they might be represented across the airwaves. The desire for a multitude of voices in a marketplace of ideas once shaped FCC policies. Today, the qualification for radio ownership appears to be determined solely on a financial basis rather than on an owner's ability to serve in the public interest, necessity, and convenience of the community. There exists a scarcity of public expression across the airwaves, if defined by independent minority ownership. Minority voices are often limited in their ability to participate economically in the high stakes game of radio ownership, regardless of the number of media outlets available for auction across the U.S.

On April 29, 2002, a decade had passed since the Los Angeles uprising and with that came a flurry of media reports that filled the airwaves, the local and national newspapers, and magazines as people reflected on the events that had erupted in South Central years earlier. It was also on this date that KJLH aired its special version of *Front Page*, inviting listeners to call into the studio to discuss the political, social, and economic progress (and lack of it) over the past decade since the uprising. Comments reaffirmed KJLH's central role in unifying and rebuilding the community.

In an editorial that was published in the *Los Angeles Times*, Slade underscored the "imperative" nature of minority-owned and -operated media to "ensure that information, specifically news, is pertinent and relevant to our culturally specific audience" (1993, p. 22). KJLH continues to be instrumental in providing public dialogue within the community. Goree had referred to his audience as his *Front Page* family. On February,

22, 2002, the Urban Issues Breakfast Forum for Greater Los Angeles brought together community leaders to discuss "Bernard Parks: Why Should the Chief of Police Be Appointed to a Second Term." Its sponsors were the Black Business Association, the *L.A. Watts Newspaper*, and KJLH. He was not reappointed.

What if any, lessons were learned by those inside and outside the community? Goree points out that there is a distinct difference between talking about an issue and working toward a solution. Racial profiling is still a major impediment toward rebuilding the social, political, and economic fabric of South Central:

> I would say some of our politicians became a little more aware of the anger and they started to address some of those issues, but addressing the issues and solving the issues are two different things. They did start to address them. Now again, racial profiling, which is a great issue in this city, it really was not addressed. It was thought to be just those whining Blacks out there because of their criminal nature. They're now crying because they're getting caught. Then you have this tape that shows up ... actually March the third of 1991 of Rodney King getting beat. Okay, now you have this tape, you know, and shockingly, other tapes started to appear from other areas in the country shortly after that — even there was one in New Jersey. I remember that surfaced where a gentleman was getting beat by police. Even as recently as a couple of years ago in Philadelphia, they showed a group of police officers beating a Black motorist for apparently nothing. Okay, but the point is that prior to March third with Rodney King, there wasn't a lot of discussion on racial profiling — so what did they learn? I can't say a whole lot other than they need to be more careful the next time; make sure there's no camera pointing at you [Goree, personal communication, 2002].

Points of Light

On April 29, 2002, President George W. Bush spoke to a group of community leaders at the First A.M.E. Church regarding the 10-year anniversary of the uprising. Ten years prior, his father "recognized the church as the 177th point of light ... for its efforts to revitalize" South Central (*Front Page*, 2002b). One listener expressed his outrage during the special anniversary edition:

> How can we allow ourselves to let some corporate America that perpetuated this uprising in the first place, sit down, and dictate what the agenda would be out here today. Bush [will] be here to talk to some community leaders. The only community leaders, the only community people that we have basically are

the ones that's really kind of [politically] conscious and listen to KJLH. And on the other hand, I feel like we really don't have a community.... So when are we really gonna sit down. We should be up there by the millions when Bush comes today to protest what he's doing; turn off the television when you hear that propaganda with Bush and [his] staff. I think we just ought to get conscious, start loving each other, stops this Eastside-Westside thing, and just sit down and really create some real dialogue and start demanding, instead of on our knees begging like Malcolm, say we will be doin' in this time had we not straightened our game out [ibid.].

In that same program, Nelson commented, the "ambers that sparked the uprising 10 years ago are there today in L.A. and a lot of people feel there could be another riot" in the South Central area. To Wonder, as he has articulated through station mission and policies and actualized in practice by discussion and moving beyond talk, radio provides a solution through information and communication and a means to unify his community through service. To others, the goodwill of this celebrity owner is quaintly unique, and only fairly representative of the situation that many African American independent owners have encountered since massive consolidation:

On one hand, there are probably more radio signals owned today by African Americans than ever before in the history of broadcast, strictly because of stellar telecommunications operations like Radio One and Inner City Broadcasting, but is that better than having a lot of individual owners? And I think your point goes to individual African American owners of radio stations, and yet, the example you're offering of KJLH is so unique, in the sense, several senses [that] a multibillionaire owns KJLH [Collins, personal communication, 2002].

Given the context of Collins's observations, he would likely concur that whether Wonder has the resources to compete nationally or internationally is not as relevant to the question of ownership and service as much as his willingness to embrace the significance of localism, as well as the idea that new technologies can be used to extend his concept of community.

KJLH is one of approximately 140 African American owned FM outlets in the U.S., and a number of these stations are dedicated to providing culturally specific programming and service to an often-neglected audience. Ownership does not guarantee commitment toward one's community of license, but historically it has tended to be the case. Wonder's public statements to the FCC have supported the ideal of preserving independently owned, Black-operated media. Corporate radio stations have bought out struggling Black-owned independents, and in some instances their urban formats continue to target African American audiences. However, some listeners and community leaders have noted a decrease in community service at the local level among a growing number of stations, as discussed in the literature review. Retired Supreme Court justice William Brennan once argued minority ownership "influenced" station content (Kleiman 1991, p. 419), and the National Telecommunications and Information Administration (NTIA, 2001) and the Black Broadcasters Alliance (BBA, 1997), among others (Ivy, 2000), have since affirmed a loss of diversity over the years as a result of deregulation and subsequent consolidation.

Will it be merely a matter of time before Black and urban radio loses its cultural edge at the hands of corporate owners? Only time will tell. But by then, it might be too late, if it is not already, to promote localism and community service activities at the grassroots level, given rumors of another round of deregulation. Imagine if African American business leaders (as individuals or in unison) in towns across America with the intent to serve in the public interest claimed one radio station for each community — a move toward increasing Black-ownership like former FCC commissioner Benjamin Hooks advocated in the 1970s ("Coming Through," 1972).

These stations, some of which already exist across the U.S., like KJLH-FM, would be dedicated to local programming and community service, and would extend that mission beyond individual neighborhoods through creative use of the Internet. These efforts might lead to one incredible lobbying force with the potential to challenge the trend toward consolidation and away from community service. Perhaps the power to transmit is in the hands of African American business leaders that are as passionate as philanthropist Stevie Wonder and who have a vision to address the often-neglected issues within communities across the U.S. The number of independently owned Black and urban stations will continue to dwindle against a corporate backdrop, especially if their owners are not allotted a financial or other competitive advantage. Wonder bought his station for 2 million dollars in 1979; and in 1999 it was valued at more than 40 million dollars, an increase of more than 38 million. The reality of ownership today is that it takes a lot of money to buy a station, let alone compete against corporate radio giants on a day-to-day basis (and add to that the burden of culturally specific market barriers for African American owners).

It would also be significant to mention that corporate radio owners must be careful to not lose sight of what made Black radio, such a community force in the first place, as in the early days of WDIA (Memphis) or more recently through KJLH-FM's outreach during the Los Angeles uprising in 1992. The perception of corporate radio, even Black-owned, is that it is driven by economics rather than public interest. Although as Newman (1988) states, Black radio is indeed a business and yet the product is community service.

Deep Roots in South Central

Black radio performs a community service for its listeners. It has deep roots in the community and social and political implications for its audience. This fact, however, often goes unnoticed during congressional hearings on telecommunications policy, especially with regards to drafting legislation in favor of minority ownership. That its significance cannot be denied was most evident in the Los Angeles uprising when Black radio rallied to alleviate the tension building in the city and the nation. KJLH halted its music programming for nearly five days during the uprising by allowing listeners to call in to the station and vent their anger and frustration. All this from a small Class A Black-owned station licensed to Compton, California. During the uprising and aftermath, KJLH worked with non-profit organizations within South Central to help residents find resources and shelter. In one sense, winning a George Foster Peabody Award (nominated by a listener) validated KJLH's coverage and public service efforts during the 1992 riots. Yet changes in federal regulatory policies since the uprising continually impact the station's ability to adequately perform those types of service activities in the future.

KJLH's connection to listeners and its historical link to area churches and neighborhoods created a political dialogue that engaged local leaders, celebrities, and public officials. The historical network among the personalities, programmers, and management of Black-targeted radio stations (some of which were formerly Black-owned) became evident when KJLH's programming aired across the nation to African American and other audiences. KJLH, since its inception in the mid–1960s, has served its audience with a consistent level of commitment and community service prior to the Los Angeles uprising. KJLH's mission was clearly articulated once again in the testimony of Wonder and Slade before Chairman Kennard during the 1999 FCC hearing on localism. KJLH staff, listeners, and community leaders shared a similar perspective within the multitude of oral and written sources gathered for this study. Moreover, the significance of Black ownership is underscored by Wonder's station's membership in the National Association of Black-Owned Broadcasters and exemplified through the station's willingness to challenge mainstream news and opinions.

Prior to Wonder's purchase of KJLH, a number of church services were broadcast over the station and many community activities were promoted over its airwaves. However, since the late 1970s, and especially with the recent decline of independent African American community broadcasters in South Central, KJLH has become known as a leader in the sponsorship of civic events as well as a vehicle for community unification, as actualized through town hall meetings, fund-raising drives for the needy, community softball games, and political rallies. KJLH responded immediately after the verdict was announced in 1992, with owner and managers already prepared to their best abilities for worst case scenarios. KJLH stopped the music and embraced dialogue from its listeners, like that of many stations decades earlier when the Reverend Dr. Martin Luther King, Jr., died. The station itself became the headquarters for media organizations and a place to drop off money for the displaced and homeless. Black churches, like the First A.M.E. in South Central, provided the meeting places for voter registration rallies.

Since 1992, its depth of investigation into issues and concerns relevant to its listeners has earned national media coverage. The one undeniable piece of evidence that KJLH has increased its commitment to its audience is *Front Page*'s expansion from a 15-minute light news and call-in segment into a 90-minute program. Moreover, KJLH has been involved in numerous community outreach projects and other efforts to rebuild Los Angeles — economically and spiritually. Financial impediments and federal regulation may potentially limit KJLH's ability to service its audience in the future. The station has managed to carve a niche out of the second largest radio market in the U.S., against a backdrop of corporate radio that dominates Los Angeles. Black radio ownership increased upward from approximately 110 stations in 2001 to 138 stations in 2006, with similar upward trends of African American representation in radio news. Even with these gains, Black-owned radio represents approximately 4 percent of the more than 10,000 stations in the U.S. African Americans comprise approximately 13.5 percent of the U.S. population, and nearly 60 percent reside in metropolitan areas. The majority of urban and African American targeted formats reside in major cities. Given all this, it would seem that radio has an obligation to broadcast culturally specific programming to minority populations, and provision should be made to those groups not served with relevant content aimed to their interests and needs in rural areas as well. The significant force that drives KJLH's community service activities and discussion is its independence. It is also people like Slade — and her present and past employees — who define the character of KJLH as a station that cares and serves its community.

When KJLH broadcast its coverage of the Los Angeles riots in 1992, the story was heard live across the world via various radio stations from Europe to Japan. Nearly 25 years later, Black radio has made its mark throughout the word, with stations in Australia, Austria, Bahamas, Belgium, Bermuda, Netherlands, Czech Republic, England, France, Germany, Haiti, Iceland, Ireland, South Africa, Sweden, and Canada. It is not only the music that permeates the world, but Black radio's message of empowerment, which can be heard through lyrics, town hall meetings, and community connections. Black radio cannot simply be packaged as a one-stop format, Black culture for a price, lots of music and some semblance of community concern. KJLH's message is also one that connects Black communities across the world, creating a bond beyond broadcast activities from its annual trips to Africa to its part in raising nearly $60,000 for Hurricane Katrina relief efforts. The KJLH story is testimony to the power of culturally specific programming; it is not the first story, and hopefully it will not be the last one either.

CHAPTER 10

Keeping the Peace
Concluding Remarks

The problems of South Central are much deeper than economics and can hardly be solved by one altruistic radio station owner and his dedicated staff. Alonso (2002), in an online neighborhood newsletter, indicated that many of the social and political problems that led to the 1992 Los Angeles unrest had not been addressed one decade later: "Historians of the Black Urban experience have concentrated on New York and Chicago, tending to ignore the nation's second largest city, Los Angeles, yet the events in 1965 and 1992, the evolution of gangster rap music, the proliferation of gangs, sensational trials, and the growth of various forms of nationalism suggest that LA is a city worthy of deeper investigation." He continues, "Gerald Horne was absolutely correct and several of these phenomena continue to shape and define Los Angeles in the 21st Century, such as the Rampart police investigation, the ouster of Chief of Police Bernard Parks, a recent significant increase in violence, and the upcoming trial of Robert Blake that will prove to have many eyes on LA for several weeks, but is the potential for another riot there?"

All the same, KJLH-FM establishes a sense of community leadership by providing a means toward social, political and economic empowerment. Perhaps Slade says it best:

> I think the key is to remember we're still, I don't like to think of us as a small broadcast facility, but we are.... We don't have full-market coverage, and we're a single outlet, so our resources are limited. Our human resources, our financial resources, however, it's worth the investment. I think it's an investment in diversification and differentiation in how we separate ourselves from our competitors and solidify our core position in the community.... Did we make a dif-

ference? I'd like to think so, to what degree, I cannot say. The difference that
we made during that period was probably, we were, I think, the best communication outlet for our community. We didn't have to travel to it — we were
already there. And because of our history in the community, they know us. They
know our numbers. They know where we're located, so they can call us, and
they checked with us first before they did anything. Once they checked with
us, they locked themselves in. So I think at that moment, if I could, without
sounding like I'm bragging, I think we were the best of what we could possibly be. We used the medium to its maximum, what it was meant to be. We
were of service to our community [Slade, personal communication, 2001].

KJLH's story underscores the significance of the small-market
approach to radio broadcasting. KJLH-FM advocates the old-fashioned
roll-up your sleeves type of grassroots activism, at a time when a number
of minority-owned radio stations are slipping into the hands of mega
media corporations. To many American broadcast station licensees, radio
station ownership has not been historically about serving in the public
interest. Radio's birth, in essence, coincided with the industrial era's drive
toward automation and consolidation.

Yet, KJLH-FM is, and always has been, a community broadcaster,
and its historic mission has been one of empowerment to its listeners
through culturally specific and locally relevant programming and activism
not unlike other independent Black-owned radio stations in the U.S., the
number of which continues to dwindle amid rampant consolidation. In
today's corporate environment, it would be nearly impossible for many of
these owners to obtain a commercial radio license. Indeed, this point was
made by Radio One founder Catherine Hughes in an earlier chapter, when
she said that she would not have been able to build her radio empire within
today's consolidated marketplace.

As a community broadcaster, KJLH-FM is defined by its owner's
willingness to serve in the public interest of its audience. Much of its past
and present community service activity has been defined by the mission
of the station owner. The future of KJLH will likely be determined by
Wonder's ability to compete within an increasingly consolidated marketplace. It would seem appropriate that radio stations with a strong desire
to serve in the community interest, beyond a juke box mentality, would
be rewarded with licenses over conglomerates designed to profit from and
appeal to masses. The granting of additional watts of power to KJLH
appears to be little consolation for its extraordinary community outreach.
In many instances, efforts to promote minority ownership through regulation has been perceived or construed as promoting the special interests

of a select group of listeners, rather than as an opportunity to ensure a diversity of independent voices in the marketplace.

KJLH's employees, indeed, have been empowered through Wonder's commitment. The employees of the past and present were strong members of the community, such as Jamaal Goree's Internet talk show on LibRadio.com. Carl Nelson bought his own commercial radio station that forwarded the notion of community broadcasting to another generation of listeners. Meanwhile Jacquie Stephens, Greg Johnson, Karen Slade, and a host of supportive African American local and national leaders continue to engage KJLH listeners and fuel a community spirit in South Central through the airwaves.

Regardless of KJLH's ability to compete against the corporate giants of Los Angeles, it has demonstrated cumulatively to millions of people for three decades how radio (and media) can potentially serve community interests. The essence of KJLH is captured within the spirit of its owner and the employees who embrace Wonder's mission of community service as their own. Slade, as the driving force behind KJLH, has served Wonder well in her implementation of his mission not only because she is a loyal employee, but also because she is loyal to her audience. It is a lesson that seems lost among many corporate owners today — in essence, that to achieve loyalty and a sense of credibility among listeners it is necessary to address their needs and concerns.

The station's economic base also appears to be dependent on the future demographics of South Central Los Angeles. Even so, KJLH has already positioned itself to compete in the national arena by streaming its community service programming. The owner's status, of course, might be one of the reasons that KJLH has attracted a number of politicians, community leaders, and celebrities to station events, town hall meetings and on-air discussions. Yet, its physical location in Crenshaw also led to its pivotal role in the coverage of the unrest, assisting national and international media; and it was the station's prior commitment to its audience that resulted in its credibility within the community whereas reporters from other news organizations were sometimes beaten.

KJLH is effective on a grassroots level, and has managed to address its audience's needs for 30 years under Wonder, and more than 14 years under Hill, Jr., with relevant information and service, similar to a handful of independent Black-owned, Black-formatted heritage stations facing extinction in the near future. Slade explains, however, the challenge behind the mission:

The difficulty is keeping it current and relevant. When you have a core block of listeners that love the station and care about the station, and they support the station, their views are a certain way — it's difficult to effect change when you have the same people recycling the same thoughts with the same information, and what we try to do is put new guests and new ideas in there to keep it current and relevant, and that's probably the challenge, to keep it fresh and relevant ... on today's topics and their impact on your lifestyle today. So that's probably the main challenge, but I don't ever see it going away because it's how we keep our hand on the pulse of our community [ibid.].

A number of White-owned media companies that have bought legendary Black-owned or Black-targeted radio stations should take care to understand that they cannot purchase credibility with an audience; it is earned over time through hard work and commitment. Soundalike formats often imitate music and personalities, like when White deejays faked Black accents in the 1940s (Barlow, 1999). In the end, the listener knows who is talking to them — and who is talking at them. As Newman (1988) points out, listeners are consumers. And as African American consumers, the concept of brand loyalty may be just as significant for a radio station as it is for a bottle of soda, if not more so.

Surely, the voices on the streets of South Central Los Angeles and across the KJLH airwaves, as well as within the music of rappers like Ice-T, made an impact on the station's decision to extend its talk and issue programming. During a lecture presentation at Southern Illinois University–Carbondale, Ice-T discussed the King trial and events leading up to the verdict. He pointed out that the problems of South Central and other urban areas were not new, just often ignored by the media and the government:

> You know, they had a riot in L.A. But Black people, we called it an uprising. We didn't call it a riot. We felt that was the day we stood up against the police. Rodney King and the LAPD — totally out of pocket. I made a song about it — a year before it happened. They tried to take my head off for it, but eventually people know and show themselves [Marrow, 2001a].

In early July 2002, a decade after "Cop Killer" was pulled off the air from many radio stations across the U.S., the community of Inglewood was tested once again when Mitch Crooks, 27, caught on videotape the violent arrest of 16-year-old Donovan Jackson at a nearby gas station across the street from Crooks' Motel. KJLH, newly located in front of the Inglewood police station, opened the airwaves to its listeners for discussion. Since then, as well, other stories of KJLH being there for its listeners — from the majors to the minors — have continued its legacy of a community station.

Epilogue

E. Steven Collins on the
Soul of Black Radio

E. Steven Collins, director of urban marketing and external relations for Radio One, hosts a weekly show at WRNB-FM in Philadelphia that features national and local guests. Collins, a 30 year broadcast veteran, connects to the African American community via the airwaves and events. WRNB-FM is owned by the corporate Black-owned radio chain Radio One. When I interviewed him in 2002, he was the national sales manager of WDAS-AM/FM. He had worked with KJLH-FM to transmit its station's signal across the East Coast and then to the world. At the time, both stations were Black-owned, and now only KJLH-FM is. It seems appropriate to end with a passage from Collins, who describes the very essence, the very soul, of Black radio, which cannot be merely packaged and sold to African Americans en masse. It also must be appreciated and preserved for its historical significance (as the voice of Black America) and understood for its relevance to future generations. Collins explained:

> I kind of live it in the sense that when there is a major catastrophe, when there is a major occurrence, certainly when 911 occurred I was in another building away from my home station. The program director and general manager called me within minutes of that first plane, asked me to get back to the station and from 9:30 A.M. until about 8:30 P.M. suspended all music and I anchored solo our coverage. And the ratings for that day were equal to, if not exceeded, our regular ratings — because African American listeners wanted information, certainly had access to the All News stations and certainly television, but felt more comfortable and probably trusting of their radio station and voices and information providers that they have known for a long, long time. So, I just think urban radio will always have a different mission. It's reflected in music,

it's reflected in commentary, it's reflected in time spent listening, and I think most importantly, in the medium of choice. Of all that's available, from satellite to digital radio, to cable television and regular TV and newsprint and all the magazines, even the most sought after ones, *Essence* and *Black Enterprise* today, radio is still king, and I just think that's a big, big, big, big factor in how African Americans not just get their news and information but shape their opinions about the community and world and how they color a variety of issues.

And every once in a while — a song stylist like Marvin Gaye will sing "What's Goin' On?" And he doesn't just sing a song about Vietnam or the '70s or whatever, there's something else there that he's giving me. You know, he's saying, "Do you hear the soul of me talk to you?" And we get that, you know. Walter Hawkins has a song called, "Goin' Up Yonder." Have you ever heard that? I just urge you to go get that song. "Goin' Up Yonder" is about goin' to see the Lord, and it's supposed to be sung at funerals, but God, it's such an uplifting song — you have to just listen and feel ... I mean, what is this brother talkin' about, you now. I'm thinking of all these great, great songs, "Oh Happy Day," the Hawkins Singers, oh my God. There's just so many, "Peace Be Still," James Cleveland, oh man, I tell you. There's a song that I heard the other day by the Winans, who are still relatively new, even though they've been around about 15 years, and it's just beautifully put together; and it's just the way they harmonize, which is also an important part of American music, if you take away the electric guitar for a moment you know, and you take away the electric amps and electronic keyboards and the strings, even though we love strings, just take that away for a moment and you listen to the soulful harmony, and it could be a blue-eyed, blond guy from Tennessee's hills somewhere, but if that harmony is there, we feel the soul of whatever it is, you know, whatever it is that they're communicating — then it's more than a song. It's the soul of man.

So when Black folks hear a song that talks about what our purpose [is] and when God talks to us through songs and gives us direction in that, and it's harmonized, and the harmony is sweet and powerful, but not overpowering, you get it, you just get it. There's something so righteous about this stuff. It's like eatin' greens and puttin' hot sauce on it. You know, it's just like my grandma would make biscuits and they'd be so good by themselves and then she'd have the audacity to put butter on them, and then add homemade jelly on top, and then, wait a minute, I can't stand it anymore, you know. It's just like, whew, there's something here. And I kinda put all of this in my way of thinking in the context of our treasure, because the trauma of Black history, the middle passage, whether we're talking about slavery or we're talking about the great slave trade, or we're talking about Jim Crow, or we're talking about just being hated simply because of your color and the kinds of horrible things that happened to our parents and their parents — you need to know that reconciliation there needs to happen.

I think a lot of why there's so much Black anger today is because so many kids, youngsters, listen to rap and they try to keep it real, but they don't connect to the great greatness of Black achievement because they don't know that in spite of all the suffering and loss, our parents persevered, often in a non-violent dignified way. You know, that it wasn't Michael Jordan slamming a basketball, although that was a great achievement. Don't get me wrong, or it wasn't merely a great speech by Dr. King, or the monumental business achievements of people like Bob Johnson or Oprah Winfrey, other great achievements, you know. But it was just the simple people like Rosa Parks, who said, "I ain't gettin' up — it's about my dignity, and I ain't gettin' up. I'm not giving up my dignity here." The simple people who marched and walked on protest and said, "I'm simply not going to compromise my dignity and my humanity over somebody's view that because I'm brown-skinned I can't somehow be equal to somebody else." The hospital workers, the sanitation workers, the mothers and fathers who sacrificed dearly to provide a better life for their children, year after year after year. Those individual acts, those individuals who went to work and worked in the fields, and worked in factories; and worked [as] bus drivers, or day workers, sanitation workers; worked in the nursing homes or worked for Ms. Millie; they paused in their lives to stand up for [them]selves and for their children. And when you know that, and you go back even a generation before that you gain that reconciliation I was discussing.

I went to Senegal. I went to the Island of Goree and I saw where our people literally were held before they got on boats and sent across the shores to South America and Europe and to the Caribbean, and here to America, and I saw and felt that for a minute, what I could, and I cried, I literally cried. I was with a group of people — Ossie Davis, Walter Foundry, Dr. Leon Sullivan and Reverend James Allen, and we just cried to know just how they suffered.... Walter — asked all of us to think deeply on how it must have been for our people, and then he sang "To Dream the American Dream" ... we cried ... we felt that [the] 13 hours that we spent on an airplane ... was just horrible. By comparison, our ancestors spent months and months and months and chained in squalor with the worst conditions imaginable and didn't speak the language and many died — and it was beyond horrible. And that they were separated for all time from their families, their mothers and their children and their husbands and wives ... I mean — damn, that would have blown my mind, I would not be any good any more — but that some of those people survived all of that, you know, and somehow pulled themselves up, somehow, and learned a new language and new ways, and took beatings and were raped and were lynched, and were just treated like cattle, and all that other, other, other indignities and somehow got through eating the worst food, from the least valued animal — pork — you know, chittlins, which we laugh about today, but chittlins were the worst and somehow they made it a delicacy; and somehow through all of that they still produced the generation that gave people like me an opportunity to attend and graduate college and become an important part of our society.

When you consider from whence we've come and that this younger generation has literally no real understanding of all of that, it is a mighty long way and it's a mighty important lesson for them to learn and to know and so, you know, not to go on and on and on, I see this in my entire career, the role that this broadcast mechanism called radio has played. It's ever present. It's every day. It's exactly why these stations are important and they can never get too far away from the expectation of their audience.

And I gotta say, in all honesty, just in closing out here, corporate ownership, with all that it is, in a mix from gospel, adult contemporary, urban contemporary, jazz to a variety of other Urban variations, talk stations, talk and oldies and so forth, Black oldies and dusties, they call them — but they've done a pretty good job of leaving the stations alone and letting them be who they are, and not become homogenized in some kind of, you know, a watered down version, and I swear, I hope that that continues and that they understand, and I think they do, 'cause the reality is, mostly all of the stations are big money makers. I know [W]DAS is, I know Power 99 is here, I know [W]GCI is in Chicago, and the Mix in Detroit, KKBT in LA, WKYS in DC and WERQ in Baltimore, and WBLS in NY — these stations are huge.... And when you really look at it, it's an amazing history. I just wish that there were more archival tapes from [these stations].... I'll tell you the absolute truth, I've been offered jobs over these years. I've been here, it will be 25 years next June and I would hate to leave this for anything, and I can certainly do a lot of other things. I just dig this so much based on it being what it's been for 25 years, albeit changes, different owners, different philosophical views, corporate views, and so on and so forth. At the core of Urban radio WDAS-FM, WUSL-FM, WPHI, and WHAT still communicate every day to each listener, with a kind of, I don't want to say altruistic concern, but a genuineness about its concern, about you know, what's important out there. I think as long as it does that it will remain vital and important to not just its listeners, but to the full circle, to advertisers, to Wall Street, to the civic community, to the political and religious communities [Collins, personal communication, 2002].

Bibliography

Abelman, N., and J. Lie (1995). *Blue Dreams: Korean American and the Los Angeles Riots.* Cambridge, MA: Harvard University Press, 1995.

Adarand Constructors, Inc. v. Pena, 515 U.S. 200 (1995).

Alcalay, R., and S. Taplin (1989). "Community Health Campaigns: From Theory to Action." In R. E. Rice and C. K. Aktin (Eds.), *Public Communication Campaigns* (2nd edition) (pp. 105–129). Newbury Park, CA: Sage Publications.

Alexander, G. (2008, August 11). "One on One with Michael Baisden: The Future of Black Radio." *Black Enterprise.* Retrieved November 23, 2008, from http://www.blackenterprise.com/lifestyle/arts-culture/2008/08/11/one-on-one-with-michael-baisden/.

Alger, D. (1998). *Megamedia: How Giant Corporations Dominate Mass Media, Distort Competition, and Endanger Democracy.* Lanham, MD: Rowman & Littlefield.

Allen, R. L., M.C. Dawson, and R.E. Brown (1989). "A Schema-Based Approach to Modeling an African-American Racial Belief System." *American Political Science Review, 83,* 426–438.

Alonso, A. A. (2002). "Los Angeles Riots 10 Years Later and the Likelihood of Another Revolt." *Streetgangs.com Newsletter.* Compton, CA: Streetgangs.com. Retrieved April 29, 2002, from http://www.streetgangs.com/topics/2002/042902tenyearslater.html.

Alston, R. (1978, July). "Black Radio: Taking to the Airwaves in a Hurry." *Black Enterprise,* p. 20.

Alvarez, F. (1992, August 2). "Simi Valley, South L.A. Ball Teams Make Pitch for Unity." *Los Angeles Times,* p. 3.

Amuleru-Marshall, O. (1989/1990). "Substance Abuse Among America's Youth." *The Urban League Review, 13* (1 and 2), 93–98.

Andersen, K. (1993, November 1). "Big Mouths." *Time,* pp. 60–66.

Anderson, R.N., K.D. Kochanek, and S.L. Murphy (1997). "Report of Final Mortality Statistics, 1995." *Monthly Vital Statistics Report, 45* (11) (2 Suppl.). Retrieved June 11, 2002, from http://www.cdc.gov/ncipc/factsheets/yvfacts.htm.

Anderson, T., and W. M. Harris (1990). "A Socio-historical and Contemporary Study in African-Americans in U.S. Corporations." *Western Journal of Black Studies, 14* (3), 174–181.

Anti-Defamation League of B'Nai B'Rith vs. FCC, 403, F 2d 169 (1969).

Appleford, S. (1992, May 31). "DJ Changes the Mix with His Aggressive Show on Santa Monica-Based KCRW-FM. Michael Mixx'in Moor Shifts His Focus from Party Music to Political Messages." *Los Angeles Times* (Valley Edition), p. 79.

Arndt, R. (1991). "Phoenix, Memphis

Elections." *Nation's Cities Weekly, 14* (40), 11.

Assessment of State Minority Health Infrastructure and Capacity to Address Issues of Health Disparity (2002, January). Washington, DC: Office of Minority Health Resources Center.

Associated Press (1993, March 10). "King Calm, Confident During Testimony." *The Record* [Bergen County, NJ], p. A07.

_____. (1992, December, 13). "Taped Beating Victim Tired of Being Judged. Jackson says King Showed Sheer Character 'Calling for Peace.'" *The Plain Dealer* (Cleveland, OH), p. 8A

Baker, B. (1992, May 31). "One Stereotype That Won't Go Away. Young Black Males Find Themselves Continually Under Scrutiny from Police and Public. 'Until You're Black, Until You Get Pulled Over ... You'll Never Understand,' One Says." *Los Angeles Times,* p. 1.

Baldassare, M. (Ed.). (1994). *The Los Angeles Riots: Lessons for the Urban Future.* Boulder, CO: Westview Press.

Barabak, M. Z. (2000, October 17). "Latimes.com: For Many Blacks, Election Isn't on Radar." Retrieved January 21, 2001, from http://www.cnn.com/2000/ALLPOLITICS/stories/10/17/latimes.campaign.

Barlow, W. (1999). *Voice over: The Making of Black Radio.* Philadelphia, PA: Temple University Press.

Barrett, D. (1999). "LARP (Los Angeles Radio People) Get Spring Report Card." LARADIO.COM Archives, July 16–31, 1999. Retrieved April 4, 2006, available at http://www.laradio.com/julyb99.htm.

Bates, K. G. (2002). "The Changing Face of Los Angeles: Ten Years On, Black L.A. Isn't the Same" (audio). Retrieved April 27, 2002, from http://www.npr.org/new.

BBA: Black Broadcasters Alliance (1997). "Minority Commercial Broadcast Ownership Overview," pp. 1–5. First Published 1997; Retrieved June 11,

2002, from http://www.thebba.org/NTIA.html.

Beauregard, R. A. (1990). "Tenacious Inequalities, Politics and Race in Philadelphia." *Urban Affairs Quarterly, 25* (3), 420–434.

Beresteanu, A., and P.B. Ellickson (2007). *Minority and Female Ownership in Media Enterprises.* Duke University. Washington DC: FCC Documents. Retrieved November 19, 2008, from http://hraunfoss.fcc.gov/edocs_public/attachmatch/DA-07-3470A8.pdf.

Berry, S., and J. Waldfogel (2001). "Do Mergers Increase Product Variety? Evidence from Radio Broadcasting." *The Quarterly Journal of Economics,* August 2001, 1009–1025.

Best, J. A. (1989). "Intervention Perspectives on School Health Promotion Research." *Health Education Quarterly, 16* (2), 299–306.

Bingham, C. (1992). "City of the Stars Under Siege and Occupation." *Los Angeles Sentinel.* [KJLH-FM file.]

Birk, T. A., and P. Johnson (1993, April 7). "Community Service: A Comparative Analysis of African-American Gospel Radio to Other Black/Urban Formats." Presented at the Radio Division (sponsored by the *Journal of Radio Studies*), Popular Culture Association, New Orleans, LA.

Black American Study. (2008). "NY: Radio One." Retrieved November 21, 2008, from http://www.blackamericastudy.com.

"Black Consumer: Myths Shattered." *Radio & Records,* June 21, 1991, p. 20.

"Black FCC Chairman Kennard's Priority." (2001). Federal Communication News. Adversity.Net, Inc. Silver Spring, MD. Retrieved December 15, 2008, from http://www.adversity.net/fed_stats/fednews_FCC.htm.

"Black International Radio." (2008). Retrieved November 26, 2008, from http://www.africanamericans.com/BlackRadio.htm

"Black Radio: On a High Wire with No

Net." *Broadcasting,* August 31, 1970, pp. 44–50.

Black Radio Today. (1996). New York: Arbitron.

Black Radio Today. (2003). New York: Arbitron. Retrieved November 11, 2008, from http://www.arbitron.com/NEWS ROOM/archive/07_14_03_a.htm.

Black World Report. (2001) Newswire. Retrieved November 21, 2008, from http://www.nnpa.org/nnpanewsite/newswire/5-21-01/RadioShow.txt.

Blackwell, L. S. (1978). *The Wings of the Dove: The Story of Gospel Music in America.* Norfolk, VA: Donning.

Bloomquist, R. (1991, November 29). "The Lack of Black Talkers: Waiting for Jackie Robinson." *Radio & Records,* p. 40.

Blumhofer, Edith L. (1993). *Aimee Semple McPherson: Everybody's Sister.* Grand Rapids, MI: William B. Eerdmans.

Bolden, J. (1992, September 17). "Briseno Says: 'It's Time to Clear Record.'" *Los Angeles Sentinel.* [KJLH-FM file].

Boyer, E. J. (1988, October 12). "Jackson Makes Last-Minute Bid on Radio to Register New Voters." *Los Angeles Times,* p.15.

Boyer, H. C. (1995). *How Sweet the Sound: The Golden Age of Gospel.* Washington, DC: Elliott & Clark.

Brandenburg vs. Ohio, 395, U.S. 444 (1969).

Braverman, H. (1974). *Labor and Monopoly Capital: The Degradation of Work in the Twentieth Century.* New York: Monthly Review Press.

Breedon, R. (1997). *The End of a Decade with WPGC. Expansions with Robin Breedon.* [newsletter.] Mitchellville, MD: All Soaring On Vision, Inc.

Briggs, J. (2002, April). "The Fire Last Time." *The Source,* pp. 120–124

"Broadcast Stations in Los Angeles, Miami Win Peabody Awards." *St. Louis Post-Dispatch,* April 4, 1993, p. 10A.

Broadcasting Yearbook. (1991). Washington, DC: Times/Mirror, Broadcasting Publications Inc.

Broadcasting Yearbook. (1992). Washington, DC: Times/Mirror, Broadcasting Publications Inc.

Broadcasting Yearbook. (1993). Washington, DC: Times/Mirror, Broadcasting Publications Inc.

Brosowsky, J. M. (2002). "Number One with a Bullet." *Business Forward.* Retrieved May 20, 2002, from http://www.bizforward.com.

Brown, J. D., K. W. Childers, K. E. Bauman, and G. G. Koch (1990, February). "The Influence of New Media and Family Structure on Young Adolescents' Television and Radio Use." *Communication Research, 17* (1), 65–82.

Brown, F., Jr. (1990). "African American Broadcaster: The Link to Their Communities." *The Pulse of Radio: Radio's Management Weekly, 5* (46), 22–24.

Bruno, T. J. (1999, May). "State of the Radio Industry." In *Changes, Challenges, and Charting New Courses: Minority Commercial Broadcast Ownership in the United States* [2001] Washington, DC: National Telecommunications and Information Administration, U.S. Department of Commerce.

Bryant, C., B. Collette, W. Green, S. L. Isoardi, J. Kelson, H. Tapscott, G. Wilson, and M. Young (1998). *Central Avenue Sounds.* Berkeley, CA: University of California Press.

Buffa, A. (2000). "Broadcast Blackout." *SFBG News:* San Francisco: Retrieved September 20, 2000, from http://www.sfbg.com/News/34/51/51radrac.html, pp. 1–2.

Bunting, E., and D. Diaz (1999). *Smoky Night.* San Diego, CA: Harcourt.

Bunzel, R. E. (1992, January 13). "AMs Take Five Top Spots in Arbitron." *Broadcasting,* pp. 84–85.

Burd, G. (1979). "What is Community?" *Grassroots Editor, 20,* 3–5.

Burke, K. (1969). *The Grammar of Motives.* Berkley: University of California Press.

Burroughs, T. S. (2002). "Charlotta Bass and the California Eagle." *Black PressUSA.com.* The Black Press of

America: National Newspaper Publishers Association. Retrieved July 1, 2002, from http://blackpressusa.com (history/timeline).

CAAM. (2007). KJLH Profile. California African-American Museum. Retrieved November 13, 2008, from http://www.caam.ca.gov/gala_2008/honorees/pages/gala_kjlh.htm.

Caffey, R. (1992, February 11). Personal communication. In P. Johnson (2003), *The Community Role of Black-Owned KJLH-FM During the 1992 Los Angeles Civil Uprising & 10 Years Later in an Era of Media Consolidation: Listening Through the Window.* Ph.D., diss., Southern Illinois University Carbondale.

Caldwell, E. (1968, April 8). "Mrs. King to March in Husband's Place in Memphis Today." *The New York Times,* p. 1.

Calhoun, C. (1992*). Habermas and the public sphere.* Cambridge, MA: MIT Press.

_____. (1994). *Introduction to Social Theory and the Politics of Identity.* Oxford, London: Blackwell.

Cannon, L. (1999). *Official Negligence: How Rodney King and the Riots Changed Los Angeles and the LAPD.* Boulder, CO: Westview Press.

Catania, S. (1996, October 4). "Maxine in Motion: Waters Vows to Make Crack Conspirators Pay." *LA Weekly,* p. 12.

Cantor, L. (1992). *Wheelin' on the Beale.* New York: Pharos Books.

Carr, E. (1993, March 14). "South KJLH Gives Youths On-The-Air Training." *Los Angeles Times,* p. 7.

Castuera, I. (Ed.) (1992). *Dreams on Fire, Embers of Hope: Los Angeles After the Riots.* Atlanta, GA: Chalice Press.

"Celebs Pitch In to Help Riot Victims." *USA Today,* May 4, 1992, p. 2D.

Chambers, S. (1997). *Stan Chambers: News at 10.* Los Angeles: Stan Chambers.

Chan, C. (2002, April 2002). "Sermon Cites Hope." *Los Angeles Times* [Dailynews.com], p. 1.

Chang, E. T., and J. Diaz-Veizades (1999). *Ethnic Peace in the American City: Building Community in Los Angeles and Beyond.* New York: New York University Press.

Chapman, W. (1991, January). "The Illinois Experience: State Grants to Improve Schools' Parent Involvement." *Phi Delta Kappan,* pp. 355–357.

Chelimsky, E., and W. R. Shadish (1997). *Evaluation for the 21st Century.* Thousand Oaks, CA: Sage Publications.

Chipty, T. (2007). *FCC Media Ownership Study #5: Station Ownership and Programming in Radio.* CRA International, Inc. Washington DC: FCC Documents. Retrieved November 19, 2008, available from http://hraunfoss.fcc.gov/edocs_public/attachmatch/DA-07-3470A6.pdf.

Chomsky, N. (1992). *Deterring Democracy.* New York: Farrar, Straus & Giroux.

"City under Siege." *USA Today,* May 1–3 1992, p. 1.

"Clinton Praises Radio Curbs on Violent Lyrics." *Radio & Records,* December 17, 1993, p. 1.

Cobo, L. (1991, January 7). "Philly Station Giving Power to the People." *Broadcasting,* p. 89. Cockburn, A. (1995). "Rebel Radio Versus the F.C.C." *Nation, 260* (7), 228.

Cohen, J., and N. Solomon (1994, November 4). "Spotlight Finally Shines on White Hate Radio." *Media Beat,* p. 1. Retrieved January 7, 2000, from http://www.fair.org/media-beat/941103.html.

Collins, E. S. (1993, June 24 and July 25). Personal communication. In P. Johnson (2003), *The Community Role Of Black-Owned KJLH-FM During the 1992 Los Angeles Civil Uprising & 10 Years Later in an Era of Media Consolidation: Listening Through the Window.* Ph.D., diss., Southern Illinois University Carbondale.

_____. (2002, August 24). Personal communication. In (P. Johnson, 2003), *The Community Role Of Black-Owned*

KJLH-FM During the 1992 Los Angeles Civil Uprising & 10 Years Later in an Era of Media Consolidation: Listening Through the Window. Ph.D., diss., Southern Illinois University Carbondale.

"Coming Through the Front Door of Ownership." *Broadcasting,* October 30, 1972, pp. 25–27.

Cosper, A. (2007). "Los Angeles Radio History." Retrieved November 14, 2008, from http://www.tangentsunset.com/laradiohistory.htm.

Cotton, P. (1992). "Medical News & Perspectives: Health Care Injustice Fuels Rage Riots." *JAMA: The Journal of the American Medical Association, 267* (20), 2719.

"Crisis in the LAPD: The Rodney King Case." *Los Angeles Times,* April 5, 1991, p. 2.

Curry, G. E. (2007). "FCC Commissioner: Declining Black Media Ownership is a 'National Disgrace.'" *NNPA News Report.* The National Newspaper Publishers Association. Retrieved November 19, 2008, from http://news.ncmonline.com/news/view_article.html?article_id=73c4c4e5c34d18d4c77770bdeb3a33a4.

Czarniawska, B. (1998). *A Narrative Approach to Organization Studies.* Thousand Oaks, CA: Sage Publications.

Dates, J. L., and W. Barlow (1993). *Split Image: African Americans in the Mass Media.* Washington, DC: Howard University Press.

Davis, A., B. B. Gardner, and M. R. Gardner (1941). *Deep South.* The University of Chicago Press.

Davis, J., and O. Gandy, Jr. (1999). "Racial Identity and Media Orientation: Exploring the Nature of Constraint." *Journal of Black Studies, 29* (3), 367–397.

Davis Broadcasting Newsletter. (Fall/Winter 1991). Columbus, GA: WOKS-AM & WFXE-FM.

Davison, W. P. (1988). "Mass Media, Civic Organizations and Street Gossip: How Communication Affects the Quality of Life in an Urban Neighborhood" [working paper]. New York: Gannett Center for Media Studies.

"The Dawn of African Independent Radio." (1993). *InteRadio, 5* (3), 1, 10.

Dawson, J., and T. Guizar (2000). "Los Angeles' Influences on American Music." *Los Angeles Music Week* (*LAMW*). Retrieved April 12, 2001, from http://www.lamusic2000.com.

Dawson, N. (1994a). "A Black Counterpublic? Economic Earthquakes, Racial Agenda(s), and Black Politics." *Public Culture, 7 (1),* 195–224.

_____. (1994b). *Behind the Mule: Race and Class in African-American Politics.* Princeton, NJ: Princeton University Press.

"Day of Music Draws Thousands to Cooper Creek." (1991). *Columbus Ledger-Enquirer.* Duplicate, Columbus, OH: WOKS-AM/WFXE-FM file.

Denzin, N. K., and Y. S. Lincoln (Eds.) (2000). *Handbook of Qualitative Research.* Thousand Oaks, CA: Sage Publications.

Devall, C. (2002). "From the Ashes" (radio series). *Marketplace.* (Aired on National Public Radio, April 23–April 29, 2002).

Di Paola, J. (2001). "Dial M for Mystik." *CityLink Online* (Ft. Lauderdale, FL). Retrieved October 3, 2001, from http://citylinkonline.com (Cover story, p. 1).

"Did you know..." (2001). *Radio Facts.* Washington, DC: National Association of Broadcasters. Retrieved April 12, 2001, from http://www.nab.org/radio/radfacts.asp.

Dizard, W. P., Jr. (1989). *The Coming Age: An Overview of Technology, Economics, and Politics.* New York: Longman.

Dominick, J. R., B. L. Sherman, and G. A. Copeland (1993). *Broadcasting/Cable and Beyond: An Introduction to Modern Electronic Media* (2nd ed). New York: McGraw Hill.

Douglas, P. (1992, May 2). "Voice of Calm Amid Chaos." *Press-Telegram,* p. A6.

Du Brow, R. (1993, April 18). "Ringmasters Keep Tight Rein on News Circus

Media: Coverage is Immediate, Reflects the Emotional Relief and Generally Goes Smoothly. By Noon, the Stations Are Back to Normal Broadcasting." *Los Angeles Times*, p. 6.

Duncan, J. (1992, June). *American Radio: Sixteenth Anniversary Issue (1976–1992): A Statistical History*. Indianapolis, IN: Duncan's American Radio.

_____. (1990). *American Radio, 15*. Indianapolis, IN: Duncan's American Radio.

_____. (1993). *Duncan's Radio Market Guide*. Indianapolis, IN: Duncan's American Radio.

_____. (1983) *Radio in the United States: 1976–1982: A Statistical History*. Duncan Media Enterprises: Kalamazoo, MI.

Dungee, R. (1995). "Celebrity Softball Game a Benefit for the Negro Leagues Pension Fund." *Los Angeles Sentinel*, September 21, 1995, p. B1.

Eardley, L., and J. Berger (1994, January 4). "Fired DJs to go Back on Air Here." *St. Louis Post-Dispatch*, p. 1.

Erlandson, D. A., E. L. Harris, B. L. Skipper, and S. D. Allen. *Doing Naturalistic Inquiry*. Newbury Park, CA: Sage Publications.

Erskine, N. L. (1991–1992, Winter/Spring). "King and the Black Church." *The Journal of Religious Thought, 48*, 9–17.

EuroWeb. (2006). "'I've Stopped Being Afraid of What I Say and Do with Black Radio' (Pt.1): Gary Taylor Explains His Letter to Black Radio." Black Web Portal. Retrieved November 11, 2008, from http://www.black webportal.com/wire/DA.cfm?Article ID=2787.

Fabrikant, G. (1994, May 31). Slow gains by minority broadcasters, *New York Times*, p. D1.

Facts on Black youth, violence, & crime. (2002). Washington, DC: Children's Defense Fund Action Council.

Farhi, P. (1999, January 13). Advertisers avoiding minority radio. FCC study cites Washington market for Black and Hispanic "dictates." *Washington Post*, p. F01.

Farrar, R. T. (1988). *Mass communication: An introduction to the field*. St. Paul, MN: West Press.

Fedler, F. (1973, Summer). The media and minority groups: A study of adequacy of access. *Journalism Quarterly, 50* (2), 109–117.

Federal Communications Commission (2004, July 14). Ownership Report for 2003, Minority Ownership. Accessed April 24, 2006, available at: http://www.fcc.gov/ownership/owner_minor _2003.pdf

Federal Communications Commission (1969). 17 F.C.C.2d 844. Retrieved November 19, 2008, available from http://www.uiowa.edu/~cyberlaw/ FCCOps/1969/17F2–844.htm.

Federal Communications Commission (2002, March 27). Comments of the National Association of Black-Owned Broadcasters, Inc. Rules and Policies Concerning Multiple Ownership of Radio Broadcast Stations in Local Markets. MM Docket No. 01–317.

Federal Communications Commission (2000, April 13). "FCC Chairman Responds To House Vote To Cut The Number Of Community Radio Stations by 80%" [News release]. Washington DC: Federal Communications Commission

Federal Communications Commission (1998, November 20). FCC Notice of Proposed Rule Making. MM Docket No. 98–204; MM Docket No. 96–16.

_____. (1992, September 4). Revision of Radio Rules and Policies. Memorandum Opinion and Order and Further Notice of Proposed Rulemaking, 7 FCC 6387 R 9.

"FCC Chief Wants Racial Quotas for Media Ownership." (1999) Federal Communication News. Adversity.Net, Inc. Silver Spring, MD. Retrieved December 15, 2008, from http://www. adversity.net/fed_stats/fednews_FCC. htm.

Federal Communications Commission Proceeding. (1999, February 12). FCC en banc: Local Broadcasting Ownership. Washington, DC: Federal Communications Commission. Available at: www.fcc.gov.

Feldman, M. S. (1995). *Strategies for Interpreting Qualitative Data.* Thousand Oaks, CA: Sage Publications.

Ferretti, F. (1970). The White Captivity of Black Radio. *Columbia Journalism Review, 9* (2), 35–39.

Fife, M. (1987). "Promoting Racial Diversity in U.S. Broadcasting: Federal Policies Versus Social Realities." *Media, Culture and Society 9,* 481–504.

Fingerhut, L. A., D. D. Ingram, and J. J. Feldman (1992). Firearm and Nonfirearm Homicide Among Persons 15 Through 19 Years of Age. *JAMA: The Journal of the American Medical Association, 267* (22), 3048–3053.

Foote, D., and A. Murr (2002, May 6). "Back on the Block." *Newsweek,* pp. 42–47.

Fornatale, P., and J. E. Mills (1980). *Radio in the Television Age.* Woodstock, NY: The Overlook Press.

Foster, L. S. (1988). "Avenues for Black Political Mobilization: The Presidential Campaign of Reverend Jesse Jackson." In L. Morris (Eds.), *The Social and Political Implications of the 1984 Jesse Jackson Presidential Campaign* (pp. 204–213). New York: Praeger.

Freeman, M. (1992, May 4). "L.A.'s Local News Takes to the Streets." *Broadcasting,* p. 11.

Front Page (1992a, April 29). Transcripts. KJLH-FM: Compton, CA.

Front Page (1992b, April 30). Transcripts. KJLH-FM: Compton, CA.

Front Page (1992c, May 1). Transcripts. KJLH-FM: Compton, CA.

Front Page (1992d, May 2). Transcripts. KJLH-FM: Compton, CA.

Front Page (2002a, January 28). Transcripts. KJLH-FM: Compton, CA.

Front Page (2002b, April 29). Transcripts. KJLH-FM: Compton, CA.

Gale, D. E. (1996). *Understanding Urban Unrest: From Reverend King to Rodney King.* Thousand Oaks, CA: Sage Publications.

Gandy, O., Jr. (1996). "If It Weren't For Bad Luck. Framing Stories Of Racially Comparative Risk." In V.T. Berry and C. L. Manning-Miller (Eds.), *Mediated Messages and African-American Culture: Contemporary Issues* (pp. 55–75). Thousand Oaks, CA: Sage.

Gandy, O. H., Jr. (2001, May). "Racial Identity, Media Use, And Social Construction Of Risk Among African Americans." *Journal of Black Studies, 31* (5), 600–618.

Garland, P. (1988). "The Black Press: Down but Not Out." In R. E. Hiebert & C. Reuss (Eds.), *Impact of Media* (pp. 337–339). New York: Longman.

Generation Rap. (1993). KPRS-FM: Kansas City, KS.

Gentzkow, M., and J. M. Shapiro (2006). "Media Bias and Reputation." *Journal of Political Economy, 114* (2), 280–316.

George, N. (1988). *The Death of Rhythm & Blues.* New York: Pantheon Books.

Ghee, K. L. (1990). "Enhancing Educational Achievement Through Awareness in Young Black Males." *The Western Journal of Black Studies, 14* (2), 77–89.

Gilliam, D. (1993, March). "Editorial Content. Is It Fair? Is It Accurate?" *Kerner Plus 25: A Call to Action* (pp. 18–20). Oakland, CA: Unity '94.

Gilje, Paul A. (1996). *Rioting in America.* Bloomington: Indiana University Press.

Ginsberg, S. (1994, January 10). "Tune-Out of Anti-Social Rap May Hit Chord on Radio Stations' Bottom Line." *Los Angeles Business Journal, 16* (1), 9.

Gold, J. (1989, December 3). "Ice-T Raps Himself In First Amendment. Ice-T: "Freedom Of Speech ... Just Watch What You Say." *Los Angeles Times,* p. 66.

Goree, J. (2002, January 28). Personal communication. In (P. Johnson, 2003), *The Community Role of Black-Owned KJLH-FM During the 1992 Los Angeles Civil Uprising & 10 Years Later in an Era of Media Consolidation: Listening Through the Window.* Ph.D., diss., Southern Illinois University Carbondale.

"Groups to Play Softball to Ease Racial Tensions." *San Francisco Chronicle,* June 22, 1992, pp. A14.

Gooding-Williams, R. (1993). *Reading Rodney King: Reading Urban Uprising.* New York: Routledge.

Gregory, D. (2002, May 13). Personal communication. In (P. Johnson, 2003), *The Community Role of Black-Owned KJLH-FM During the 1992 Los Angeles Civil Uprising & 10 Years Later in an Era of Media Consolidation: Listening Through the Window.* Ph.D., diss., Southern Illinois University Carbondale.

Gronau, K. (2001). "Stevie Wonder Takes KJLH to Higher Ground." *Radio Guide Magazine.* Retrieved April 18, 2001, from http://www.radioguide.com, pp. 1–5.

Gwalthney, J. L. (1981). *Drylongso: Self Portrait of Black America.* New York: Vintage Books.

Haederle, M,. and C. Heredia (1993). "When 'Enlightened' People Make Racist Remarks." *Los Angeles Times* (Home Edition), May 27, 1993, p. 2.

Hale-Benson, J. E. (1986). *Black Children: Their Roots, Culture, and Learning Styles.* Baltimore, MD: John Hopkins University Press.

Halonen, D. (1992, February 24). "Court Axes FCC's Gender Policy." *Electronic Media,* p. 4.

Halper, D. (2004). "Hats Off to a Happy Cowboy: A Salute to Herb Jeffries." Retrieved November 16, 2008, from http://www.bjmjr.net/jeffries/salute2.htm.

Hammond IV, A. S. (1999). "Measuring the Nexus: The Relationship Between Minority Ownership and Broadcast Diversity After Metro Broadcasting." *Federal Communications Law Journal, 51* (3), 627–637.

Hangen, T. J. (2002). *Redeeming the Dial: Radio, Religion, and Popular Culture in America.* Chapel Hill: University of North Carolina Press.

Hare, B. R. (1988–1989, Summer/Winter). "African-American Youth at Risk." *The Urban League. Review, 12* (1 and 2), 25–28.

Harvey, W. B., P. F. Bitting, and T. L. Robinson (1989–1990, Summer/Winter). "Between a Rock And a Hard Place: Drugs and Schools in African-American Communities." *The Urban League Review, 13* (1 and 2), pp. 113–128.

Hausman, C., L. M. O'Donnell, and P. Benoit (2002). *Modern Radio Production: Production, Programming and Performance.* Belmont, CA: Wadsworth

Hawkins, S. (2000, June 23). "Issues and Answers on 'Front Page.'" *Los Angeles Times: Our Times.* Retrieved February 20, 2001, from http://www.kjlhradio.com/frontpage/our_times.html.

Head, S. W., and C. H. Sterling. *Broadcasting in America: A Survey of Electronic Media.* Boston, MA: Houghton Mifflin, 1956; 6th edition, 1990.

Head, S. W., C. H. Sterling, and L. B. Scholfield (1994). *Broadcasting in America,* 7th ed. Boston, MA: Houghton Mifflin.

Heckler, M. M. (1985). *Report of the Secretary's Task Force on Black & Minority Health, Volume I: Executive Summary.* Washington, DC: U.S. Department of Health and Human Services.

_____. (1986). *Report of the Secretary's Task Force on Black & Minority Health, Volume IV: Homicide, Suicide, and Unintentional Injuries.* Washington, DC: U.S. Department of Health and Human Services.

"Herenton Elected First Black Mayor of Memphis." *Jet,* 81, October 21, 1991, p. 4.

Hick, V. (1992). "Radio Response, Listeners Call in on LA Verdict." *St. Louis Post-Dispatch,* May 1, 1992, 25A.

Hill, K. (1990). "Politics and Participation in the Black Church." *Western Journal of Black Studies, 14* (2), 123–135.

Hilliard III, A. G. (1987–1988/Summer/Winter). "Reintegration for Education: Black Community Involvement with Black Students in Schools." *The Urban League Review, 11* (1 & 2), 200–208.

Hilmes, M. (1990). *Hollywood and Broadcasting : From Radio to Cable.* Bloomington: University of Illinois Press.

Hochman, S. (1992, August 30). "Pop Eye." *Los Angeles Times,* p. 63.

Holland, B. (1999, February 24). "Removal of Radio/TV Ownership Rules Assessed." *Billboard, 111* (9), 7, 86.

Hollenweger, W. J. (1997). *Pentecostalism: Origins and Developments Worldwide.* Peabody, MA: Hendrickson.

"Homicide Among Young Black Males — United States, 1978–1987." (1991). *JAMA: The Journal of the American Medical Association, 265* (2), 183–184.

Hopkins, R. B. (n.d.) *Growth of the Black Community in Los Angeles from 1890–1930.* Ph.D., diss., University of California, Santa Barbara: UCLA Oral History Program.

Horne, G. (1997). *Fire This Time: The Watts Uprising and the 1960s.* New York: Da Capo Press, Inc.

Hoover, D. W. (1970). "Black History" (pp. 32–49). In M. Ballard (Ed.), *New Movements in the Study and Teaching of History.* Bloomington: Indiana University Press.

Horowitz, R. (1990). "Sociological Perspectives on Gangs: Conflicting Definitions and Concepts." In C. R. Huff (Ed.), *Gangs in America* (pp. 37–54). Newbury Park, CA: Sage Publications.

Hughes, L., and A. Bontemps (Eds.) (1983). *Book of Negro Folklore.* New York: Dodd, Mead and Company.

Hunt, D. M. (1997). *Screening the Los Angeles 'Riots': Race, Seeing, and Resistance.* Cambridge, UK: Cambridge University Press.

Hurston, Z. N. (1983). *Tell My Horse.* Helena, MT: Bedrock Books.

Hutchinson, E. O. (1999). "Endangered Black Radio." *Black Journalism Review Online.* Washington, DC: Retrieved May 2, 2001, from http://www.black-journalism.com/news.htm, pp. 1–2.

Hutton, F. (1992). "Social Morality in the Antebellum Black Press." *Journal of Popular Culture, 26* (2), 71–84.

Iving, L. (1999). "The Impact of Convergence in the Media." Conference of Broadcast, Cable, and Media Industry Union. National Telecommunications and Information Administration: U.S. Department of Commerce (Washington, DC). Retrieved June 11, 2001, from http://www.ntia.doc.gov/ntiahome/speeches/bcmiu41999.htm.

Ivy Planning Group LLC. (2000, December). *Whose Spectrum Is It Anyway? Historical Study of Market Entry Barriers, Discrimination and Changes in Broadcast and Wireless Licensing—1950 to Present.* Prepared for the Office of General Counsel. Washington, DC: Federal Communications Commission.

Jackson, H. (1992, Summer). "We Weren't Listening: By Not Tapping Into Rap's Message of Violence, Media Failed to Prepare Public for Rampage." *Nieman Reports, 46* (2), 15–16.

Jackson, J., Sr. (2002a). "One Thousand Churches." Retrieved September 27, 2002, from http:// www.10000churchesconnected.org.

Jackson, J., Sr. (2002b). "Rainbow Push Coalition." Retrieved September 27, 2002, from http://www.rainbowpush.org [History].

Jacob, J. E. (1987–1988/Summer/Winter). "Taking the Initiative in Education: The National Urban League Agenda." *The Urban League Review, 11* (1 & 2), 13–17.

Janowitz, M. (1952). *The Community Press in an Urban Setting.* Chicago: University of Chicago Press.

Jenkins, D. (1972). *Job Power: Blue and White Collar Democracy.* Garden City, NY: Doubleday.

Jet National Report. (2008, August 4) Press Release. Retrieved November 18, 2008, from http://www.blackamericastudy.com/press/RadioOnePDF8.13.08.pdf.

Jeter, J. P. (1981). *A Comparative Analysis of the Programming Practices of Black-Owned Black-Oriented Radio Stations and White-Owned Black-Oriented Radio Stations.* Ph.D. diss., University of Wisconsin.

"John L. Hill, Jr." (1998). Obituary. Angelus Funeral Home, Inc. (2006). Los Angeles, LA. Retrieved July 19, 2006, from http://www.for-success.com/angelus/arhome.html.

Johnson, C. S. (1941). *Growing Up in the Black belt: Negro Youth in the Rural South*. New York: Schocken Books.

Johnson, G. (2002, January 28). Personal communication: Interview. KJLH-FM: Compton, CA.

Johnson, P. (1995, November). "Black Radio's Role In Sports Promotion: Sports, Scholarships, and Station Sponsorships." *Journal of Sport and Social Issues, 19* (4), 397–414.

Johnson, P. (1992). Black/urban radio is in touch with the inner city: What can educators learn from this popular medium? *Education and Urban Society, (24)* 4, 508–518.

_____. (2003). *The Community Role of Black-Owned KJLH-FM During the 1992 Los Angeles Civil Uprising & 10 Years Later in an Era of Media Consolidation: Listening Through the Window.* Ph.D., diss., Southern Illinois University Carbondale.

Johnson, P., and T. A. Birk (1993a). "Black/Urban Radio's Community Service Mission: Participation in Education Issues and Events." *Equity and Excellence in Education, 26* (2), 41–47.

_____. (1992, October 9). "Gospel Radio and the African-American Church, Partnerships in Community Service." Presented at the Religion and American Culture, Midwest Popular Culture Association/American Culture Conference in Indianapolis, IN.

_____. (1996). "Pride and Profit in Black Radio Promotions." In V.T.. Berry and C. L. Manning-Miller (Eds.), *Mediated Messages and African-American Culture: Contemporary Issues* (pp. 218–240). Thousand Oaks, CA: Sage Publications.

_____. (1993b). "The Role of African-American Owned Radio in Health Promotion: Community Projects Targeting Young African-American Males." *Urban League Review, 16* (2), 85–93.

Julian Bond, 69 FCC 2d 943 (1978).

Keith, M. C. (1987). *Radio Programming: Consultancy And Formatics*. Focal Press: Boston.

Keith, M. C., and J. M. Krause (2000). *The Radio Station* (5th edition). Stoneham, MA: Butterworth.

Kennard, W. (2002, January 14). *Statement on Martin Luther King, Jr.*, pp. 1–2. Washington, DC: Federal Communications Commission. Retrieved May 29, 2002, from http://www.fcc.gov

Kennedy, T. R. (1980). *You Gotta Deal With It*. New York: Oxford University Press.

"KGFJ Celebrates Birthday." (1992, July 10). *Radio & Records*, p. 32.

"King is 'Tired' of Being Judged." *Buffalo News* [Final Edition], December 13, 1992, p. A12.

KJLH. (2008). Web site. Retrieved November 26, 2008, from http://www.kjlhradio.com.

"KJLH, Black Parents to Host Adoption Radio-Thon." *Los Angeles Sentinel*, March 21, 1991, p. A3.

"KJLH Communicates Unity." (1993, January). *The L. A. Watts*, p. 18.

Kleiman, H. (1991). "Content Diversity and the FCC's City and Gender Licensing Policies." *Journal of Broadcasting & Electronic Media, 35*(4), 411–429.

Koch, E. (2000). "Pioneer DJ Gibson, Who Helped Many to Stardom, Dies." *Las Vegas Sun*. Accessed April 4, 2006, available at http://www.lasvegassun.com/sunbin/stories/obits/2000/feb/01/509788857.html.

KMJM Listener. Phone call, April 30, 1992. St. Louis, MO: KJLH-FM

KMJM Newscast. (1992, April 30). St. Louis, MO: KMJM-FM.

KMJM Transcript. (1992, April 30). St. Louis, MO: KMJM-FM.

Krech III, S. (1981). *Praise The Bridge That Carries You Over: The Life of Joseph L. Sutton*. Cambridge, MA: Schenkman.

Krugman, D. M., and L. E. Reid. (1980, Summer). "The Public Interest as

Defined by FCC Policy Makers." *Journal of Broadcasting*, pp. 1–16.

"L.A. Enjoys Calm after Denny Trial Series." *St. Petersburg Times* (City Edition), October 22, 1993, p. 4A.

L.B. Report. (2004). "Hunter Hancock Dies, 1950s-era DJ Heard on LB Station (and Others) Broke Taboos, Showed Mainstream Appeal Of R&B Music." LBReport.com. Retrieved November 13, 2008, from http://www.lbreport.com/news/aug04/hunter.htm.

Lacey, M., and S. Hubler (1992, April 30). "Rioters Set Fires, Loot Stores; 4 Reported Dead." *Los Angeles Times*, pp. 1, A21.

Langlois, S. (1993, May 12–18). "Shocking Behavior." *The Riverfront Times*, p. 6.

Lasar, M. (2007). "Black Broadcasters Call FCC Media Ownership Proceeding 'Grossly Deficient.'" Retrieved November 19, 2008, from http://www.lasarletter.net/drupal/node/307

Lazarsfeld, P. F., and H. Dinerman (1979). "Research for Action." In P. F. Lazarsfeld & F. N. Stanton (Eds.), *Communication Research 1948–1949* (pp. 73–108). New York: Arno Press.

Lee, J. (2002, May). "Of Riots and Rebellion." *Vibe*, pp. 125–128.

"Legacy of the Riots: 1992–2002; Charting the Hours of Chaos." *Los Angeles Times*, April 24, 2002, pp. 1–8. Retrieved April 26, 2002, from http://www.latimes.com.

Legette, C. (1994). "Key Strategies for Smart Marketing to African Americans." *Public Relations Journal, 50* (7), 38–39.

Leigh, A. (1992, May 15). "KJLH Shines as Crisis Heartbeat," pp. 1, 7. [KJLH-FM file.]

Letter to Lonnie King, 36 FCC 2d 636 (1972).

Life & Times Transcript. (2003, August 8). *Life & Times*, Program LC030808. Los Angeles: KCET-TV. Accessed at April 4, 2006, available at http://www.kcet.org/lifeandtimes/archives/200308/20030808.php.

Lincoln, Y., and E. G. Guba (1985). *Naturalistic inquiry: The Paradigm Revolution*. Beverly Hills, CA: Sage Publications.

_____. (1995). *Naturalistic inquiry: The Paradigm Revolution*. Beverly Hills, CA: Sage Publications.

Logan, J. (1989, January 31). "Why Radio Plays What It Plays." *The Philadelphia Inquirer*, p. 1F. Lornell, K. (1988). *Happy in the Service of the Lord: Afro-American, Gospel Quartets in Memphis*. Urbana and Chicago: University of Illinois Press.

Love, W. (1991a, January 25). "A Profile in Commitment." *Radio & Records*, pp. 36, 62.

_____. (1991b, May 10). "Cool Fun in the Summertime." *Radio & Records*, p. 8.

_____. (1990, October 5). "Ganging Up on Gangs: Radio Fights Crime." *Radio & Records*, p. 50.

_____. (1992a, July 10). "KGFJ Celebrates Birthday." *Radio & Records*, p. 32.

_____. (1991c, December 20). "The Year in Review." *Radio & Records*, p. 42.

_____. (1999a, August 27). "Black Consumers: $532 Billion & Growing." *Radio & Records*, p. 93.

_____. (1999b, January 15). "The Dream of Dr. King Lives On." *Radio & Records*, p. 48.

_____. (1999c, November, 12). "It's Working Like a Charm." *Radio & Records*, p. 60.

_____. (1996, November 22). "KJLH Brings Issues to the 'Front Page.'" *Radio & Records*, p. 41.

_____. (1999d, July 9). "KKBT/Los Angeles is Rolling' with New Changes." *Radio & Records*, p. 52.

_____. (1992b, May 21). "KJMZ Heats Up Dallas Battle." *Radio & Records*, p. 41.

_____. (1992c, January 17). "Keeping the Dream Alive." *Radio & Records*, p. 46,

_____. (1998, December 4). "The Need for Community Involvement." *Radio & Records*, p. 50.

_____. (2000, May 26). "Owning Up to Diversity: Conversations with the Top

Minority Owners." *Radio & Records*, pp. 36–40.

_____. (1999e, February 5). "Today's Lesson: Teach the Value of Your Audience." *Radio & Records*, pp. 56.

_____. (1999f, February 19). "WDIA-AM/Memphis — Yesterday and Today." *Radio & Records*, p. 64.

_____. (1991, June 14). "WXYV's Winning Ways." *Radio & Records*, p. 41.

MacDonald, J. F. (1979). *Don't Touch That Dial! Radio Programming in American Life*. Chicago, IL: Nelson-Hall.

MacManus, S. A. (1990). "Minority Business Contracting with Local Government." *Urban Affairs Quarterly, 25* (3), 455–478

Marable, M. (1991, November). "Black American in Search of Itself." *The Progressive*, pp. 18–23.

Marion, J. C. (2001). "Historical R & B Radio Moments." Retrieved April 11, 2002, from http://home.earthlink.net/~jaymar41/radionotes.html.

Marrow, T. (2002a, February 22). "An Evening with Ice-T." Lecture Series. Shryock Auditorium: Southern Illinois University, Carbondale.

Marrow, T. (2002b, February 22). Personal communication with Ice-T: Interview; guest lecture. Southern Illinois University, Carbondale.

Maycock, J. (2002, July 20). "Loud and Proud." *The Guardian*. Accessed April 4, 2004, available at http://www.guardian.co.uk/weekend/story/0,3605,757376,00.html.

McAdams, J. (1996, March 16). "Winston is Committed to R&B at Wonder's KJLH." *Billboard, 108* (11), 102.

McCoy, Q. (1999). *No Static*. San Francisco, CA: Backbeat Books.

_____. (2000). "The Stand-Alones: A Fight for Survival." *Gavin*. Retrieved September 3, 2000, from http://gavin.com/industry/features/black_radio.shtml.

"MeasureCast Announces Top 50 Streaming Radio Stations for June; Internet-Only Streaming Up, Terrestrial Streaming Down." (2001, June). *Market Guide: Significant Developments*. MeasureCast, Inc.

Meeske, M. D. (1987). "Specialization and Competition in Radio." In A. Wells (Ed.), *Mass Media and Society* (pp. 112–135). Lexington, MA: Lexington Books.

Metro Broadcasting, 497 U.S. 547 (1990).

Meyer, A. J. (1971). *Black Voices and Format Regulations: A Style in Black-Oriented Radio*. Stanford, CA: Institute for Communication Research.

Meyer, R. J. (1970). "Blacks and Broadcasting." In A. E. Koenig (Ed.), *Broadcasting and Bargaining: Labor Relations in Radio and Television* (pp. 203–227). Madison, WI: The University of Wisconsin Press.

Michaelson, J. (1995, October 4). "The Simpson Verdicts: Callers to Talk Radio Span the Dial with Debate; Reaction; About the Only Person to Claim No Opinion is Kato Kaelin, Even Though This Station Billed His Afternoon Show as a 'Worldwide Exclusive.'" *Los Angeles Times*, p. 9.

"Minority Stations Get Fewer Ads." (1999). *Quill 87* (2), 1–6.

Mitchell, J. L. (1989, December 28). "Group Retains Its Mission as Face of Needy Changes Homeless: Helpers for the Homeless and Hungry Has Provided Groceries and Shelter to the Poor Since 1972. Today, Only the Clientele Has Changed." *Los Angeles Times*, p. 1.

MMTC: Minority Media & Telecommunications Council. (2002). "MMTC Unveils Proposal to FCC for 'Free Speech' to Break Deadlock Over Local Radio Ownership Regulation and to Promote Minority Ownership" [www.wifp.org/communicationnews.html]. Washington, DC: MMTC.

Moldovan, R. (1999). *Martin Luther King, Jr.: An Oral History of His Religious Witness and His Life*. San Francisco: International Scholars Publications.

Montague, M. (2005, August 7). "The Yelp that Burned L.A." *Los Angeles*

Times, accessed April 4, 2006, available at latimes.com.

Montague, Magnificent, and Baker, Bob. (2003). *Burn, Baby! Burn!* Champaign: University Illinois Press.

Mundy, A. (1999, January 11). "FCC's Ad Study to Hit Hard." *Media Week, 9* (2), 1–2.

"NAB Announces Marconi Award Winners: Power 106 and Big Boy Take Home Radio's Highest Honor." (2002). *Business Wire* (Seatle Ed.). Retrieved September 24, 2002, from http://Eurweb.com.

NABOB. (2002a, March 27). *Comments on the Rules and Policies Concerning Multiple Ownership of Radio Broadcast Stations in Local Markets,* pp. 1–16. MM Docket No. 01–317, 2002. Washington, DC: Federal Communications Commission.

———. (2002b). Home page. Washington, DC: National Association of Black-Owned Broadcasters. Retrieved March 27, 2002, from http://www.nabob.com.

NAHJ. (2006). News. Washington DC. Retrieved November 19, 2008, from http://www.nahj.org/nahjnews/articles/2006/april/ntiaresponse.shtml.

NASDAQ (2002). Home page. New York: NASDAQ. Retrieved June 2, 2002, from http://www.nasdaq.com.

Napoli, P. M. (2001). "The Localism Principle in Communications Policymaking and Policy Analysis: Ambiguity, Inconsistency, and Empirical Neglect." *Policy Studies Journal, 29* (3), 372–387

National Telecommunications and Information Administration. (1995). *Capital Formation and Investment in Minority Business Enterprises in the Telecommunications Industries* (capital formation report). Washington DC: The U.S. Department of Commerce.

———. (1996). *Minority Broadcast Ownership in the United States.* Washington DC: The U.S. Department of Commerce.

———. (1998). *Minority Broadcast Ownership in the United States.* Washington, DC: The U.S. Department of Commerce.

———. (2001). Changes, *Challenges, and Charting New Courses: Minority Commercial Broadcast Ownership in the United States.* Washington DC: The U.S. Department of Commerce.

National Women Organization Foundation. (NOW). (1998). "Attack on Affirmative Action in Broadcasting." Retrieved June 4, 2002, from http://www.nowfoundation.org/communications/tv/affirmative.html.

Nelson, C. (1993, February 18). Personal communication. In (P. Johnson, 2003), *The Community Role of Black-Owned KJLH-FM During the 1992 Los Angeles Civil Uprising & 10 Years Later in an Era of Media Consolidation: Listening Through the Window.* Ph.D., diss., Southern Illinois University Carbondale.

———. (2001, October 10 & November 20). Personal communication. In (P. Johnson, 2003), *The Community Role of Black-Owned KJLH-FM During the 1992 Los Angeles Civil Uprising & 10 Years Later in an Era of Media Consolidation: Listening Through the Window.* Ph.D., diss., Southern Illinois University Carbondale.

"New TV Comedy Centers Around Black Radio Station: Radio News Update." *J. R. Reynolds.* [undated]. [KJLH-FM file] Newman, M. (1988). *Entrepreneurs Of Profit and Pride: From Black Appeal to Radio Soul.* New York: Praeger.

Newscast. (1992, April 30). KMJM-FM: St. Louis, MO.

News Release. (2005). "Inglewood Mayor Partners with National Conference of Black Mayors, KJLH Radio and Recycling Black Dollars Raising Over $58,000." Retrieved November 26, 2008, from http://www.cityofinglewood.org/civica/press/display.asp?layout=1&Entry=118.

Oberholza-Gee, F., and J. Waldfogel (2001). "Electoral Acceleration: The Effect of Minority Population on Minority Turnout." Working Paper 8253.

Cambridge, MA: National Bureau of Economic Research. Retrieved April 29, 2001, from http://www.nber.org/papers/w8252.

O'Connor, D., and G. Cook (1975). "Black Radio: The Soul Sellout." In T. C. Smythe & G. A. Mastroiani (Eds.), *Issues in Broadcasting — Radio, Television and Cable.*

Ofori, K. A. (2002, March). *Radio Local Market Consolidation and Minority Ownership.* Washington, DC: Minority Media & Telecommunications Council.

_____. (1999). *When Being No. 1 is Not Enough; The Impact of Advertising Practices In Minority-Owned and Minority-Formatted Broadcast Stations.* Prepared by the Civil Rights Forum on Communication Policy. Washington, DC: Office of Communications Business Opportunities, Federal Communications Commission.

O'Neill, S. (1992, July/August) "L.A. Stories: A City Ablaze Casts a Glaring Light on the Press." *Columbia Journalism Review*, pp. 23–25.

Papper, B. (2005, July 26). "Running In Place: Minorities & Women in Television See Little Change, While Minorities Fare Worse in Radio." Retrieved November 19, 2008, from http://www.rtnda.org/research/research.shtml.

_____. (2008, July/August). "Issues: Cover Story: 2008 Women and Minorities Survey." *Communicator.* Retrieved November 19, 2008, from http://www.rtnda.org/pages/media_items/the-face-of-the-workforce1472.php.

Parker, E. (1998, October 21). "John Lamar Hill Dies at age 75." *Los Angeles Sentinel*, p. A3.

Parenti, M. (1993). *Inventing Reality: The Politics of News Media* (2nd edition). New York: St. Martin's Press.

Paterno, S. (1992, August 15). "Under Fire at Hearings On L.A. Riots, Critics Blast the Media on Coverage, and Lack of Coverage, of Minorities, Cities." *Editor & Publisher*, pp. 18–19.

Patterson, D. R. (n.d.). *Breaking the Line: Black radio pioneers.* Retrieved November 14, 2008, from http://rockradioscrapbook.ca/black.html.

Pember, D. R. (1993). *Mass Media Law.* Madison, WI: Brown & Benchmark.

"The Phone Company Rings Through with No Charge." *Los Angeles Sentinel*, May 14, 1992. [KJLH-FM file].

Postman, N. (1986). *Amusing Ourselves to Death.* New York: Viking Penguin.

Powell III, A. (1993). "You Are What You Hear." *Media Studies Journal*, 7 (3), 71–76.

"President Clinton and Rev. Jesse Jackson Join NABOB to Promote Vote Turnout." (2000, October 31). Washington, DC: National Association of Black Owned Broadcasters. Retrieved April 11, 2001, from http:// www.nabob.org

"Problem Officers' Get Counseling/L.A. Police Comply With Civilian Panel's Recommendation." *Houston Chronicle*, December 13, 1992, p. 5.

Pulse interview, Pierre M. Sutton. (1990, November 19). *The Pulse of Radio 5* (46), 18–22.

"Radio Format Special Report, Part 3." *Radio Business Report*, July 2, 1990, p. 14.

Radio & Records Directory (1999). Radio & Records: Los Angeles, CA.

Radio & Records Directory (2000). Radio & Records: Los Angeles, CA.

Radio & Records Directory (2001). Radio & Records: Los Angeles, CA.

Radio & Records Directory (2002). Radio & Records: Los Angeles, CA.

"Radio One Profits Plummet." (2008, November 7). *The A-List Magazine*, 117. Retrieved November 19, 2008, from http://thealistmagzine.blogspot.com/.

"Radio Station's Serving Minorities Lag in Revenue Performance." (2001). *The Chicago Reporter*, pp. 1–5. Retrieved March 29, 2001, from http://www.chicagoreporter.com/2001/3–2001/radio/radio1/htm.

Ramaprasad, J. (1996). "How Four Newspapers Covered the 1992 Los Angeles

'Riots.'" In V. T. Berry and C. L. Manning-Miller (Eds.), *Mediated Messages and African-American Culture: Contemporary Issues* (pp. 76–95). Thousand Oaks, CA: Sage Publications.

"Rappers Speak Out on 102.# KJLH." *Los Angles Sentinel.* February 10 [no year]. [KJLH-FM file.]

Rathburn, E. (1996, March 11). "$8 Billion Loose in Station Markets; Radio and Television Station Trading in 1995." *Broadcasting & Cable,* p. 40+ (Special Edition).

Reagan, J., and J. Collins (1987). "Sources for Health Care Information in Two Small Communities." *Journalism Quarterly, 64* (2 & 3), 560–563.

Reed, E. (2001, October 12 and November 21). Personal communication. In P. Johnson (2003), *The Community Role of Black-Owned KJLH-FM During the 1992 Los Angeles Civil Uprising & 10 Years Later in an Era of Media Consolidation: Listening Through the Window.* Ph.D. diss., Southern Illinois University Carbondale.

"Riordan Speaks Out on KJLH." *Los Angeles Sentinel,* February 3, 1994.

Riot. (1997). Documentary. Showtime Network Inc.

Robins, J. M. (1992, May 4). "Chopper Heaven in L.A. Hell." *Variety,* pp. 111, 115.

Rollins, M. (1993, April 11). "Trucker Case is the Big One that L.A. Blacks Worry About." *The Oregonian,* p. A01.

Rose, H.M. (1986). "Can We Substantially Lower Homicide Risk in the Nation's Larger Black Communities?" In M.M. Heckler (Ed.), *Report of the Secretary's Task Force on Black & Minority Health, Volume V: Homicide, Suicide, and Unintentional Injuries* (pp. 185–223). Washington, DC: U.S. Department of Health and Human Services.

Rosenfeld, M. (1991, November 15). "WPGC's Robin Breedon, Urging Listeners to Stop the Violence." *The Washington Post,* pp. F1, F4.

Routt, E., McGrath, J. B., and Weiss, F.

A. (1978). *The Radio Format Conundrum.* New York: Hastings House.

Rubel, R. J. (1980). "Extent, Perspectives, and Consequences of Violence and Vandalism in Public Schools." In K. Baker and R. J. Rubel, *Violence and Crime in the Schools* (pp. 17–28). Toronto, Canada: Lexington Books.

Sanders, T. (2002, May). "Statistical Market Summary of KJLH: 1976–2002." Indianapolis, IN: Duncan's American Radio.

Sanjek, R. (2000, Fall). "Keeping Ethnography Alive In An Urbanizing World." *Human Organization, 59* (3), pp. 280–289.

Schatzman, D. (1994, September 8). "KJLH Must Move Station." *Los Angeles Sentinel,* p. A1.

Schwerin, J. (1992). *Got To Tell It.* Oxford, UK: Oxford University Press.

Schiller, J. (1970). *Mass Communication and American Empire.* New York: A. M. Kelley.

Schuyler, J. (1990, November 19). "Black-Owned Radio in the 90s." *The Pulse of Radio, 5* (46), pp. 14–16, 22.

Scott, J. W., and Black, A. (1989). "Deep Structures of African-American Family Life: Female and Male Kin Networks." *The Urban League Review, 13* (1), 17–23.

Scott, M. S. (1993, June). "Can Black Radio Survive an Industry Shakeout." *Black Enterprise, 23* (11), 254.

Settel, I. (1967). *A Pictorial History of Radio.* New York: Grossett & Dunlap.

Shank, B. (1996, Fall). "Fears of the White Unconscious: Music, Race, and Identification in the Censorship of 'Cop Killer.'" *Radical History Review,* pp. 1–17. Retrieved February 4, 2001, from http://chnm.gmu.edu/rhr/66.htm.

Shaw, D. L., and M. E. McCombs (1989). "Dealing with Illicit Drugs: The Power — and Limits — of Mass Media Agenda Setting." In P. J. Shoemaker (Ed.), *Communication Campaigns about Drugs, Government, Media, and the Public* (pp. 113–120). Hillsdale, NY: Lawrence Erlbaum Associates.

Shepard, A.C. (2001, November). "Empire of the Air." *Washingtonian 37*(2), pp. 39–47.

Sheppard, N., Jr. (1983, March 15). "Black-Oriented Radio: A Key in Chicago's Election." *The New York Times*, p. 24.

Sherard, R. G. (1988). "The Emergence of Blacks on Television." In R. E. Hiebert & C. Reuss (Eds.), *Impact of Media* (pp. 328–337). New York: Longman.

Shiver, J., Jr. (1990, August 8). "Charting the Rise of 'Urban Contemporary' Radio: KKBT's New Format Has Launched it Into Southern California's Top 20." *Los Angeles Times*, p. 1.

Sharkey, B. (1997, April 21). "There's a 'Riot' Going On." *MediaWeek, 7* (16), pp. 24–27.

Shingles, R. (1981). "Black Consciousness and Political Participation: The Missing Link." *American Political Science Review, 75* (1), 76–91.

Shoemaker, P. J. (Ed.) (1989). *Communication Campaigns about Drugs, Government, Media, and The Public*. Hillsdale, NJ: Lawrence Erlbaum Associates.

Shweder, J. (1998, September 18). "AWRT Confab Studies Consolidation's Effects on Both Women and Minorities." *Radio & Records*, pp. 3, 12, 28.

Siegelman, P., and J. Waldfogel (2001, October 24). *Race and Radio: Preference Externalities, Minority Ownership, and the Provision of Programming to Minorities*. Washington DC: Federal Communications Commission, Retrieved October 24, 2001, from http://www.fcc.gov.

Silberman, S. (1997, September 18). "This Revolution is Not Being Televised." *Wired News*. Retrieved May 18, 2001, from http://www.wired.com/news/print/0.1294,6816,00.html.

"Simpson Lashes at His Critics." *Cincinnati Post*, March 1, 1996, p. 2A.

Sitton, T., and W. Deverell (2001). *Metropolis in the Making: Los Angeles in the 1920s*. Berkeley, CA: University of California Press.

Slade, K. (1993a, March 21). "Commentary on Local Issues, Viewpoints of Residents and Community Leaders, and Letters. A Voice-and Ear-to the Community KJLH-FM's General Manager Says Minorities Want Information That Is Relevant to Their Lives." *Los Angeles Times*, p. 22.

Slade, K. (1993b, March 2). Personal communication. In P. Johnson (2003), *The Community Role of Black-Owned KJLH-FM During the 1992 Los Angeles Civil Uprising & 10 Years Later in an Era of Media Consolidation: Listening Through the Window*. Ph.D. diss., Southern Illinois University Carbondale.

_____. (2001, December 10). In P. Johnson (2003), *The Community Role of Black-Owned KJLH-FM During the 1992 Los Angeles Civil Uprising & 10 Years Later in an Era of Media Consolidation: Listening Through the Window*. Ph.D. diss., Southern Illinois University Carbondale.

_____. (2002, January 28). Personal communication. In P. Johnson (2003), *The Community Role of Black-Owned KJLH-FM During the 1992 Los Angeles Civil Uprising & 10 Years Later in an Era of Media Consolidation: Listening Through the Window*. Ph.D. diss., Southern Illinois University Carbondale.

Slaughter, D. T., and V. S. Kuehne (1987–1988, Summer/Winter). "Improving Black Education: Perspectives on Parent Involvement." *The Urban League Review, 11* (1 and 2), 59–74.

Smith, A. (1988/1989). "Responsibility of the African-American Church as a Source of Support for Adolescent Fathers." *The Urban League Review, 12* (1 and 2), 83–90.

Smith, A. D. (1994). *Twilight: Los Angeles, 1992 — On the Road, the Search for American Character*. New York: Anchor Books/Doubleday.

Smith, R. C. (1988). "From Insurgency Toward Inclusion: The Jackson Campaigns of 1984 and 1988." In L. Morris (Ed.), *The Social And Political Implications of the 1984 Jesse Jackson Presiden-*

tial Campaign (pp. 215–230). New York: Praeger.

Smith, W. (1989). *The Pied Pipers of Rock-'n'Roll: Radio Deejays of the '50s and '60s.* Marietta, GA: Longstreet Press.

Smith, W. D. (1985/1986). "Improving Black Health Care: A Neverending Campaign." *The Urban League Review,* 9 (2), 3–12.

Snow, R. P. (1983). *Creating Media Culture.* Beverly Hills, CA: Sage Publications.

Soul of America (2001). Retrieved October 3, 2001, from http://www.soul ofamerica.com/cityfldr/la3.html (Los Angeles).

"Southern Folklore Celebrates Radio Pioneers." *The* [Memphis] *Downtowner,* 2 (1), February 10–11, 1992, pp. 10–11.

Spaulding, N. W. (1981). *History Of Black Oriented Radio in Chicago, 1929–1963.* Ph.D. diss., University of Illinois at Urbana-Champaign.

Spencer, Jon Michael. (1992). "Rapsody in Black: Utopian Aspiration." *Theology Today* 48 (4), 444–451.

Spergel, I. A., and G. D. Curry (1990). "Strategies and Perceived Agency Effectiveness in Dealing with the Youth Gang Problems." In R. C. Huff (Ed.), *Gangs in America* (pp. 208–399). Newbury Park, CA: Sage Publications.

Squires, C. R. (2000). "Black Talk Radio." *Harvard International Journal of Press/Politics,* 5 (2), 73–93.

St. James, T. (1992, February 11). Personal communication. In P. Johnson (2003), *The Community Role of Black-Owned KJLH-FM During the 1992 Los Angeles Civil Uprising & 10 Years Later in an Era of Media Consolidation: Listening Through the Window.* Ph.D., diss., Southern Illinois University Carbondale.

Stake, R. (1995). *The Art of Case Research.* Thousand Oaks, CA; Sage Publisher.

"Stars Join KJLH in Food Drive for the Homeless" (1998). *Los Angeles Sentinel,* November 5, 1998, p. A1.

Stamm, K. R., and L. Fortini-Campbell (1983). "The Relationship of Community Ties to Newspaper Use." *Journalism Monographs,* pp. 1–27.

Stavitsky, A. G. (1993). "Ear on America." *Media Studies Journal,* 7 (3), 71–76.

Stein, M. L. (1993, February 27). "Limited Access." *Editor & Publisher,* pp. 12–13.

Stephens, J. (2002, January 28). In P. Johnson (2003), *The Community Role of Black-Owned KJLH-FM During the 1992 Los Angeles Civil Uprising & 10 Years Later in an Era of Media Consolidation: Listening Through the Window.* Ph.D. diss., Southern Illinois University Carbondale.

Sterling, C. H., and J. M. Kittross (1990). *Stay tuned: A Concise History of American Broadcasting* (2nd edition). Belmont, CA: Wadsworth.

Stern, H. (1993). *Private Parts.* New York: Simon & Schuster.

Stewart, J. (2002). "Can Conservative Black Speak Out in America: Ask KABC Talk Show Host Larry Elder, the Target of a Black National Group in L.A." *New Times/Los Angeles,* pp. 12–21. Retrieved May 20, 2002, from www. larryelder.com/ainteasy/freethisman. htm.

Straight from the Hood (documentary). New York: Music Television Network (Aired April 24, 2002.

Strauss, A., and B. Glaser (1967). *The Discovery Of Grounded Theory: Strategies For Qualitative Research.* Chicago, IL: Aldine.

Surlin, S. H. (1972). "Black-Oriented Radio: Programming to a Perceived Audience." *Journal of Broadcasting,* 16 (3), 289–298.

_____. (1973). "Black-Oriented Radio's Service to the Community." *Journalism Quarterly, 50,* 556–560.

Sweeney, J. (1975). "Radio Stations Dial "A" for Automation." In T. C. Smythe and G. A. Mastroianni (Eds.), *Issues in Broadcasting* (pp. 395–412). California State University: Mayfield.

Synan, Vinson (2002). "The Orgins of the Pentecostal Movement." Tulsa, OK: Oral Roberts University Holy

Spirit Research Center, January 4, 2002). Retrieved October 2004, from http://www.oru.edu/university/library/holyspirit/pentorg1.html.

Tanter, Kirk. (2004). "Chuck Johnson 1938 – 2004." New Soulbeat, Inc. Hollywood, CA. Retrieved November 14, 2008, from http://soulbeattv.com/about.htm.

Telecommunications Act of 1996. Washington, DC: FCC. Retrieved June 1, 2000, from http://www. fcc.gov.

Tellis, W. (1997, July). "Introduction to Case Study." *The Qualitative Report, 3*(2), 1–9 [on-line serial]. Retrieved April 12, 2001, from http://www.nova.edu/ssss/QR/QR3–2/tellis1.html.

Thomas, S. B. (1990). "Community Health Advocacy for Racial and Ethnic Minorities in the United States: Issues and Challenges for Health Education." *Health Education Quarterly, 17* (1), 15.

Thompson, H. A. (2000, March). "Understanding Rioting in Postwar Urban America." *Journal of Urban History, 26* (3), 391–493.

Thompson-Sanders, V. L. (1990). "Factors Affecting the Level of African American Identification." *Journal of Black Psychology, 17* (1), 19–35.

Thompson, T. L., and L. P. Cusella (1991). "Muddling Through Toward Small Wins: On the Need for Requisite Variety." In L. Donohew, H. E. Sypher, & W. J. Bukoski (Ed)., *Persuasive Communication and Drug Abuse Prevention* (pp. 313–333). Hillsdale, NJ: Lawrence Erlbaum Associates.

Totten, G. O., and H. E. Schockman (Eds.) (1994). *Community in Crisis: the Korean American after the Los Angeles Civil Unrest of April 1992.* Claremont CA: Regina Books.

"Traffic Reporter Sues in Nickname Dispute; Infinity Execs to Get Sensitivity Training." *Billboard,* May 14, 1994, p. 98.

Treadwell, D. (1992, April 30). "Violence Erupts in Atlanta as Other Cities Brace for Trouble." *Los Angeles Times,* p. A-9.

Tyson, T. B. (1999). *Radio Free Dixie: Robert Williams and the Roots of Black Power.* Chapel Hill: The University of North Carolina.

Understanding the Riots: Los Angeles and the Aftermath of the Rodney King Verdict. (1992). Los Angeles, CA: Los Angeles Times.

Van Arnem, H. (2002, July 18). "Stevie Wonder: Technology, Music and Being Blind." Retrieved July 18, 2002, from http://www.ican.com.

Vongs, P. (2006). "Minorities are a Small Percentage of Media Owners." New America Media. Retrieved November 19, 2008, from http://news.newamericamedia.org/news/view_article.html?article_id=c968d077fd3d6b7561b623d230c5326f.

"WPGC/DC Purchase Protest Dropped." (1994). *R&R Hot Fax NewsFlash.* Los Angeles, CA: *Radio & Records,* p. 1.

Wade, M. (2008, August 6). "FCC Hearing Broaches Media Ownership for Minorities: Panelists Outline Strategies to Improve Minority Ownership." *Black Enterprise.* Retrieved November 21, 2008, from http://www.blackenterprise.com/diversity/diversity-news/2008/08/06/fcc-hearing-broaches-media-ownership-for-minorities/.

Waldfogel, J. (2001, October 29). *Comments on Consolidation and Localism.* Prepared for FCC Roundtable. Washington, DC: Federal Communications Commission [www.fcc.gov].

Wall, B. (1996). *The Rodney King Rebellion: A Pyschopolitical Analysis of Racial Despair And Hope.* Chicago, IL: African-American Images.

Wallace, A., and D. Ferrell (1992, April 30). "Verdicts Greeted With Outrage and Disbelief." *Los Angeles Times,* pp. 1, A24.

Wallis, D. (1998). *All We Had Was Each Other.* Bloomington: Indiana University Press.

Ward, B. (1998). *Just My Soul Responding: Rhythm & Blues, Black Consciousness, and Race Relations.* Berkeley: University of California Press.

Watson, W. H. (1989). *The Village*. Atlanta, GA: Village Vanguard Inc.

Weinstein, S. (1993, April 2). "KJLH Earns Peabody for Riot Coverage." *Los Angeles Times*, p. 13. Werner, C. (2004). *Higher Ground: Stevie Wonder, Aretha Franklin, Curtis Mayfield, and the Rise and Fall of American Soul*. New York: Crown.

"What's Happening in SoCal Radio." *Call Letters*. Los Angeles, CA: Southern California Broadcasters Association.

White, H. L. (2008). "Rich Mosaic of African American Life." *The Charlotte Post*, 33 (45), p.1A, 6A. Retrieved November 18, 2008, from http://thealist-magzine.blogspot.com/2007/01/52.html [Feature: Black media ownership & the FCC; An A-List Analysis. *A-List Magazine*].

Whiteman, D. L. (1997, January). "Contextualization: The Theory, the Gap, the Challenge." *International Bulletin of Missionary Research, 21* (1), 2–7.

Williams, G. A. (1998). *Legendary Pioneers of Black Radio*. NY: Praeger.

Williams, G. A., and G. Alan-Williams. *A Gathering of Heroes: Reflections on Rage and Responsibility: A Memoir of the Los Angeles Riots*. Chicago, IL: Academy Chicago.

Wittebols, J. H. (1993). "News from the Non-Institutional World: U.S. and Canadian Television News Coverage of Social Protest." Presented at the 1992 Association for Education in Journalism and Mass Communication Conference, Kansas City, MO, August 1993.

Yin, R. (1993). *Applications of Case Study Research*. Beverly Hills, CA: Sage Publications.

_____. (1984). *Case Study Research: Design and Methods* (1st edition). Beverly Hills, CA: Sage Publications.

_____. (1994). *Case Study Research: Design and Methods* (2nd edition). Beverly Hills, CA: Sage Publications.

_____. (1989). *Case Study Research: Design and Methods* (Rev. ed.). Beverly Hills, CA: Sage Publications.

Yu, E. (Ed.) (1994). *Black-Korean Encounter: Toward Understanding and Alliance: Dialogue Between Black and Korean Americans in the Aftermath of the 1992 Los Angeles Riots*. Regina Books: Claremont, CA.

Zerbinos, E. (1995/1996). "The Talk Radio Phenomenon: An Update." *Journal of Radio Studies, 3,* 11–22.

Zimbalist, A. S. (1979). *Case Studies on the Labor Process*. New York: Monthly Review Press.

Ziegler, D., and Dickerson, B. J. (1993). "Breaking Through the Barriers: Using Video as a Tool for Intercultural Communication." *Journal of Black Studies, 24* (2), 159–177.

Zorn, E. (1983, September 12). "Chicago Listens as Blacks Talk Back." *Chicago Tribune* (Section 5), pp. 1, 8.

Index

211